W9-ADO-720

LUDENDORFF

GENIUS OF WORLD WAR I

✠

BOOKS BY
D. J. GOODSPEED

THE CONSPIRATORS
NAPOLEON'S EIGHTY DAYS
LUDENDORFF:
GENIUS OF WORLD WAR I

DD 231
L8
G6

D. J. GOODSPEED

Ludendorff

GENIUS OF
WORLD WAR I

113630

ILLUSTRATED WITH
PHOTOGRAPHS AND MAPS

HOUGHTON MIFFLIN COMPANY BOSTON
The Riverside Press Cambridge
1966

FIRST PRINTING W

COPYRIGHT © 1966 BY D. J. GOODSPEED
ALL RIGHTS RESERVED INCLUDING THE RIGHT TO
REPRODUCE THIS BOOK OR PARTS THEREOF IN ANY FORM
LIBRARY OF CONGRESS CATALOG CARD NUMBER: 66–17175
PRINTED IN THE UNITED STATES OF AMERICA

TO TED

"Why these murders and horrors? It will be shown that war is a business, divine in itself, and as needful and necessary to the world as eating and drinking or any other work."

MARTIN LUTHER, *Whether Soldiers Can be in a State of Grace*

CONTENTS

ILLUSTRATIONS
following page 210

MAPS

LUDENDORFF

GENIUS OF WORLD WAR I

✠

CHAPTER I

THE RED HOUSE ON THE KÖNIGSPLATZ

T HE TWO MEN standing on the hilltop looked carefully around before producing a map which they spread out on the bonnet of their open touring car. Below them the Belgian countryside lay exposed like a panorama. On their right the Meuse River flowed north towards the misty flatness of the Dutch frontier, and on their left hills and forests tumbled away in rugged confusion to the south and southeast. In the foreground, columns of black smoke rose from innumerable ironworks and factories where a dozen undistinguished villages clustered around the city of Liège like grimy children clutching their mother's skirts.

The year was 1911, and the two men were looking down on the Liège Gap, the ten-mile-wide passageway between Holland and the Ardennes which was the most important route leading from Germany into France. Running east-west through this narrow corridor, the four tracks of the main Paris-Berlin railway glinted in the morning light, and in an irregular circle around the city the smooth mounds of the Liège forts guarded with their guns the white roads that converged from the German frontier thirty kilometers away.

✠

The next afternoon in Berlin the same two men walked in step along Unter den Linden. They looked very smart in their tight-fitting gray uniforms, with brass buttons twinkling on their tunics and broad crimson stripes glowing on their trousers. As they turned into the unpretentious red-brick building on the

Königsplatz which housed the Prussian General Staff, the sentries at the entrance crashed to attention. The two officers made their way up to the first floor where one of them knocked on a door with a gloved hand. A voice shouted *"Herein!"* and they entered, clicked their heels and saluted with correct little bows.

The man behind the desk remained seated but nodded to them pleasantly. In many ways Lieutenant Colonel Erich Ludendorff looked a typical Prussian, no different from hundreds of others who came from the same windy East Elbian plains. He was a thick-set man of forty-six, bullet-headed and heavy jowled, with a roll of fat at the back of his neck above his collar. He had the usual large moustache and close-cropped hair, but his eyes were cold and intelligent and he emanated an air of brutal vigor that was impressive and a little chilling. As Chief of the Second, or "German," Section of the General Staff, he was responsible for the mobilization and deployment of the army in war.

He fixed a monocle in his eye and looked at the officers in front of him.

"Well," he said, "can it be done?"

They allowed small discreet smiles to flicker across their faces.

"We think so, yes," one of them replied.

Ludendorff stood up and walked over to a map-case set against the wall. Seated, he had appeared tall but now he was seen to be of only medium height, for his long trunk was set on a pair of curiously short legs. Soon the three were deep in technical conversation, with Ludendorff asking curt questions and the others answering.

✠

In the summer of 1911, Ludendorff was desperately interested in the Liège fortifications, for they were the key to the entire German war plan. And since Europe was in the middle of its third international crisis in six years, that plan might have to be implemented at any moment. In July, because of an unimportant difference with France over trading concessions in Morocco, Kaiser Wilhelm II had suddenly dispatched the gun-boat *Panther* to Agadir. France and Germany had faced each other with nakedly revealed hatred; warning orders had been sent to the British fleet; and military precautions had been taken along European frontiers.

The German people were more excited than alarmed by the Agadir incident. All things military filled them with a joyous exaltation of spirit, for they had never outgrown the mood of those miraculous years between 1864 and 1871 when Denmark, Austria and France had each been defeated in turn. Memories burned bright of Königgrätz and Sedan and of returning heroes marching through the Brandenburger Tor with captured guns and colors. Now, whenever a detachment of soldiers goose-stepped by in the new field-gray uniforms that had been introduced in 1910 to replace the old Prussian blue, men and women in the open-air cafés and beergardens along the street would smile proudly. The army belonged to the nation and only the Germans really understood the trade of arms.[1]

In common with most General Staff officers, Ludendorff took a more sober view of Germany's strategic position. To superficial observers, Germany was the most powerful nation on the continent; her people were clever and industrious; her trade was expanding; her army unexcelled. Wise social legislation, a high level of prosperity, and the patriotism of the workers mitigated the bitterness of the class struggle and ensured an impressive degree of national unity. Granted a reasonably adequate direction of affairs, Germany seemed destined to become even stronger, richer, and happier.

The trouble was that all this fair future depended on continued peace in Europe, and in the past twenty years the international situation had steadily deteriorated. Ever since 1890, when the newly crowned Kaiser had dismissed Chancellor Otto von Bismarck, German diplomacy had been disastrously unsuccessful. Although France had not forgiven the war that had been forced on her in 1870 or the conqueror's peace imposed on her, she had presented no serious threat to Germany by herself. But when Germany had made an alliance with Austria, Russia had been estranged and in 1894 had joined France in the Dual Alliance which threatened Germany from the east and the west. Italy's lukewarm attachment to Germany and Austria in the Triple Alliance was no compensation for this diplomatic defeat, and from the moment of the signing of the Dual Alliance the Brocken specters of war had loomed above the nations of Europe.

This was bad enough, but it was worse that Germany faced the gathering storm with presumptuous overconfidence. When the Kaiser frivolously decided he wanted a High Seas Fleet powerful enough to challenge the navy of his detested uncle, King Edward VII, Britain grew hostile. Both the British and German naval building programs were fantastically expensive — in 1909 Britain had laid down the keels of no less than eight Dreadnoughts — but Germany was paying by far the higher price for the Kaiser's whim. Not only did the new German navy make friendship with Britain impossible, but it also drained off money, labor and materials which could have been used much more effectively by the army.

War had almost come in 1908, when Russia objected to the Austrian annexation of Bosnia and Herzegovina, but the Kaiser had ranted in fine dramatic style, pledging a "Nibelungen oath of fidelity" to Austria and declaring that he stood behind his ally "in shining armor." Although Tsar Nicholas II had prudently given way, Wilhelm's diplomatic victory had not been as cheap as it appeared, for henceforth there was a war party in Russia as well as in France.

Ludendorff, whose daily concern was that Germany should be ready for *Der Tag,* sometimes thought he was living in a nightmare. The terrible images of war were constantly before his eyes, and occasionally his nerves suffered. Every morning, at exactly seven o'clock, he rode briskly along the same path in the

Grunewald in a losing battle with his thickening waistline, but the exercise gave him no escape from his thoughts and he never noticed the scenery. At home he would sometimes sit for long periods without speaking, his face stern and grim. His wife and four step-children would tiptoe around the house, taking care not to disturb him.

"Be careful," the children would say to one another. "Look out! Today father looks like a glacier." [2]

To meet the dangers pressing in around her Germany had a plan. It had been drawn up in 1905 by Count Alfred von Schlieffen, the Chief of the General Staff, and was based on the premise that when faced with a war on two fronts, Germany should first concentrate to defeat one enemy decisively, then turn with all her strength and defeat the other. Three considerations had decided Schlieffen to strike first at France: the Russian concentration might take place too far to the East for a German attack to reach; the Russians might in any case retire into "the interior of [their] enormous empire," [3] thus depriving Germany of a quick decisive victory; and finally, since France could mobilize much more rapidly than Russia, France was initially more dangerous and should be defeated first, in the interval between the outbreak of hostilities and the completion of Russian mobilization.

A campaign of annihilation against France presented serious difficulties. The French frontier with Germany was only some 150 miles long and nearly half of it was covered by the Vosges mountains. The gaps in France's natural defenses were strongly guarded by fortresses at Belfort, Epinal, Toul and Verdun, so that the chances of a breakthrough were uncertain. Moreover, Schlieffen believed that frontal attacks could never achieve more than limited success, that the enemy, even if defeated, would fall back to fight again. From his study of military history* he concluded that a battle of annihilation was possible only if the en-

* Schlieffen had served for a time as director of the German Army Historical Section.

emy could be outflanked and enveloped. Hannibal's victory at Cannae was for him the classic example of this doctrine.

How then to outflank the French army? A swing to the left around the French fortress line would have to pass through the mountainous terrain of Switzerland and the advance would be delayed. Time was the one thing Germany could not afford, for all the while German divisions were fighting their way through the Jura mountains, huge Russian forces would be gathering in the East. However, intensive studies carried out on staff rides convinced Schlieffen that it would be possible to turn the other French flank by swinging wide to the right through neutral Belgium and Luxembourg. Because a German advance north of the Ardennes would run into the defile of the deep-cut Meuse valley, and because this defile was guarded by the formidable Belgian fortress of Liège, Schlieffen decided to turn the right flank of the Liège forts by marching to the north, across the strip of Dutch territory known as the Maastricht Appendix.

The morality of this course of action troubled Schlieffen not at all, nor did it worry his hero-worshiping subordinates like Ludendorff. They came to believe that France would certainly violate Belgian neutrality no matter what Germany did, but this was a later rationalization, discovered after they had decided to go through Belgium in any case. Schlieffen hoped that the German concentration on the Belgian border would lure the French into crossing Belgium's southern frontier to take up the natural defensive position in the Meuse valley south of Namur, so that the onus for the breach of neutrality would be placed on France. He hoped that Belgium would do no more than protest against the German invasion and that Holland too would acquiesce. None of these pious afterthoughts can absolve Schlieffen and his staff from deliberately forming a plan which, in violation of Germany's express treaty obligation, would outrage three inoffensive neutral nations and kill and injure many thousands of their citizens.

If these consequences of his plan did nothing to deter Schlieffen, still less did the practical consideration that a violation of Belgian neutrality would almost certainly bring Britain into the war against Germany. He considered his plan of campaign and its momentous political implications from the narrowest of military viewpoints. The only questions he asked himself were how large was the British regular army and how would it be employed. Since he believed that for economic reasons no great power could fight anything except a short war, he dismissed both the Royal Navy and the possibility of a greatly expanded British army from his calculations. He had read and admired Bismarck's witty comment that, if British forces ever invaded Germany, he would have them arrested. In Schlieffen's opinion a British Expeditionary Force of 100,000 men could easily be shut up in Antwerp along with the remnants of the Belgian Army. They would, he wrote, be "securely billeted in the fortress much better than on their island. . . ." [4]

The German right wing, which would pivot on Metz, had to be "as strong as possible," and accordingly Schlieffen allotted a total of 79 divisions to it, while the remainder of the German front from Metz to Switzerland would be held with only nine divisions, some Landwehr forces and the garrisons of Metz and Strasbourg. East Prussia would be left practically undefended against a Russian advance; Schlieffen allotted only ten divisions to the Eastern Front.

The Schlieffen Plan had its critics within the German Army and even a junior officer like Ludendorff had reservations about it on purely technical grounds, but the Kaiser, the Chancellor, and the Foreign Office agreed to it without a murmur.[5] This is not surprising, for in Kaiser Wilhelm's Germany whimsy rather than policy directed the state. In theory, ultimate responsibility rested with the monarch, but Wilhelm was neither an absolute nor a constitutional sovereign. He was a vain, impulsive man who hated to read even the briefest of state papers and who was apt to fill the margins of those he did read with schoolboyish comments.[6] Consequently, much was kept from him and much of what he was told he did not properly understand. As a result, there was little co-ordination among Government departments. The Army, the Navy and the Foreign Office went their separate ways, often with completely contradictory policies. Under the glitter and splendor of official Berlin was something not far removed from administrative chaos.

This was the more dangerous because the high competence of the General Staff did not extend beyond technical, tactical, and strategic matters. In the realm of grand strategy, where political and military factors interact, the General Staff was naïve, old-fashioned, and unrealistic. Because competence in grand strategy can be tested only by war, not on staff rides or maneuvers, this weakness was largely unsuspected.

When Schlieffen retired in December 1905, the Kaiser had insisted that Colonel General Helmuth von Moltke, the nephew of the great Field Marshal of 1870, replace him. Moltke had been reluctant to accept, saying that he was "too reflective, too scrupulous, and, if you like, too conscientious for such a post," [7] but the Kaiser, attracted by the famous name,[8] had insisted.

Moltke's appointment was fateful in several ways. One of the least obvious but more momentous results was that Ludendorff, although then only a major, became an extraordinarily important staff officer.[9] Moltke trusted him implicitly and relied on his advice. The two men complemented each other. Moltke had a far broader outlook and a more general culture, but he lacked Ludendorff's energy and will. In time of war the head of the Second Section traditionally became Chief of Operations — a vital appointment — but Ludendorff would have had decidedly less influence in peacetime under anyone other than Moltke.

The new Chief of the General Staff had soon begun to modify the Schlieffen Plan. He did so, not on the advice of the Foreign Office or the direction of the Kaiser, but because he considered the Plan as it stood altogether too much of a gamble. Ludendorff, as Chief of the Second Section, was fully aware of the changes made and probably even initiated some of them. Certainly he agreed with the most important alteration, which was that as new divisions became available they should be used to strengthen the left wing from Metz to Switzerland rather than the wheeling right wing that would pass through Belgium. Technical considerations caused Ludendorff to favor this change of relative strength, for there was little room on the right for the concentration of more divisions and the railways in the area were already fully committed.[10] Another important change Moltke made was to cancel the proposed invasion of Dutch territory. After Ludendorff had informed him of what the two staff officers had discovered by their reconnaissance of Liège, Moltke wrote:

. . . A hostile Holland at our back could have disastrous consequences for the advance of the German army to the west, particularly if England should use the violation of Belgian neutrality as a pretext for entering the war against us . . .

Furthermore it will be very important to have in Holland a country whose neutrality allows us to have imports and supplies. She must be the windpipe that enables us to breathe.

However awkward it may be, the advance through Belgium must therefore take place without the violation of Dutch territory. This will hardly be possible unless Liège is in our hands. I think it possible to take it by a *coup de main*. Its salient forts are so unfavorably sited that they do not overlook the intervening country and cannot dominate it. I have had a reconnaissance made of all roads running through them into the center of the town, *which has no ramparts*. An advance with several columns is possible without their being observed from the forts. Once our troops have entered the town I believe that the forts will not bombard it but will probably capitulate. Everything depends on meticulous preparation and surprise. The enterprise is only possible if the attack is made at once, before the areas between the forts are fortified. It must therefore be undertaken by standing troops immediately war is declared. The capture of a modern fortress by a *coup de main* would be something unprecedented in military history. But it can succeed and must be attempted, for the possession of Liège is the *sine qua non* of our advance. It is a bold venture whose accomplishment promises a great success. In any case the heaviest artillery must be at hand, so that in case of failure we can take the fortress by storm. I believe the absence of an inner rampart will deliver the fortress into our hands.[11]

Ludendorff worked out the tactical details of the seizure of Liège. In spite of Moltke's optimism, the problem was a difficult one, for the city was girdled by a ring of twelve modern forts that had been built by the world's foremost fortress engineer, Henri Brialmont, between 1888 and 1892. Ludendorff allotted the capture of Liège to a special force of six regular brigades and two cavalry divisions which would be stationed in the vicinity of Strasbourg and trained for this specific task.

Yet even if Liège fell quickly and imposed no check on the German divisions pouring into Belgium, Ludendorff was concerned that the Schlieffen Plan might fail.[12] The margin of time, after all, was desperately small. The great scythe of the German right wing had to sweep around the French left, swing west of Paris to encircle it, bring the French Army to battle, completely defeat it, and drive it against the Swiss frontier — all in six weeks. Then the victorious German troops would have to entrain for the East to halt the invading Russians. The Plan was certainly brilliant but was also bold to the point of rashness.

Moreover, Schlieffen had stipulated that 94 equivalent divisions would be needed for the West, and in 1911 Germany could produce only 65. The German Army, in fact, was only slightly larger than the French, for France enforced conscription rigorously, calling up 82 per cent of her available manpower as against Germany's 52 per cent.* When the British Expeditionary Force and the Belgian Army were taken into account, the Germans would have no numerical superiority at all. Worse still, six or seven army corps would have to be left behind to invest the "gigantic fortress" of Paris. Schlieffen had always rec-

* In his Plan of 1905 Schlieffen had indignantly pointed out that France, with a population of 39 millions, provided 995 battalions for her field army, while Germany, with a population of 56 millions, provided only 971 battalions.[13]

ognized that he had too few troops to implement his plan, but he had been something of a fatalist and had made little attempt to force his ideas upon the Kaiser, the Chancellor or the Reichstag.

There was nothing of the fatalist about Ludendorff, and he worried incessantly over Germany's unpreparedness. He was utterly convinced of the superiority of German troops over any opponents they would have to meet — at least at the beginning of a war — but it was nevertheless disquieting that, after Paris had been by-passed, the decisive battle in the West would be fought with an absolute inferiority of force.

When Russia was considered, the situation looked even blacker. Russia had a vast army of one and a quarter millions, supported by over three million reserves,[14] and ever since the Russo-Japanese War, obsolete Russian equipment had slowly but steadily been replaced by modern French designs. Even more sinister was the fact that Russia, with the aid of French loans, was year by year extending her railway network westward toward the German frontier. No matter how Ludendorff looked at it, he always arrived at the same answer — Germany and Austria-Hungary would sooner or later be forced to fight against desperate odds.

In war the character of military leaders is as important as the strength of the forces they command, and during the crisis of 1911 the more knowledgeable officers in the German Army watched General von Moltke a little apprehensively. A tall broad man of 63, Moltke lacked his uncle's Prussian singlemindedness for soldiering. His friends, for some reason, all called him "Julius," and the Kaiser, who liked his sad charm, always referred to him as *"der traurige Julius."* Everything had gone surprisingly well in the six years since Moltke had become Chief of the General Staff, but his responsibilities still weighed heavily on him. That may have been why he allowed his wife, Elisa, to interest him in spiritualism and theosophy. These were not the usual hobbies of a Prussian general, and when rumors began to circulate that seances were held in the von Moltke home, the officers in the Red House on the Königsplatz were not reassured.

The Army felt quite differently about Moltke's assistant, Ludendorff. He was promoted to full colonel in 1911, but of course he was still too junior to be considered for high command and besides he was not of the nobility. In fact, it was rumored that his father, who had been a small landowner near Kruschevnia in Posen, had gone bankrupt in the 1880's and before his death early in the new century had taken to selling insurance. However, his mother's family, the von Tempelhoffs, was patrician enough, although impoverished.

Erich Ludendorff had been the third of six children, and as a child was distinguished by only two unusual characteristics — his excessive cleanliness (he would not play with other children if he thought he might dirty his shoes) and his passion for mathematics. In 1877, at the age of twelve, he went to the Cadet School at Plön where, as a result of the brilliant marks he made on his entrance examination, he was admitted to a grade two above that of his age group. There, among boys who were all older than himself, he excelled in everything except gymnastics.[15]

In due course, at the age of seventeen, he passed out of Plön to the Military Academy at Lichterfelde near Berlin where again he consistently headed his class. He had had his way to make in the world, and by then hard work had become a habit. At Lichterfelde Ludendorff learned to swear on his sword-knot, to love his country, serve his Kaiser, and think like a soldier. The riding circle, the drill square, the bare lecture rooms, the long day's work and the evenings of study had no more serious purpose. The creed he was taught had its own ethics, making virtues from necessities, but the virtues were real enough for all that — discipline, courage, loyalty to comrades, all that would be of assistance in war. Like most virtues, these were not practiced perfectly, and this made them tolerable.

When he had been posted from Lichterfelde to the 57th Infantry Regiment at Wesel as a second lieutenant, he had usually remained in camp with his books and his maps while his wealthier or more carefree comrades drank Moselle and ate sausages with dubious female companions in bars and night-clubs.[16] He served as a lieutenant in the 2nd Marine Battalion at Kiel and Wilhelmshaven and with the 8th Grenadier Guards at Frankfurt on the Oder. Although he was respected and well enough liked, Ludendorff made no close friends at Plön, Lichterfelde, or in regimental service. He was too intent on his career to experience those happy times whose remembrance binds young men together.

In 1893 he attended the Kriegsakademie, where General Meckel, the reorganizer of the Japanese Army, recommended him for the General Staff. He was promoted to captain in 1895, and after commanding an infantry company at Thorn, held staff appointments with the 9th Division at Glogau and the 5th Corps at Posen. In 1900 he was promoted to major and in March 1904 went to the Second Section of the General Staff in the Red House on the Königsplatz. There he received much of his practical staff training under Schlieffen, whom he regarded as "one of the greatest soldiers who ever lived." [17] In 1907 he was promoted to lieutenant colonel and the following year he became the head of the Second Section. He and Wilhelm Gröner, a rival of long standing, had both been considered for this coveted post, but it had gone to Ludendorff because Gröner was a Württemberger rather than a Prussian and because Gröner's father had not been an officer, while Ludendorff's father had been a Rittmeister in the reserve cavalry.

In theory, and to a large extent in practice, the officers of the General Staff lived sequestered from the main currents of German life, aloof from politics and untouched by the ferment of industrial expansion and prosperity in the Reich. In many ways they were as withdrawn and dedicated as members of a religious order. Like a religious order, too, they managed to combine the opposing principles of autocracy and democracy, exacting the best from both systems. They regarded rank less highly than in-telligence; they debated military problems freely and often heat-edly until the moment of decision; and although a junior was expected to carry out any positive order scrupulously, he was expected as well to advise honestly and without subservience. This was why it was possible for Ludendorff to be one of the most important staff officers in Germany.

He spent long hours in his office, and every afternoon after he went home, an orderly with a bulging brief-case appeared sharp at five o'clock to deliver the work to be done that evening. His wife, Margarethe, looked on this as a necessary evil, but her husband always awaited the brief-case impatiently.[18]

Ludendorff had married suddenly at the age of 44, and, al-though the marriage was successful, with real affection on both sides, it had done nothing to help his career. Instead of choos-ing the aristocratic daughter of some Prussian Junker, he had, for once in his life, yielded to a romantic impulse. Coming home from the Red House one rainy evening, he had seen a lady sheltering in a doorway, had instantly been attracted to her and had persuaded her to share his umbrella. He had seen her home through the rain and not long afterwards, in August of 1909, had married her. Before this was possible, however, Frau Mar-garethe Pernet had to divorce her first husband, a businessman whom she had married on leaving school. The snobbish and strait-laced raised their eyebrows, but this background was not the handicap it would have been a few decades earlier. Nearly half the General Staff now came from the middle classes,[19] and, although the social code of the officer corps was strict — the Kaiser, for instance, forbade his officers to dance the tango in uniform — divorce no longer brought ostracism in Lutheran North Germany. In any case, many staff officers felt that on Der Tag it would be important to have the self-confident, ener-getic Ludendorff standing at Moltke's elbow.

Nevertheless, in spite of his spiritualism and self-doubt, Moltke had done far more than Schlieffen to increase the size of the German Army. Much of this had been due to Luden-dorff's influence in the background, but Ludendorff was still deeply dissatisfied with what had been accomplished. The train-ing estimates for 1912 revealed that 540,000 able-bodied Ger-mans who were eligible for military service would not be called to the colors because of lack of money and training facilities. And yet Schlieffen had plainly set out in his Plan that for the final battle in France everything depended on an overwhelm-ingly superior right wing. "Only when 25 army corps* have been made available left of the Moselle for this battle, for which one cannot be too strong, can one await the result with a calm conscience," he had written.[20] Therefore at the time of the Aga-dir Crisis Ludendorff pressed strongly for the creation of addi-tional army corps. He wanted three more corps authorized im-mediately and another three to be raised in 1913 and 1914.

Moltke showed little enthusiasm for the political in-fighting this would entail. The strong Social Democrat Party in the Reich-stag would oppose any increase and the cost of the program would make it unpalatable to other parties as well. Moreover, a matter such as this, which was concerned primarily with finance, was really more the business of the War Ministry than of the Chief of the General Staff. And the War Minister, General von Heeringen, disapproved of the increases Ludendorff wanted. In fact, one of Heeringen's subordinates, General Wandel, Director of the General War Department, argued strongly against a rapid enlargement of the Army, claiming it would disrupt organiza-tion and lower training standards. Ludendorff brushed such talk aside, for he felt — possibly rightly — that these arguments were mere excuses and that the War Ministry's real concern was to avoid unpleasantness.

The Agadir Crisis passed slowly; the British Navy maintained its state of alert until nearly the end of September; and no agree-

---

* A German army corps was composed of two infantry divisions, each with an independant cavalry regiment and two infantry brigades (each of two regi-ments of three battalions). Divisional artillery consisted of 54 field guns and 18 howitzers.

ment was reached between France and Germany until November. Even then European tensions were not greatly relieved. A final reckoning was only postponed.

In the autumn of 1911 Italy launched a war against Turkey in Tripolitania, and not long afterwards the Italian General Staff informed Moltke that, because a strong expeditionary force had to be retained in North Africa, Italian troops could not be sent to Germany under the terms of the Triple Alliance. Moltke still believed that, when the time came, Italy would honor her commitments and "come to the rendezvous," but the deletion of Italian formations from the initial German order-of-battle was serious. He commented: "This means that Germany loses five army corps and two cavalry divisions against the French." It also meant that Ludendorff increased his efforts to raise new formations.

The debate between the War Ministry and the General Staff continued for months with increasing bitterness. Von Heeringen and Wandel rightly guessed that their real opponent was Colonel Ludendorff, not Colonel General von Moltke, and they resented this. They resented, too, Ludendorff's uncompromising attitude and acrimonious tone. Ludendorff put all his immense energy into the fight, for he felt that only his efforts could provide Germany with the extra troops. Day after day he returned home exhausted from stormy meetings. One afternoon he sank into an armchair in his living room and said to his wife: "I have to make Moltke stand his ground by gripping him like a vice, otherwise I think his weakness would bring him to utter ruin." [21]

The outcome of Schlieffen's great battle would be a matter of life or death for Germany. The entire future of the nation would be at stake. Yet never for a moment did either Ludendorff or his chief, von Moltke, seek a non-military solution to their dilemma. Like Schlieffen, Ludendorff did his best with the materials at hand but never viewed the military problem in any wider context. Ludendorff, indeed, went further than Schlieffen had ever done to obtain the military resources he considered necessary, but in Wilhelm's Germany it was inconceivable that the Army chiefs should bluntly tell either the Kaiser or the Chancellor that a two-front war had to be avoided at all costs and that the diplomats must therefore ensure it never occurred.

Since Ludendorff came from a bourgeois background, he cared less for the taboos of the officer class than an aristocrat might have done. When he found he was not carrying his point with the War Ministry and was unlikely to get the additional corps by working through the regular channels, he did something von Schlieffen would never have considered doing — he sought political allies. He approached General Keim, a retired officer who was a supporter of Heinrich Class, the president of the nationalist Pan-German League. Herr Class at once began agitating for the additional corps, much to the annoyance of the War Ministry. Heeringen and Wandel suspected that Ludendorff was behind the political agitation and were incensed that a staff officer should so far have forgotten the traditions of the service.

General Wandel reproached Ludendorff angrily for his intransigence, telling him that if he got all the troops he was demanding he would "drive Germany to revolution." Wandel was wrong in this. At that time it would have taken more than a rigorous application of conscription to have brought Germany to revolution. But the comment did show a remarkable insight into Ludendorff's personality and its ultimate consequences.

In 1912, while the argument over the army increase was still going on, the international situation deteriorated further when Serbia, Bulgaria, Greece and Montenegro suddenly attacked Turkey and quickly defeated her. A general war almost occurred when the Serbs claimed Northern Albania; both Austria and Russia ordered partial mobilization; and only the combined efforts of Germany, France and Britain saved the peace. Albania became an independent state; and Serbia, left without her share of the spoils, went to war with Bulgaria over the division of Macedonia. Serbia was joined by Greece and Roumania, and Bulgaria was defeated.

The principal result of the Balkan Wars was that Serbia almost doubled her population and territory. The Serbian South-Slav extremists, led by a secret terrorist society known as the *Ujedinjenje ili Smrt* (Union or Death), or Black Hand, now looked forward confidently to the liberation of Bosnia and Herzegovina. This could hardly be achieved without a general European war, for it would presage the disintegration of the Austro-Hungarian Empire. Foreseeing the danger, the Austrian Chief of Staff, Conrad von Hötzendorff, urged a preventive war against Serbia. Peace was kept only because the German Kaiser flatly refused to support Austria in such a venture.

But it was a very precarious peace. Now there were war parties in France, Russia, Serbia, and Austria. Russia pressed on with the modernization of her army; Britain continued to build Dreadnoughts; France lengthened her term of conscript service from two years to three; and the German General Staff, with Ludendorff as its spokesman, continued to demand more army corps.

After prolonged debate in the Reichstag, two additional corps were finally authorized in April 1913, which meant that the peacetime strength of the German Army was fixed at 870,000 men, but a third corps was disallowed, and the Government postponed the raising of any further troops until 1916–1921.

There was another, almost unnoticed result of the behind-the-scenes struggle between the General Staff and the War Ministry. In January 1913, Ludendorff was abruptly posted away from the Red House and relegated to regimental duty at Düsseldorf. This meant that he would not now act as Moltke's Chief of Operations when war broke out. The consequences of this may well have been fateful for Germany.

The Ludendorffs said their good-byes in Berlin soon after the New Year. It was cold and dark in the capital; raw north winds drove snow and sleet in from the Baltic; the street lights were turned on by four o'clock each afternoon; the trees rattled their bare branches along the wide sweep of Unter den Linden; and snowflakes whirled and eddied around the Victory Column and the massive base of the Brandenburger Tor. Their friends told the Ludendorffs how much pleasanter it would be on the Rhine.

Nevertheless, the posting to Düsseldorf was a sort of exile. For nine years Ludendorff had immersed himself in his work at the Red House. He had planned the concentration of the seven great armies Germany would deploy in the West, the timings of the troop trains that would run to the frontier, the march-tables of corps and divisions, the crossings of the Meuse, the Somme and the Seine. It had been work suited to his talents and had promised a brilliant future. Also he had cherished his status as a General Staff officer, who wore the coveted crimson trouser stripes and moved among the great.

At first he could not conceal his disappointment, at least from his wife. Secretly he had hoped to be given a Brandenburger regiment, which would not have been too painful a social demotion, but when the posting order came he was appointed to command the 39th Lower Rhenish Fusiliers. He must have irritated the War Ministry more seriously than he had thought. It was unjust, too, that he should be punished for doing his duty. What was especially annoying was that many of those who had opposed him over the army estimates were rewarded with orders and decorations. General Wandel, who had professed to think that Germany could be driven to revolution by the raising of a few more soldiers, had actually been promoted to the nobility and given a "von" to put in front of his name.

After his first sense of outrage, Ludendorff put a good face on it. At least he could show he possessed the military virtue of obedience.

"The soldier has no personal ends to pursue," he declared to his wife. "He goes where he is sent. That's enough about it."

When Margarethe was packing for their journey to Düsseldorf she came across two helmet plumes, a black one her husband had worn when he had been in the Grenadier Guards and a white one he had worn with the General Staff.

"And which plume will you be wearing with your new regiment, dear?" Margarethe asked him.

Ludendorff looked at her in affectionate exasperation. "My

child, you must be quite mad," he said. "How long have the line regiments worn a plume?" [22]

Margarethe, for her part, would miss the tattoos before the Royal Palace, the Guards Cavalry parades at Potsdam when every trooper was magnificent in the silver and gold of his dress uniform, the receptions Berlin gave to foreign royalty, the Opera Ball each winter when princes and royal dukes, ministers, diplomats, high officials and army officers sat in the boxes or danced the Lancers before the Emperor and Empress. She would miss, too, her own circle of friends, most of them the aristocratic wives of General Staff officers. [23]

Before Ludendorff left Berlin he heard that Count von Schlieffen had passed peacefully away in his 80th year. The Field Marshal had spent a pleasant Christmas with his two daughters, his son-in-law, and his small granddaughter, Anna Josepha. There was a Christmas tree decked with candles and glass ornaments, and the front door and windows were decorated with wreaths of evergreen. Schlieffen played with his little granddaughter and joined in the family prayers and Bible reading on Christmas Eve. But the holy day was no sooner over than he went quietly off to his own room to compose a final memorandum on the subject of his Plan. Perhaps he felt the chill of approaching death settling upon him and wished to complete his military testament before the end. [24]

The old man's mind had been as keen as ever. Neither his advanced age nor the nearness of death, any more than the spirit of Christmas, caused him to modify his views. His wrinkled white hand moved slowly across the paper as he advocated for the last time the invasion of a small neutral country whose only offense was that it provided the easiest pathway into France. Indeed, the only new suggestion in Schlieffen's memorandum of the 28th of December 1912, was that if Belgium were threatened with terror she would more readily grant the German armies free passage through her territory.

". . . It will," von Schlieffen wrote, "be advisable to confront the Belgian Government with the choice of a bombardment of its fortified towns, particularly Liège, as well as a considerable levy — or of handing over all fortresses, railways, and troops. But to turn the threatened bombardment into reality if necessary, the heavy artillery must be suitably equipped. The latter will also prove necessary in the further course of the campaign. To begin with, the great industrial town of Lille offers an excellent target for bombardment . . ." [25]

The very evening he finished this memorandum Schlieffen was stricken with his final illness. For a week he lay near death, fortified no doubt by the consciousness of an upright life. Just before he died on the 4th of January 1913, he is said to have opened his eyes and spoken very distinctly:

"It must come to a fight. Only make the right wing strong."

In Düsseldorf, among his 39th Rhenish Fusiliers, Ludendorff had exactly the same conviction, but now he could do no more about it than the dead Field Marshal.

Margarethe, rather to her surprise, found Düsseldorf enchanting, with its magnificent public gardens laid out along the river, its excellent theaters and concert halls. Because it was inhabited by Rhinelanders rather than Prussians, its atmosphere was easier and more friendly than that of Berlin. Within a few days of their arrival the Ludendorffs found a large roomy house with a spacious garden near the Royal Park and the Rhine bridge. Although Ludendorff tended to restrict his acquaintances to the officers of the garrison, Margarethe's beauty and gaiety soon drew Düsseldorf's foremost artists, professors and industrialists to her drawing room. She said later that the months in Düsseldorf were the happiest of her life and she came to look back on that time in 1913 as the end of a gracious epoch which would never come again. Within little more than a year, most of the young officers who were always in and out of her house had been killed and her own life had been permanently marked with sorrow and anxiety.[26]

Her husband devoted himself conscientiously to his regimental duties, but his thoughts kept turning back to the General Staff, the Red House on the Königsplatz and the great map sheets there which showed in the minutest detail the roads, railways, and bridges of Belgium and Northern France. However, he kept these thoughts to himself. Once when a friend asked him if he would not rather be in Berlin, he fixed his monocle in his eye and replied: "I'm nearer the enemy where I am." He was silent and glowering at breakfast rather more frequently, but even he, with all his sense of urgency, had no idea how close the moment of trial really was. Meanwhile, the long summer slowly faded, the grapes ripened in the vineyards along the Rhine valley, the hillsides turned a darker brown, the golden days drew in, and the old world, happy and unheeding, spent its last autumn of peace.

CHAPTER II

. . . AND HAPPY SUMMER DAYS

W HILE THE TRAIN was still miles away, Margarethe Ludendorff saw the spire of Strasbourg Cathedral tall in the April sunlight and knew at that moment she would like the place. Her husband had just been promoted to major general and given command of the 85th Infantry Brigade, which was stationed in the ancient Alsatian city. Normally, promotions were gazetted early in the New Year, but in 1914, for some reason, Ludendorff's promotion had been delayed until the spring. Perhaps it was another evidence of the displeasure of the War Ministry. At all events, one result of the delay was that the new brigade commander could not find a suitable house to live in; he had to make do with a large flat that had no balcony, bow window or garden.

The absence of a garden was not too important, for, as Margarethe said, all Alsace was a garden at this time of year. She was enchanted by Strasbourg's narrow twisting streets, its gabled houses covered with purple clematis and rambler roses, and its palatial French-style buildings standing proudly along the Place Broglie. As dusk closed in she loved to watch the peasants' carts, piled high with vegetables and fruit for the Strasbourg market, lumber into the city from the neighboring town of Rupprechtsau, looking as though they belonged in some old painting of another century. Every so often a hay wagon would go by in a cloud of fragrance with its driver perched high on top of his swaying load.[1]

Ludendorff had little time to appreciate the beauty of Alsace, although he was glad his wife had a feeling for that sort of thing. He concentrated on the work before him, feeling that that was enough for any soldier. The 85th Brigade had one Prussian and one Saxon regiment, but Ludendorff found he had little contact with the officers or troops under his command. In the German system the brigade was an administrative rather than a tactical echelon and as brigade commander he was at once plunged into problems of organization and supply.[2] He was not unhappy with these tasks, for they were staff problems, although of a very different kind from the ones he had resolved in the Red House.

In May, along with several other senior officers, he took part in a staff ride from Freiburg-im-Breisgau to Cologne. They were accompanied by a fair slender young man with a vacuous face and a general's uniform. Everyone was most respectful to this officer, clicked their heels in front of him, called him "Hoheit" punctiliously, laughed at his jokes and listened even to his military opinions. This was because he was Frederick Wilhelm, Crown Prince of the German Empire and the Kaiser's eldest son.

If the Crown Prince's presence did not contribute substantially to the military lessons learned, the staff ride was a success for all that. Such exercises always were a success, for they were conducted with the intelligent hard-headed diligence that distinguished the German from all other peacetime armies. In Germany no one, except royal visitors, played at the business of soldiering.

In June two of Ludendorff's stepsons, Franz and Erich Pernet, returned home on leave from their cadet school at Lichterfelde. The other stepson, Heinz, an ensign in the 31st Infantry Regiment, remained with his unit at Altona, and the stepdaughter, Margot, was visiting relatives in Berlin. While Ludendorff was engrossed in military affairs, Margarethe, Franz, and Erich explored the lovely countryside of the Vosges, visited Molsheim, Schirmeck and Schlettstadt and climbed the mountains at Donon and Hohkönigsburg. Once they went to Zabern where riots had broken out the previous November between the Alsatian townspeople and German troops. The soldiers, under Lieutenant Graf von Förstner, had behaved in such an arrogant, brutal manner that even the Reichstag had been scandalized. An official court of inquiry had exonerated the garrison, but the more perceptive Germans had realized with a shock that, even after forty years, the "Reichsland" of Alsace-Lorraine had not changed its old allegiance. Nevertheless, in 1914 Zabern seemed to Margarethe and her boys only a quiet sleepy place, basking under the summer sun.

✠

At Kiel on the Baltic, Sunday, the 28th of June, was a lovely sunny day. A fresh wind hurried a few puffs of white cloud across a bright blue sky and filled the sails of the Kaiser's yacht, *Meteor,* driving her along splendidly over the sparkling sea. Wilhelm felt at his jovial best, for it was Regatta Week at Kiel and he hoped the *Meteor* would win his own prize for the fastest sailing ship. He also had another and better reason for his high spirits. For the first time in years a British naval squadron was paying a courtesy visit to a German port. British and German sailors drank together in the pleasant beergardens of Kiel and walked arm in arm through the town. Banquets were held in the wardrooms of both fleets; and if the officers watched each other closely and listened intently whenever the conversation took a technical turn, both sides were impressed. Some real friendships were formed, and when a German naval aviator was killed while flying a British airplane, officers and ratings of both navies stood bareheaded together at the open grave.

The Kaiser hoped this visit would be the beginning of a better understanding between the two nations. Perhaps the British were at last accepting the fact that Germany was a power on the sea as well as on land. That would be wonderful. Wilhelm saw himself being treated with new respect on his next visit to his mother's family at Windsor. In his mind's eye he pictured a series of splendid naval reviews in which the High Seas Fleet definitely outshone the Royal Navy.

The telegram was brought out to the *Meteor* shortly after two o'clock. The motor launch which carried it came up in a swirl of spray, throttling back as it pulled alongside, while the naval officer on the loud-speaker announced that he had a priority message for His Majesty. The telegram was passed to the *Meteor,* and a few minutes later the yacht put about and headed back for Kiel harbor.

At eleven o'clock that morning the Heir Apparent to the Austrian throne, the Archduke Franz Ferdinand, and his wife, the Duchess Sophia of Hohenburg, had been shot and killed in the Bosnian town of Sarajevo. The assassin and some of his accomplices had been caught, and the Austrian police were investigating. The actual murderer was said to be a young Bosnian Serb by the name of Gabriel Princip.

When the Kaiser came ashore from his yacht he looked pale and haggard. That evening he cancelled the regatta and left Kiel, and the British squadron, after listening to the wireless messages that crackled out in code from the Admiralty in London, raised anchor and sailed for home. The next day the shopkeepers of Kiel took down the Union Jacks and lowered to half-mast the black, white and red imperial flags which had decorated their storefronts. The brief period of fraternization was over.

Wilhelm was genuinely distressed at the deaths of Franz Ferdinand and Sophia. He had always liked them both. Only a few weeks before he had visited them at Konopischt, walked with the Archduke among the famous rose gardens and talked hopefully with him about the future of their countries. As well as being the heir to the Austrian throne, Franz Ferdinand had been a personal friend. Moreover, he had always been touchingly grateful for the small courtesies Wilhelm had punctiliously paid the Duchess.

Now Franz Ferdinand was dead, and Sophia was dead beside him, both lying under sheets in the Sarajevo Town Hall while arrangements were being made to transport the bodies back to Vienna.

The Kaiser was outraged, too, that royal blood had been shed — and by the Serbians, who only eleven years before in the Konak in Belgrade had hacked their king and queen to pieces with sabers and thrown their mutilated bodies from a second-story window. Wilhelm very rightly suspected that the same men who had murdered King Alexander and Queen Draga in 1903 were responsible for this later assassination. No one could blame Austria if she determined to teach Serbia a lesson.

In Vienna, Colonel General Conrad von Hötzendorff was already pressing for war. The son of a colonel of hussars, Conrad was a fiery old man who had spent most of his life serving his Emperor. With all the fervor of his passionate nature he loved the moribund disintegrating Empire and the older, more gracious world for which it stood. He dreamed of saving both from the enemies he saw gathering like vultures beyond the frontiers. For years he had been a voice crying in the wilderness but now at last there were people in Vienna ready to listen to him. And the most important of these was Count Leopold Berchtold, the vain and irresponsible Austrian Foreign Minister.

✠

The news of the Sarajevo murders made little impression in Germany. It was, of course, a terrible thing, but the Archduke was little known outside his own country. Ludendorff and Margarethe remembered vaguely that he was a friend of the Kaiser's and were reminded that his marriage to the Czeck countess, Sophia Chotek, had been a love match, bitterly opposed by his uncle, the old Emperor Franz Joseph. One detail of the assassination was certainly touching. Just before he died, the mortally wounded Archduke, shot through the neck from three yards range and aware only that his wife too had been hit, gasped out: "Sophia, live for the sake of our children!"

As they read these details in Monday's newspapers, people shook their heads at the wickedness there was in the world.

But Margarethe and her boys had not the slightest presentiment of personal tragedy. The holiday season was just beginning. Families were packing to go to the seaside; university students were setting out in leather shorts and hobnailed boots to climb mountains; sailboats were skimming along the Rhine and the Baltic coast; beaches were crowded with bathers; and the Black Forest was being invaded by throngs of happy hikers. It was a time for relaxation, for flirtations, for enjoying the goodness of life. Few Germans thought for a moment that the murder in Sarajevo could possibly touch their own lives. There had been so much talk of war and so many crises that the frightful had ceased to frighten. In any case, Bosnia was far away, and had not Bismarck once said that the Balkans were "not worth the bones of a single Pomeranian grenadier"?

Many observers who lived through June and July 1914 and later looked back across the gulf of the war have claimed that there was something different about that summer, especially after the murder of the Archduke. "The light had grown more livid," was the way Theodor Wolff, the editor of the *Berliner Tageblatt*, put it,[3] and Winston Churchill said that "there was a strange temper in the air." [4]

If this was so, it was certainly not evident in Strasbourg. Military bands, playing in the evenings in the municipal gardens and on the lawns of the barracks, blared out *Heil Kaiser Dir* and *Was blasen die Trompeten?*, but no one felt there was anything particularly sinister in such tunes resounding through the city where the *Marseillaise* had been composed.

Margarethe, Franz, and Erich left for Lucerne in Switzerland, while Ludendorff went on a "supply ride" which was held along the Rhine to test the administrative system of an army. The location of ammunition dumps, the supply of rations, the evacuation of the wounded, the requirements for forage and billeting, the provision of reinforcements and the capacity of railroads all

had to be calculated. After the supply ride there would be the
annual maneuvers, when the troops as well as the staff would
be exercised. The maneuvers would be held after the harvest
was in, when the soldiers could practice their trade among the
golden stubble fields. Regular officers of every grade were expected to conform their plans to these duties, and the commander of the Strasbourg garrison, General von Deimling, was a
dedicated soldier, who took no account of holiday seasons.

In Paris Madame Caillaux, the wife of a French cabinet minister and former premier, walked into the editorial offices of *Le
Figaro,* took out a pistol and killed Gaston Calmette, the editor,
because he had been printing details of her private life. The
murder was a godsend to the press during the slack summer season. Through the first three weeks of July, in Berlin as well as
Paris, Madame Caillaux's trial was far more prominent front-
page news than the international situation. At the Oval in London, Hobbs was piling up fantastic scores whenever he came to
bat, and what attention the British public gave to anything other
than cricket was centered on Ireland, where the Protestants of
Ulster were threatening to resist Home Rule by civil war. In Germany the Conservative candidate was unexpectedly defeated in
a by-election in Labiau-Wehlau, and the Kaiserin was presented
with an ornament made of gold and diamonds from the German
colonies. The sad-faced General von Moltke went off to Karls-
bad with his wife and daughter to take the waters, and the
Kaiser set out as planned in the royal yacht, *Hohenzollern,* for a
tour of the Norwegian fiords. The old Austrian Emperor was at
Ischl, and Conrad von Hötzendorff in the Tyrol.

Count Berchtold, unfortunately, remained at his desk in the
Ballplatz, busily preparing the diplomatic stroke with which he
would astound the world. His first move was to sound out German official opinion. The answer was entirely satisfactory, and
when Conrad was informed, his seamed, old soldier's face
creased up in a happy smile. The German Government agreed
that Serbia would have to be punished and promised Austria full

support. The Kaiser gave his opinion that "Russia will not enter the lists for Serbia, which has stained itself by an assassination"; Austria would soundly thrash Serbia in a brisk little war confined to the two of them; honor would be satisfied; and Germany would improve her international position and increase her prestige. Chancellor Bethmann-Hollweg shared these views.

While Ludendorff was in the field with his brigade on the annual maneuvers, he had little time to read the newspapers. However, like everyone else, he probably noticed that on the 14th of July unpleasant rumors began to circulate in Vienna. Some people said that Austria was preparing to attack Serbia, and some that civil war had broken out in Albania. A mild panic set in on the Vienna stock exchange and prices dropped on the Berlin bourse. Although the markets soon rallied, they remained nervous.

On the 23rd of July, almost a month after the Sarajevo murders, Austria finally delivered an ultimatum to Serbia. The terms had deliberately been made so severe as practically to preclude Serbian acceptance. One reason why Berchtold had moved so slowly in the matter — apart from a Viennese aversion to hurry — was that President Poincaré of France and his Foreign Minister, Viviani, were visiting St. Petersburg. The Austrian ultimatum was delayed until they put to sea on their return journey. Berchtold was smugly complacent about this trick. It was, he told himself, exactly the sort of thing that revealed true diplomatic finesse. Although Bethmann-Hollweg had not even asked to see the terms of Berchtold's ultimatum before it was delivered, the Wilhelmstrasse now reiterated its support of the Austrian stand.

The reaction to the Austrian ultimatum was sharp and immediate. Sazonov, the Russian Foreign Minister, said bluntly: "Russia cannot allow Austria to crush Serbia and become the predominant power in the Balkans, and secure of the support of France, she will face all the risks of war." Within a day or two the situation had become exceedingly ominous.

On the 26th the Kaiser at last cut short his Scandinavian cruise and returned to Berlin. He was met on the station platform by Bethmann-Hollweg. The Chancellor's big figure looked somehow crumpled and his anguish showed on his face. Wilhelm stepped over to meet him and asked: "Well, how did it happen?" Bethmann-Hollweg, very subdued, admitted that he had miscalculated and offered his resignation. The Kaiser refused it brusquely but added: *"Sie haben mir die Suppe eingebrockt."* [5]

While events were slipping out of control in Berlin, Margarethe and her two sons were blithely enjoying themselves in Switzerland. The Swiss newspapers, sensitive to the tourist trade, withheld much of the disturbing international news. Early one morning towards the end of July, Margarethe was called downstairs to the telephone. Ludendorff's voice came crackling over the wire from Strasbourg. He curtly informed his wife that the situation seemed menacing and that she and the boys should return to Germany at once by the shortest route.

As Margarethe, thoroughly alarmed, put down the receiver and attempted to hurry from the room, the landlady of the pension stopped her, taking her by the arm and begging her to say nothing to the other guests.

"If you do, the whole season will be ruined."

Margarethe shook her arm free. "Let me go! I must leave at once." She ran upstairs to pack, while the landlady stood in the hall below, wringing her hands and grieving over the revenue that would be lost to the pension.

Margarethe and the boys caught the next train out of Lucerne. At Basle they found a milling crowd of Germans who, like themselves, were hurrying back to the Fatherland. The train was packed and passengers and luggage jammed the corridors. Ludendorff was waiting for them at Strasbourg station with the news that the annual maneuvers had been cancelled and the troops returned to their garrisons. War appeared almost a certainty.

The boys were delighted.

"Hurrah! War! We shall soon get to the front."

Ludendorff smiled a trifle grimly at this enthusiasm, and that night, although she was tired from her journey, Margarethe lay tense and sleepless until morning. The next day Ludendorff sent Franz and Erich back to Lichterfelde so that they would be at their posts if war came. That same afternoon at two o'clock an official telegram arrived from Berlin. The message consisted of only two letters — "D.K.," standing for *"drohende Kriegs-gefahr"* ("imminent danger of war").

With general mobilization possibly only hours away, Ludendorff decided he could not leave his wife alone in Strasbourg when he proceeded to his war station at Aachen. The German General Staff had long ago guessed that the French would open hostilities by an attack on Alsace-Lorraine, and Strasbourg was near the border. Since Schlieffen's master plan, even as amended by Moltke, provided only relatively light defenses for the German left wing, it was possible that Strasbourg might soon be in French hands.

"You must leave before I do," Ludendorff told Margarethe, "so that I can know you are safe and be easy in my mind."

The trip to Berlin was Margarethe's first mild foretaste of what the war would bring. General Ludendorff's uniform and commanding air managed to secure her a seat, but more than this could not be done. The coaches were packed so tightly with Germans evacuating Alsace that many passengers fainted in the heat. Sharp at six the train began to move. While it pulled away, Margarethe stood by the carriage window looking mutely at her husband, who raised a gloved hand in farewell, then turned back to his duties.

When Margarethe reached Berlin she found that everyone seemed to share her own mood of apprehensive excitement. The streets were filled with people who wandered aimlessly up and down, hoping to catch the latest rumor or hear some official announcement. The tension had built up slowly. When Serbia had rejected the Austrian ultimatum, Conrad had mobilized eight corps along the Serbian border, but for the time being nothing else had been done. Vienna's military preparations, like its diplomacy, moved in waltz time and no Austrian troops had been ready to invade. The Austrian declaration of war had not been delivered in Belgrade until the 28th of July.

On the 29th, in St. Petersburg, the Tsar had been persuaded by his generals to sign two mobilization orders, one for partial mobilization against Austria and one for general mobilization, but Nicholas could not make up his mind which to issue. Late on the afternoon of the 29th the Russian Chief of the General Staff, General Yanushkevitch, felt that he had "a perfect right" to give the German military attaché his word of honor that general mobilization had not been decreed, although Yanushkevitch neglected to mention that he had already sent warning telegrams to the commanders of military districts, advising them that the 30th of July would be the first day of general mobilization.

The attempted deception failed. In the Red House on the Königsplatz, General Staff officers, working under Lieutenant Colonel Nicolai, the head of military intelligence, studied a large number of unconfirmed but converging reports from Russia. They were able to deduce that the Tsar either had declared, or was about to declare, general mobilization. At six o'clock on the evening of the 29th the German ambassador to St. Petersburg, Count von Pourtalès, delivered a note from Bethmann-Hollweg to Sazanov: "Further continuation of Russian mobilization measures will force us to mobilize and in that case a European war can scarcely be prevented." [6]

In truth, once the scarlet posters announcing general mobilization were pasted up in Russia, nothing could save the peace, for Germany, faced with enemies on two sides, felt that she could not afford to wait until the Russian steam-roller began to move. In the last fateful days of July the dead hand of Count von Schlieffen did more to guide German policy than did the Kaiser or Bethmann-Hollweg. Since the Schlieffen Plan called for the defeat of France while Russia was still assembling her armies, Russia could not be allowed to mobilize in peace. Conversely, if war was declared on Russia, France would have to be invaded. Or so at least General von Moltke believed. The Plan called for it. No alternative plan existed. And even if France declared herself willing to abandon her ally and allow Russia to face Germany alone, could she be counted on to resist the temptation of attacking her old enemy once the German armies were deeply committed in Russia?

On the 30th of July an erroneous report from Prince Lichnowsky, the German ambassador in London, made it appear that Britain would remain neutral and guarantee French neutrality. The Kaiser was delighted. "So we march only to the East," he exclaimed to Moltke. *Der traurige Julius,* looking gloomier than ever, declared this to be impossible — "The mobilization plans of an army of a million men cannot be improvised overnight." Wilhelm turned angrily away saying: "Your uncle would have given me a different answer."

None of it mattered in any case, for the report from London was false. France had no intention of standing aside and losing her only ally.

The afternoon of the 31st of July was bright and sunny but not uncomfortably hot. At three o'clock the people who thronged Unter den Linden saw the Kaiser and Kaiserin drive by in an open car on their way to the Palace. As usual, the Emperor's chauffeur sounded the musical motor-horn at intervals to clear the streets. The socialists used to say that the four notes of the horn stood for *"Das Volk bezahlt"* ("The people pay"), but if anyone still entertained such thoughts today he was careful not to express them. As the Kaiser went by, the crowds along the Linden were extraordinarily enthusiastic, cheering and waving their handkerchiefs, but Wilhelm, who usually responded readily to any display of popular affection, did not change his grave expression. He stared fixedly ahead, and the hand he touched to his helmet rose and fell automatically.

That evening the *Norddeutsche Allgemeine Zeitung* came out

on the streets of Berlin with an extra edition, announcing the German ultimatum to Russia. If all Russian mobilization measures did not cease within twelve hours, Germany would declare war.

Moltke and Ludendorff also shared with the dead von Schlieffen some of the responsibility for the terrible rush of events. The amended Schlieffen Plan called for the capture of Liège by a *coup de main* immediately on the outbreak of war. The Plan stipulated that, nearly three weeks before the armies of the powers were fully mobilized, the Liège forts had to be taken and the railways passing through the Liège Gap put in working order. Two entire German armies had to move by this route into France. This was an additional reason why mobilization meant war and why the time for negotiation was so drastically reduced.

As the summer evening drew in, 200,000 people gathered quietly before the Royal Palace. When the Kaiser appeared on a balcony, there was a great burst of cheering, followed by a deadly hush as the Berliners waited for his words.

"The sword is being pressed into our hand," Wilhelm declared. "And now I commend you to God. Go now to the churches, kneel before God, and pray to Him for help for our gallant army." [7]

None who heard him could doubt his sincerity and very few questioned his belief that war was being forced on Germany. As the crowd before the Palace dispersed, patriotic demonstrations broke out spontaneously throughout the city. Bands appeared and groups of young men marched singing through the streets behind the black, white, and red Imperial colors. The sound of strong young voices filled the twilight —

> *Lieb Vaterland kannst ruhig sein,*
> *Fest steht und treu die Wacht,*
> *Die Wacht am Rhein . . .*

The 1st of August was a Saturday and the fine weather continued into the weekend. In the afternoon Margarethe, her daughter Margot, and her brother-in-law, Gustav Jahn, walked in the Kurfürstendamm like thousands of other anxious Berliners. Today no one was going with picnic lunches to the Grunewald or to the forests about Potsdam. No one left the capital to sail along the Havel or on the Müggelsee.[8] Suddenly above the noise of the busy city came the sound of bells booming out from the Memorial Church of the Emperor Wilhelm. War had been declared on Russia.

That day the patriotic press was exultant. The Pan-German newspaper, *Alldeutsche Blätter,* declaimed: "This is the moment we have longed for." Similar comments appeared in French and Russian newspapers, and in England the young poet Rupert Brooke would soon write:

Now God be thanked Who has matched us with His hour.

Margarethe Ludendorff, the wife and mother of soldiers, received the news differently. As she listened to the church bells tolling out their message of war, big tears began to roll down her cheeks. Her brother-in-law comforted her. "You simply must not be so unhappy. A modern war is finished in four or five months at the most. No country could go on longer than that. You will soon have your dear ones with you again."

All across Germany the reservists at once began to report to their mobilization depots. They walked through the streets in civilian clothes, their faces grave or gay depending on their temperament and imagination. They were surrounded by wives, sweethearts, parents, and children who carried parting gifts in paper parcels — a cake to eat in the barracks, a bundle of books, some sausages or home-made jam. At the depots they exchanged their civilian clothes for field-gray, were issued with rifles, bayonets and ammunition, with large packs, two blankets and a mess-tin, and then they were formed up and marched to the railway stations. Crowds followed them on this journey too, pressing flowers on them which were pinned to tunics, stuck in

rifle barrels or fastened to spiked helmets. The march to the
station was more cheerful than the walk to the depot had been,
for it was organized. They were all in it together. As they
marched they sang, and the people who watched them go sang
too —

> *Gloria Victoria!*
> *Ja, mit Herz und Hand*
> *Fürs Vaterland. . . .*

At the railway stations the soldiers were quickly loaded into
troop trains, some of which were already chalk-marked on the
outside with slogans — *"Nach Paris," "Nach Petersburg."* The
reservists leaned out the windows and waved at their friends and
relations, as, punctual to the second, the long trains pulled away.

The mobilization plans, which Ludendorff had prepared with
so much detailed labor in the Red House on the Königsplatz,
worked without the slightest hitch. Battalion after battalion, division after division, corps after corps were formed up to full
strength, equipped with every last item needed, and entrained
for predetermined localities. The marvelous German railway
system, with four double lines running right across the country
from East to West and with every subsidiary line designed with
mobilization in mind, handled the troop movements smoothly
and efficiently. If there were military errors in the first weeks of
war, they were not in the technical staff work of the Second
Section.

Ludendorff left Strasbourg early on the morning of the 2nd
of August, after turning over the command of his brigade to
another officer. It was one thing for the War Ministry to have
punished Ludendorff by relegating him in peacetime to regimental duty, but the German Army had no intention of allowing his staff-trained talents to go to waste in time of war. He was
posted as Deputy Quartermaster General (Deputy Chief of
Staff) to General von Bülow's Second Army, one of the five
armies that were to form the wheeling German right wing.

Ludendorff was in no particular hurry to reach Army Headquarters at Aachen. For several days, while mobilization was
in progress, there would be little for him to do. All the necessary staff work had been completed long ago. Accordingly, he
set out from Strasbourg on horseback, sending his personal
equipment along by rail with his batman. At Cologne he was
able to see part of his mobilization plan in action. Every ten
minutes, with clockwork regularity, a fully loaded troop train
thundered across the Hohenzollern Bridge, bringing up the soldiers who would invade Belgium. Those troop trains ran with
the same unvarying precision, day and night, for the first four-
teen days of mobilization.

That evening when he reported in at Army Headquarters,
Ludendorff was given a temporary new assignment. Because he
had made the plan for the capture of Liège, he was told to join
General von Emmich, who was to command the six brigades to
be used for the *coup de main*. Ludendorff was perfectly content
with his task. He took up his quarters at the Union Hotel in
Aachen and awaited developments. He had no doubts as to
what these would be. "No one," he said, "believed in Belgian
neutrality." [9]

That night while Ludendorff sat in his hotel room waiting for
the signal to advance, King Albert of the Belgians and his Cabinet were meeting in the Royal Palace in Brussels to consider
the German ultimatum they had just received. The text of the
ultimatum had been drafted by von Moltke. For the past few
days the sad-faced Chief of the General Staff had moved as
though in a nightmare, implementing terrible decisions taken
long ago in times of peace. His demands to the Belgian Government were for free passage for German troops, the surrender of
the Belgian Army and the handing over of Belgian fortresses.
To justify these terms Moltke claimed that France was about
to invade Belgium, and to soften the harshness to which he
was committed he promised the restoration of Belgian sovereignty at the end of the war and an indemnity which would

cover all the costs of a German occupation. In his original draft, Moltke had wanted to bribe the Belgian Government by an offer of French territory, but the Wilhelmstrasse, belatedly displaying some political acumen, had deleted this shameful suggestion.

What remained, of course, was shameful enough. In his heart Moltke knew it and cringed at the thought. Perhaps it was this as much as anything that broke his spirit in the first few weeks of war.

King Albert did not cringe. Only once, for a few seconds, did he lose his composure. When he received a personal letter from the Kaiser, urging acceptance of the German terms and reminding him that he was a German prince, he indulged in a brief outburst of profanity, a rare thing with him, for he was a religious man. When he and his Cabinet met at nine o'clock in the evening, they found little to debate.[10] They were fully aware of the peril confronting them; they knew that Germany was desperately in earnest and that a rejection of the ultimatum would bring countless horrors upon their people; but they nevertheless replied bravely to the German note:

> . . . Belgium has always been faithful to her international obligations; she has accomplished her duties in a spirit of loyal impartiality . . . Were the Belgian Government to accept the propositions conveyed to it, it would be sacrificing the nation's honour and betraying its engagements to Europe . . .[11]

After rejecting the ultimatum, the Belgian Government sent a note to Britain, reminding that country of the commitment it shared jointly with France and Germany to maintain Belgian neutrality. And from the grave, Count von Schlieffen unified the British nation and its Empire in a wholehearted resolve.

General von Emmich arrived at the Union Hotel in Aachen on the morning of the 3rd of August. He and Ludendorff, who had not met before, eyed each other closely as they talked. Ludendorff's mission, which was typical of the German employment of senior staff officers, was vague but important. He had no command of troops and did not form part of Emmich's own staff, but was the personal representative of the Second Army commander, General von Bülow, to whom he would report directly. His report would be frank and comprehensive and might easily contain criticism of the local commander. It was certain to be listened to with respect and its recommendations would very probably be acted upon. In fact, Ludendorff was to act as a sort of military commissar, although this was politely disguised by the wording of his directive, which ordered him "to coordinate General von Emmich's plans with General von Bülow's probable dispositions." [12] For the time being Bülow would remain at Hanover, but when the situation developed, Second Army Headquarters would move forward to Montjoie in the concentration zone. Supreme Headquarters, under Moltke, was still in the Red House in Berlin but would move to Coblenz soon.

That afternoon, after the French Government had rejected an impossible ultimatum to abandon Russia and surrender the fortresses of Toul and Verdun as a pledge of good behavior, Bethmann-Hollweg declared war on France. That day too, as part of the deployment plan worked out by the Second Section, German forces invaded Luxembourg to seize the railways leading into Belgium.

At first light on the 4th of August the order for which Ludendorff had been waiting went into effect. In the gray dawn German cavalry patrols, the vanguard of the special force designated for the capture of Liège, pushed across the Belgian frontier and moved towards the fortress that was the key to all the German plans.

CHAPTER III

LIÈGE

THE GRASS and hedgerows still gleamed with dew when the Uhlans clattered down the cobbled roads that ran across the Belgian frontier near Aachen. The horsemen, from the 2nd and 4th Cavalry Divisions, under the command of General von der Marwitz, were conducting a reconnaissance in force for the troops who would attack Liège.

No one opposed the Uhlans as they rode into Belgium. The peasants working in the fields looked curiously at their queer square-topped helmets and long lances, but no Belgian soldier was to be seen. Later in the day a squadron rode into the little village of Battice. It was no more than a row of houses on each side of the road, with an inn, a shop, and a small white church whose spire showed above the tall green poplar trees. By now the sun was well up and the Uhlans were riding at ease, their lances slung and their tunics unhooked at the collar. They were relaxed and almost careless, for they believed that the Belgians would not fight.

Almost certainly the shots that cracked out in the stillness of the morning came from one of the houses. No one actually saw a muzzle-flash or could be sure which cottage harbored the riflemen, but there was no other cover. It took the Germans a moment to realize this, and by then three or four of them had tumbled from their saddles and were lying in the street. They may have been the first casualties of the war.

The Uhlans had little trouble in capturing Battice. They killed several Belgians in civilian clothes, and when they discovered no enemy soldiers, decided that they had been attacked by *franc-*

tireurs. They found it outrageous that men in uniform should be fired on by civilians, for they had been brought up on legends of the war of 1870 and hated *franc-tireurs* with a patriotic passion. They drove the inhabitants of Battice out of their homes and burned the village. A similar incident occurred that day at Warsage where the Germans shot six hostages. By nightfall the cavalry had closed to the Meuse at Visé and were engaged in a sharp little fight for the crossings of the river.

Early on the 4th of August, Ludendorff had ridden north to visit von der Marwitz's cavalry and see how the invasion was going. Near Visé, for the first time in his life, he came under fire, but he returned unharmed late in the afternoon to report that so far the Uhlans were meeting little resistance. With this the infantry were ordered forward.[1]

Allied aviators flying towards the German frontier at sunset that evening saw that all the roads converging on Liège from the east, south and north were crowded with troops. From the air it looked as though a horde of gray ants was pouring remorselessly into Belgium.

Von Emmich's six mixed brigades designated for the *coup de main* belonged mainly to the VIIth and Xth Corps of von Bülow's Second Army and consisted chiefly of Hanoverian and Westphalian battalions. Each brigade was strengthened by the attachment of a cavalry squadron, a field artillery battery and a Jäger battalion. Dusk was closing in when von Emmich's scouts, trudging along the side of the road with rifles at the ready, first made contact with Belgian patrols. The Belgians fired a few shots, then retired in the direction of Liège.

When Ludendorff had drawn up the plan of attack, he had possessed exact details of the fortifications. The Liège Gap was guarded by twelve forts grouped in an irregular circle at an average distance of about four miles from the city's outskirts. The forts were between 4000 and 7000 yards apart and had a garrison of rather more than 20,000 men to serve their 400 guns. Six forts were large pentagonal structures, sunk below the ground with only a low mound of earth appearing above the surface and with disappearing cupolas to house the six- and four-inch guns of the main armament. The other six forts were smaller and triangular in shape but almost as well equipped with artillery. All could withstand the fire of any guns of up to 210 mm. caliber. Ludendorff had not been dismayed by these facts, for once the Germans had determined to invade Belgium in case of war they had begun secretly to build huge siege howitzers of the unheard-of-caliber of 420 mm. (16.5 inches). The existence of these giant guns was the first technical surprise of a war that was to produce many innovations.

What Ludendorff had not been able to foresee was how valiantly the Belgians would fight or how much assistance Liège would get from the Belgian field army. That army was still in the process of reorganization when war broke out. Its six infantry divisions and one cavalry division had establishments totalling 150,000 men, but only 117,000 soldiers were actually available. Much equipment was obsolescent, especially in the infantry and artillery; there were not enough trained officers; and Belgium had not adopted a field uniform. When the church bells pealed out their message of alarm on the night of the 2nd of August, Belgian reservists flocked to the colors, each in his peacetime uniform. By modern standards the army thus assembled looked readier for light opera than for war. The infantry of the line wore blue and white; the *chasseurs à pied* were picturesquely dressed in green and yellow, with flowing capes and peaked caps; and the Civil Guard turned out in high round hats and red facings. On mobilization one of the Army's first tasks was to collect the dogs that hauled the tiny Flemish milk carts — they were needed to pull the *mitrailleuses*.

The Belgian constitution provided that on the outbreak of war the King became commander-in-chief. As it happened, Albert was a king out of legend, good, wise, simple, and courageous, a hero from the Song of Roland, and he intended to exercise his powers, not merely to function as a royal figurehead. However, the mobilization plan had been drawn up by the Chief of Staff, General le Chevalier de Selliers de Moranville. The General's name was reminiscent of the flags and battles of the age of chivalry, but the General himself was of a cautious disposition. His plan called for a concentration of the entire Belgian Army behind the line of the River Gette, so that it could retire into the fortress of Antwerp if it were defeated in the field. King Albert, a far shrewder soldier than his Chief of Staff, wanted the army to concentrate along the Meuse between Liège and Namur, resting its flanks on the two fortresses, so that it could delay the German advance until the French and British came to Belgium's aid. It was too late to change the mobilization plan, but the King did insist that one division and one brigade be sent to strengthen Liège and that another division be sent to Namur.[2]

The whole course of the war might have been different if King Albert's plan had been put into effect. This, at least, was the opinion of the commander of the German First Army, Colonel General Alexander von Kluck, who commented later:

> Events would have transpired very differently had the Belgian Army been successful in offering, or even intended to offer, a vigorous resistance to the advance of the First and Second Armies with its whole force, basing its operations on Liège, Huy, and Namur, and preventing the bursting open of the line of forts; a most serious loss of time would thus have been imposed on the German flank armies.[3]

As it was, only the 3rd Division and the 15th Infantry Brigade from the Belgian field army went to Liège. They reached the city on the 4th of August, bringing its total garrison up to about 40,000 men. To command the defenses of Liège, King Albert chose General Gérard Leman, a quiet reserved officer of 63, who had formerly been the commandant of the Belgian War College. In the short time at his disposal Leman positioned his infantry between the forts and ordered them to dig in. It was too late to do much more. Extensive wire entanglements could not be erected; minefields could not be laid; and only the most vital fields of fire could be cleared by demolitions. Belgium was to pay dearly for neglecting her defenses but if the price was needlessly high, at least it was paid gallantly. General Leman's written instructions from King Albert read: "I charge you to hold to the end with your division the position which you have been entrusted to defend." [4]

At eleven o'clock German time on the night of the 4th of August, Great Britain declared war on Germany.

Ludendorff spent that night at Emmich's headquarters in Hervé. For the first time he slept as an invader on foreign soil, comfortably billeted in the railway inn of the Belgian village. He might almost have been some stodgy commercial traveler, waylaid the night because of a missed train, except that his rest was broken once by the sound of small-arms fire farther down the village street. He woke briefly at the sound, concluded it was the work of *franc-tireurs* who would be suitably dealt with, and went back to sleep. In the morning after breakfast he went out to visit the troops.[5]

Early that same morning a German staff car carrying a white flag drove up to Liège. The Belgian outposts allowed it to proceed under escort to General Leman's headquarters in the Rue Sainte-Foi. There it stopped and a smartly dressed young officer got out. From his spiked *Pickelhaube* to his mirror-bright boots, Captain Brinckmann was immaculate; his field-gray uniform fitted beautifully and his sword hilt sparkled in the sun. Only two days before he had been military attaché in Brussels and was accustomed to being fastidious about his toilet, as befitted a German representative in a foreign capital. A week ago he had been received as a welcome guest into Belgian homes and had had many Belgian friends.

Captain Brinckmann was ushered in to General Leman. He clicked his heels, saluted and said what he had been sent to say: General von Emmich demanded the immediate surrender of Liège. The Belgian commander curtly refused. Brinckmann then threatened that, if the fortress was not handed over, the city would be destroyed by aerial bombardment. General Leman had the German envoy ushered out.

Within an hour of Brinckmann's departure, the German field artillery, deployed in the countryside east of Liège, opened fire. Von Emmich's guns began to drop high explosive shells on the forts on the right bank of the Meuse and to sweep the city's approaches with shrapnel. The Belgian forts replied but their fire did little damage since the German gun positions were well concealed. The artillery duel was militarily ineffective, although some Belgian civilians who were slow in seeking refuge in their cellars were killed or wounded.

In the late afternoon the German infantry, who had been halted while the artillery bombardment was laid down, were ordered to resume their advance. Ludendorff's plan called for a three-pronged attack, with two brigades, the 34th and 27th, moving down from Visé in the north, two brigades, the 14th and 11th, attacking in the center from the east, and two brigades, the 38th and 43rd, closing in from the south along the valley of the Ourthe River.[6]

As the infantry shook out for its attack, Ludendorff found that the men were nervous and that their officers had little faith in the operation. This was understandable, for his plan for the capture of Liège was an extraordinarily bold one. He had allotted only six brigade groups for the assault of one of the most strongly fortified positions in Europe. And now that the fortress garrison had been reinforced by a division and a brigade, the attackers were not, in fact, significantly stronger in numbers than the defenders.

Ludendorff watched the infantry with a calm detached eye as they pushed down the roads that led to Liège. Almost at once they came under the fire of General Leman's riflemen and machine-gunners deployed between the forts. At first the German columns presented wonderful targets. The defenders squinted down their rifle-barrels and fired again and again into the center of

the gray mass that filled their sights. They could hardly believe
that any of this was happening. The feel of the wooden stock
along the cheek, the kick of the butt against the shoulder, the
sharp cordite smell and the tiny wisps of smoke trickling out the
muzzle were all more like practice camp than war. But out there,
four hundred yards away, the Germans were dying in the August
sunlight, and in the intervening fields wounded cattle bellowed
and ran in crazy circles until they fell.

The guns of the forts also poured a deadly fire into the advancing troops. None of those young Hanoverians and Westphalians
had ever been under fire before, but they behaved with a gallantry
worthy of a better task. Singing their martial songs as though
contemptuous of the death that struck everywhere around them,
they pressed on until their columns withered away and their line
of march could be traced on the ground by scattered heaps of
writhing bodies. The fire from the Belgian rifle-pits was terrible,
and although the defenders also suffered loss, mostly from the
raking shrapnel of German field batteries, very little ground
changed hands. Nevertheless, the heroic attacks continued. As
soon as one column was shot to pieces another formed up to take
its place. As daylight faded and the Belgian riflemen had more
difficulty in taking aim, von Emmich's troops pressed in more
closely. At some spots on the blazing perimeter of Liège a few
Germans actually reached the Belgian trenches, and there were
bloody hand-to-hand encounters with bayonet and rifle-butt before the attackers were killed, captured, or driven back.

On this day the Germans burned Visé and the village of Argen-
teau. In other towns and villages German soldiers were busily
pasting up posters which had been printed days ago, before it was
known that the Belgians would resist. With horrible irony, the
posters proclaimed General von Emmich's message to the Belgian nation:

I feel the greatest regret that German troops find themselves obliged
to cross the frontier of Belgium. They act according to the dictates

of inevitable necessity, Belgian neutrality having already been violated by disguised French officers who crossed Belgian territory in
a motor car in order to penetrate into Germany . . . I give formal
guarantees to the Belgian population that it will not have to suffer
any of the horrors of war; that we will pay in gold for the food it
will be necessary to take in the country; that our soldiers will show
themselves the best friends of a people for whom we feel the highest
esteem and the greatest sympathy . . .[7]

The sun went down at last, sinking into a fiery August sky,
and the night closed in, cool and cloudless. A bright moon
climbed above Liège, and by its light the Germans came on
again. From the forts searchlights stabbed out, cutting the darkness with probing beams until an advancing column was picked
out and thrown into relief. Then the rifles and machine-guns,
still hot from the execution they had done during the day,
crackled out again. The Germans could see only the spitting
line of muzzle-flashes in the darkness ahead. For many, those
little flickering lights, like a thousand fire-flies, were the last
thing they saw on earth. In some places the German dead were
piled three feet high, but their comrades clambered over them
to press the attack.

A Belgian officer who witnessed this night assault from one
of the eastern forts later wrote: "They made no attempt at de-
ploying but came on . . . until, as we shot them down, the
fallen were heaped on top of each other in an awful barricade
of dead and wounded that threatened to mask our guns and
cause us trouble. So high did the barricade become that we did
not know whether to fire through it or to go out and clear open-
ings with our hands . . . But would you believe it? — this ver-
itable wall of dead and dying enabled those wonderful Germans
to creep closer, and actually to charge up the glacis." [8] On the
glacis they were cut down by small-arms fire from the fort's
parapet.

At midnight von Emmich and Ludendorff rode from Hervé
to Micheroux, a village a little more than a mile to the northeast

of Fort Fléron. On arrival, they found the troops of Major General von Wussow's 14th Brigade falling in along the dark main street. The soldiers were making far too much noise and there was a good deal of confusion. Ludendorff expected the guns of Fort Fléron to sweep the roadway at any moment, but they remained unaccountably silent, even when someone in a house on the south side of the street fired a rifle at the Germans and thereby touched off a great burst of answering fire from the nervous troops.

At one o'clock the attackers were at last ready to move off. They were supposed to go north of Fort Fléron through the village of Retinne, and then west to the heights of La Chartreuse on the outskirts of Liège. The Germans trudged away into the night by companies, each sub-unit taking with it the new mobile field-kitchens that had been issued for the first time at the mobilization depots. General von Emmich and his staff brought up the rear of the column.

The brigade had not been moving very long when it came to a sudden halt. When Ludendorff pushed his way to the head of the column to find out what was the trouble, he discovered that the only reason for the halt was a misunderstanding of orders. He got the troops in motion again, leading them in person. While going through Retinne in the darkness he took the wrong road and immediately came under heavy fire. Men began to fall on all sides of him and two or three attempts to rush the invisible Belgian line failed with heavy loss. "I shall never forget hearing the thud of bullets striking human bodies," Ludendorff later wrote.[9] He made up his mind to retreat, although he was uncomfortably certain that the men would think he was afraid. It would have gone better for the Germans that night if more officers had made the same decision.

In Retinne Ludendorff reassembled what men he had left and found the right road to La Chartreuse. At the crossroads in the village General von Wussow's orderly was waiting, holding two of the General's horses by their bridles. When the orderly

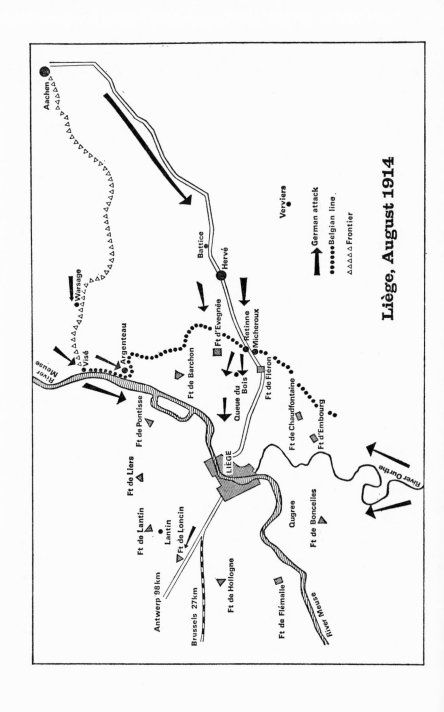

Liège, August 1914

→ German attack
••••• Belgian line
△△△△ Frontier

reported that von Wussow had been killed, Ludendorff decided to assume command of the brigade himself.

On the outskirts of the village of Queue-du-Bois, Ludendorff's group came under machine-gun fire but the stream of bullets was high and passed harmlessly over their heads. A little farther along the road, they discovered a grisly heap of dead and wounded Germans who had been von Wussow's advance party. The immaculate Captain Brinckmann, who like Ludendorff had decided to take part in the fighting, crept forward with a handful of men through the hedges and farmyards flanking the road and captured the Belgian machine-gun post.[10]

While Ludendorff was inching his way towards Liège with the 14th Brigade, another group of Germans was actually penetrating the Belgian defenses. In the pre-dawn blackness of the 6th of August a raiding party of about forty men crept through a gap in the Belgian lines and entered the city. They made their way silently through the dark streets to the house in the Rue Sainte-Foi where General Leman had his headquarters. The door was barred, but when the Germans pounded on it, a staff officer, Colonel Marchand, opened it and looked out. Half a dozen shots struck him and he fell dead on the threshold. At the sound of the firing, the Belgian headquarters defense platoon rushed up and General Leman and his staff came running down the stairs of the house with their service revolvers in their hands to join the fray. Within minutes it was all over. Some twenty raiders lay dead or wounded in the street and the remainder fled into the darkness.

Morning found the Belgian lines everywhere holding firm. An hour or two after daylight Captain Brinckmann's threat of the day before was carried out. The inhabitants of Liège looked up to see a long silvery shape floating above their ancient city. It was the army Zeppelin *L-Z* which had been sent from Cologne at dawn to drop its load of thirteen small bombs.[11] The bombs killed nine Belgian civilians, the first of countless thousands who were to die by this new form of warfare.

Everywhere the Belgians were fighting back desperately, but they lacked the German training and discipline. Often Belgian troops were caught in the open and slaughtered by the well directed German field guns. Along one stretch of winding road that ran uphill between the hamlets of Sart-Tilman and Bressoux, Belgian bodies lined both sides of the pavé, so close together as to be almost touching. A Belgian gunner officer who drove up that road with his battery later remembered the terrible impression those staring dead men made on the troops: "A little chasseur, quite a child, not yet twenty, was among them, almost kneeling on the bank, with his head hanging down, so that he looked as if he was sobbing. Opposite him lay a man of the reserve class, with gray hair and clutching hands. All along it was the same spectacle. Bodies, still more bodies. On their backs, their arms crossed, mouths open, eyes closed, their skulls smashed, their hands bleeding. I remember one man who had put his elbows on the edge of the ditch to die and whose fixed eyes watched us curiously as we passed." [12]

Most Belgian soldiers had had nothing to eat for the past thirty-six hours except the coffee and crusts of bread pressed into their hands by weeping women in the shattered villages. Civilians would run alongside marching columns of Belgian troops, giving them the news — what villages had fallen to the invader, where the Germans were, how the fight was going. Priests worked in shell-swept fields and streets, their black cassocks tucked up above their knees while they tended the wounded and carried stretchers. The Hanoverians and Westphalians of von Emmich's force took exception to these ministrations and shot a number of priests in cold blood on this day.

At least some German senior officers disapproved of such brutalities. Major General Karl von Bülow, the brother of the ex-chancellor, gave orders to his cavalry division that no priest in soutane should be summarily executed but should be sent to Aachen for trial.[13] Others, however, took the view that war was necessarily a cruel business. Von Moltke wrote to his Austrian

counterpart, Conrad: "Our advance in Belgium is certainly
brutal, but we are fighting for our lives and all who get in the way
must take the consequences." [14] Ludendorff blamed it all on the
fact that some Belgian civilians had "broken the rules of war"
by firing on the invading Germans. It was true, he admitted,
that innocent people might have had to suffer, but "the Belgian
Government can alone be held responsible. For my part, I
had taken the field with chivalrous and humane conceptions of
warfare. This *franc-tireur* warfare was bound to disgust any soldier. My soldierly spirit suffered bitter disillusion." [15]

By the afternoon of the 6th of August, the Belgian countryside about Liège, which only forty-eight hours before had been
tranquil with eighty years of unbroken peace, was a scene of horror and ruin. The smoke of burning villages and farmhouses pil-
lared up into the hot August sky; white puffs of high explosive
shell and black bursts of shrapnel dotted every horizon; and everywhere — in village streets, in farmyards, along pleasant country
lanes — dead bodies of soldiers and civilians lay where they had
fallen, for no one had had time to bury the dead.

In the midst of all this General Leman's soldiers fought on as
best they could. They were filled with a terrible helpless anger
and with almost unbearable grief. The thing that had happened
to them was so sudden, unexpected, and inexpressibly frightful
that their minds had not yet adjusted to it. But already, after
less than two days of fighting, it was quite apparent that Field
Marshal von Schlieffen had been wrong in at least one of his calculations. Terror, fire, horror, and murder were not forcing the
Belgians to capitulate.

During the first day's fighting a number of German prisoners
had been captured. Eight hundred of these were sent back to
Brussels where the excited population hailed their arrival as
proof of victory. The most wildly exaggerated accounts of the
fighting at Liège appeared in British, French, and Belgian newspapers. Most amateur military critics (and many professional
ones) claimed that the German Army's reputation had been

shattered in this first clash of arms. The Kaiser, trained as he presumably was in military affairs, displayed no better judgment than the Allied journalists. He complained petulantly to Moltke: "I expected as much. And your invasion of Belgium has brought England in against us." [16]

General Leman looked at the prisoners taken with a colder eye. He did not know that von Emmich's force was composed of mixed brigades, with soldiers drawn from different German formations, and apparently Belgian intelligence was not able to extract this information in time for it to be of use to him. What Leman did learn was that five German corps were represented among his prisoners. From this he concluded that the attacking force was many times its actual size. He believed that the mobile troops deployed between the forts could not long withstand the fury of the German attacks and he knew that, if the 3rd Division and the 15th Brigade were annihilated, the Belgian Field Army would have lost nearly a fifth of its infantry force. No help was to be expected from the French or British. The French commander-in-chief, General Joffre, refused to move so much as a brigade into Belgium before his mobilization was completed,[17] and the British Expeditionary Force was still in the United Kingdom. On the other hand, General Leman had reason to hope that the Liège forts themselves could hold out indefinitely. In the Russo-Japanese War, Port Arthur, a far weaker fortress, had withstood assault for nine months.

Therefore at noon on the 6th of August, General Leman ordered the 3rd Division and the 15th Brigade to abandon their positions and march west to join the rest of the Belgian Army on the Gette. This decision was contrary to the letter of King Albert's order that Leman was to hold Liège to the end with his division, but if the General was mistaken, it was an honest mistake and a courageous one. That afternoon Leman moved his headquarters from the Rue Sainte-Foi to Fort Loncin.

The mobile troops of the Liège garrison were already somewhat disorganized before the order for retirement reached them.

With the retreat came chaos. In the Belgian Army the standard of training and staff work was lower than the standard of valor. Orders were not delivered or were delivered only to be countermanded; batteries took up positions and were moved again within minutes; infantry, guns, ammunition columns, and baggage and ration wagons in no sort of order began to file westward along every available road. Many units marched back through Liège, finding the narrow streets deserted, the shutters closed and the boulevards empty. Some of the reserve cavalry were seen riding off with sacks for saddles and string for stirrups. On being ordered to retire, some soldiers, with bitterness in their hearts, picked up their rifles and walked silently away in the opposite direction to die fighting.

By mid-morning Ludendorff's group had cleared the village of Queue-du-Bois and advanced toward the heights north of Liège. The German soldiers had little stomach for more fighting, for they were tired and had suffered heavy casualties. Ludendorff walked among them, urging them forward.

"Surely you will not leave me to go on alone?" he would ask. "We are nearly there. Tomorrow we will be in Liège." [18]

The weary troops fell in behind him again and the advance continued. They passed between Fort Fléron and Fort d'Evegnée and by early afternoon were less threatened by their guns. All the time, too, Ludendorff's force was being strengthened by the arrival of stragglers and units that had been left behind. General von Emmich came up with his headquarters before the 14th Brigade reached the heights west of La Chartreuse at two o'clock. From the escarpment the German soldiers could look down on the old Carthusian monastery of La Chartreuse and on the city of Liège which lay spread below them like a map. The narrow streets of the old town climbed steeply up the far hillside to the north; the ancient Citadel on the west bank of the Meuse was plainly visible; but no human beings could be seen. Liège, which two days before had held 160,000 persons, looked as empty and deserted as a city depopulated by the plague.

Suddenly from the top of the Citadel a white flag fluttered out in the sunlight. General von Emmich sent a captain down to accept the surrender but he returned at sunset to report that the white flag had been broken out against General Leman's will. Liège was not capitulating.

By now it was too late in the day to take the troops down the escarpment. There was nothing for it but to wait until morning. Ludendorff's guns were trained on the city and a few shots were fired, partly to intimidate the inhabitants and partly to notify the other German columns of the 14th Brigade's position. However, since ammunition was scarce, Ludendorff soon ordered the desultory bombardment to cease.

He did not, of course, know that the Belgian mobile force had already been withdrawn and as night fell he feared that he had led the 14th Brigade into a trap. It was the only German formation to have penetrated the girdle of forts and now it was apparently cut off there. Moreover, nearly a thousand Belgian prisoners had been collected and these needed close watching. When Ludendorff discovered that an old abandoned fort immediately below them in La Chartreuse was empty, he sent the prisoners there with an infantry company to keep them in order.

That night Ludendorff suffered badly from nerves. He kept listening for the sound of fighting which he hoped would tell him that other brigades had broken through the fortress ring. Surely at least one other brigade would get through. But the night remained unnaturally silent, except for an occasional howitzer shell falling into Liège. One of the brigade officers, Major von Marcard, noticed Ludendorff shivering in the August air and lent him his cloak. By ten o'clock the suspense had become unbearable. Ludendorff could stand it no longer. He ordered a Jäger captain to take a company down the hill to seize the bridges over the Meuse. The captain, who did not relish marching off into the hostile darkness against an enemy that had fought so ferociously the previous night, looked at Ludendorff expressively but went without a word.

Shortly after first light on the 7th, Ludendorff's brigade moved down the height of land and marched unopposed into Liège. Colonel von Oven, in command of the advance guard, was to occupy the Citadel, but when he heard that the Belgian mobile forces had been withdrawn he very rightly went instead to the northwest exit of the city and took up a position on the road to Fort Loncin to intercept any stragglers escaping by that route. Ludendorff, believing that von Oven had taken the Citadel, drove boldly up to the place in a commandeered Belgian car with only the brigade adjutant beside him. When he found the great gates closed and locked, he banged upon them — with the hilt of his sword, so the story goes — until they were opened. Inside were several hundred Belgian soldiers who surrendered.

Ludendorff's act had only symbolic significance. Liège had, in fact, been abandoned when General Leman sent the mobile troops back to the Gette. But the power of symbolism is strong, and when the Kaiser, the General Staff, and the German nation heard of the incident they transmuted it into romance. Frightened people, facing the deadly test of war, always clutch at heroes. In the public mind, Ludendorff had captured Liège single-handed with the hilt of his sword.

In this case at least, the process of hero-making was materially assisted by the hero himself. As soon as he had given orders to put the Citadel in a state of defense, Ludendorff requested von Emmich to release him. He was in a fever to get back to Second Army Headquarters to make his report. There was credit to be had for this day's work and he intended to be the first to tell the story to General von Bülow.

While Ludendorff was making his way back to Aachen in another commandeered Belgian car with an impressed Belgian driver, other German brigades were marching to Liège. By evening, elements of the 34th, 11th, and 27th Brigades had joined von Emmich. But the forts were still holding out and while they did so the right wing of the German Army was unable to move.

Ludendorff reached Aachen late on the 7th of August, only

to find that von Bülow and the headquarters of the Second Army were still on the train from Hanover. There would be time for a night's sleep; he could change his uniform which he had not had off for nearly ninety hours; and he would be able to put his thoughts in order. The first thing to be done was to get the heavy siege howitzers into position. Ludendorff was glad to turn himself over to his batman, Rudolph Peters, who insisted on regarding him as someone who had returned from the dead but who drew his bath and laid out his pajamas while he chattered.

When von Bülow turned up at Aachen on the morning of the 8th, Ludendorff made his report in person. The Second Army commander was uneasy about the safety of von Emmich's force and agreed that the siege guns would have to be ordered up at once.

On the 9th, Chancellor Bethmann-Hollweg tried once again to stop the fighting in Belgium. He had never wanted it and his conscience — like a good many consciences in Germany that week — was uneasy. In the Reichstag five days previously he had admitted that the invasion of Belgium was contrary to international law but had declared: "The wrong — I speak openly — that we are committing we will make good as soon as our military aims have been attained." [19] Now he asked the American ambassador in Brussels to deliver a note to the Belgian Government. When the ambassador refused, the message was sent through the Hague. It read in part:

> The fortress of Liège has been taken by assault after a courageous defense. The German Government regrets that as a consequence of the attitude of the Belgian Government against Germany such bloody encounters should have occurred. Germany does not want an enemy in Belgium. It is only by the force of events that she has been compelled, by reason of the military measures of France, to take the grave decision to enter Belgium and occupy Liège as a base for her further military operations. Now that the Belgian Army has, in an heroic resistance against greatly superior forces, maintained the honor of its arms in the most brilliant fashion, the Ger-

man Government prays his Majesty the King and the Belgian Government to avert from Belgium the further horrors of war. The German Government is ready for any agreement with Belgium that can be reconciled in any conceivable way with its conflict with France. Once more Germany offers her solemn assurance that she has not been actuated by any intention of appropriating Belgian territory, and that that intention is far from her. Germany is always ready to evacuate Belgium as soon as the state of war will permit her.[20]

At this time, of course, the fortress of Liège had not been taken by assault, although because of the newspaper accounts of Ludendorff's capture of the Citadel perhaps even the Wilhelmstrasse was under the impression that it had. In any case, the Belgian Government curtly rejected Bethmann-Hollweg's appeal.

The Germans had a better card to play. On the night of the 9th of August the heavy siege artillery began to move towards the Belgian border, each huge black gun being drawn in two sections by 36 horses. Two types of howitzer were available, a Skoda 305 mm. and a Krupp 420 mm., and shells of either caliber could crush the Liège forts like eggshells. Before the big guns were in their firing positions, von Emmich actually took two of the forts by storm. On the night of the 9th/10th, German infantry crept up the glacis of Fort Barchon northeast of the city and gained the parapet. There was sharp hand-to-hand fighting in the underground galleries and tunnels, but the exhausted and outnumbered defenders were soon slaughtered or captured.

The next night Fort d'Evegnée was taken, and at six o'clock on the evening of the 12th the siege howitzers opened fire from surveyed gun positions in and about Liège. After a few ranging rounds, the monstrous shells began to strike the forts, smashing through the concrete cupolas and bursting with terrible effect inside.

Within twenty-four hours Forts Pontisse, Chaudfontaine, and

d'Embourg were reduced to rubble and occupied. On the 14th, Forts Liers and Fléron fell and the right bank of the Meuse was cleared. On the 15th, Forts Loncin and Boncelles were captured. Late that afternoon a direct hit on its magazine blew Fort Loncin to pieces. When the Germans arrived at the site, they found most of the defenders dead. The few tattered men who survived crawled out of the debris with their hands above their heads, calling out *"Ne pas tuer! Ne pas tuer!"* [21] Only one shot was fired — by a Belgian soldier who used his left hand because his right had been blown away. Under a pile of tumbled concrete and twisted girders the body of General Leman was discovered. At first he was thought to be dead, but medical examination established that he was still alive, although nearly asphyxiated by noxious fumes. Ludendorff and General von Emmich were both present when the fort was occupied, and von Emmich, who had met Leman on maneuvers a year or two previously, congratulated the Belgian commander on his gallant resistance and returned his sword.[22]

From his stretcher General Leman had only one request: "I ask you to bear witness that you found me unconscious."

The next day Forts Flémalle and Hollogne were silenced and the resistance of Liège was at an end. President Poincaré's government, which had concurred in Joffre's refusal to send so much as a brigade to the relief of Liège, awarded the city the Grand Cross of the Legion of Honor.

On the 14th, as soon as the right bank of the Meuse had been cleared, General von Kluck's First Army and General von Bülow's Second Army had begun to cross the Belgian frontier. German mobilization had not been completed until the 13th of August, so if the gallant defense of Liège had delayed the German timetable at all, it had been for no more than a few hours. Nevertheless, if Ludendorff's plan for the *coup de main* had in the end been successful, the political consequences, completely unforeseen by the German General Staff, were most unfavorable.

The German people hailed the battle as a great victory and

Ludendorff as the victor. The Kaiser bestowed on him Germany's highest award for valor, the *Pour le Mérite*. "Of course," Ludendorff commented later, "General von Emmich received it too, as General Officer in Command, for his was the responsibility." [23]

At the Westens Hospice in Berlin, Margarethe Ludendorff heard of the capture of Liège on her birthday. General von Stein, the Quartermaster General who worked in the Red House on the Königsplatz, brought her the news before it appeared in the newspapers. The old general bowed low as he kissed her hand, announced the capture of the city and finished by saying: "And now, gracious lady, I have kept my real bit of good news to the end. Your husband is the hero of Liège. The Kaiser has conferred the *Pour le Mérite* on him and General von Emmich."

Half an hour later Margarethe's friends in the hospice came to her room, bringing flowers and congratulations. General von Stein made an appropriately patriotic speech and ended by calling for cheers for the Kaiser, the Fatherland, and General Ludendorff. But that night, after her friends had gone, Margarethe sat alone, wondering what would become of her family in the days ahead.[24]

At the end of the first three weeks of war, French offensives in Lorraine and the Ardennes had been repulsed with heavy loss and the Germans were advancing through Belgium on schedule with the First, Second and Third Armies grouped under General von Bülow. The Belgian Army had withdrawn from the line of the River Gette to take up entrenched positions about Antwerp. On the 20th of August the Germans goose-stepped into Brussels behind banners and bands. The next day the fortress of Namur came under the fire of the huge siege howitzers. So far the Schlieffen Plan, even as modified by Moltke, appeared to be doing all that was expected of it.

The German Supreme Command found the situation in the East much less satisfactory. Austria, for whose sake Germany had gone to war, was already calling for help. Two Austrian armies which had invaded Serbia had been counterattacked and ignominiously thrown back across the frontier, and Russian forces were gathering in Galicia for an offensive. Even worse, the soil of the Fatherland had been invaded. A large Russian army under General Rennenkampf was already in East Prussia, moving ponderously west towards Königsberg, while a second army under General Samsonov was advancing north from Warsaw against the German rear. There was real danger that the German forces in East Prussia would be caught in a gigantic pincers and annihilated.

The defense of East Prussia was entrusted to the German Eighth Army under the 66-year-old General von Prittwitz, a coarse, indolent man, nick-named *"der Dicke"* ("the Fat"). He was not an inspiring commander. Supreme Headquarters had little confidence in him, for he was nervous and lacked self-confidence, traits von Moltke found especially irritating because he himself suffered from the same failings. When Prittwitz telephoned Coblenz in a panic to say that he would have to retreat to the Vistula and perhaps even beyond, Moltke decided to remove him. The Eighth Army Chief of Staff, General von Waldersee, would also have to go.

But who could replace them? Moltke did not worry unduly about an army commander. Any respectable figurehead would do. What was urgently needed was a really good Chief of Staff, someone who was tough, confident, and a highly competent staff officer. He at once thought of Ludendorff who had been such a strong support to him in the Red House during the struggle over the army estimates and who had just received the *Pour le Mérite* from the All Highest. Ludendorff would be the very man.

At nine o'clock on the morning of the 22nd of August, a staff car from Coblenz arrived at Second Army Headquarters half-way between Wavre and Namur. A staff captain dismounted and asked for General Ludendorff. When he found him, he handed over personal letters from Moltke and General von Stein. Ludendorff was to report to Coblenz immediately to be given instruc-

tions prior to his assuming the post of Chief of Staff of the Eighth
Army in East Prussia.

Von Moltke's letter read in part:

> You have before you a new and difficult task, perhaps even more
> difficult than that of storming Liège . . . I know no other man in
> whom I have such absolute trust. You may yet be able to save the
> situation in the East. You must not be angry with me for calling
> you away from a post in which you are, perhaps, on the threshold
> of a decisive action, which, please God, will be conclusive. This is
> yet another sacrifice you are called upon to make for the Father-
> land. The Kaiser, too, has confidence in you. Of course, you will
> not be made responsible for what has already happened, but with
> your energy you can prevent the worst from happening. So answer
> this new call, which is the greatest compliment that can be paid any
> soldier. I know that you will not belie the trust reposed in you.[25]

Ludendorff closely questioned the staff captain who brought
him this message but learned little except that a retired General
of Infantry by the name of Paul von Beneckendorff und von
Hindenburg was being considered for army commander. So far,
however, Supreme Headquarters did not know where Hindenburg
lived or whether he would accept the post offered him.

A chance such as this came only once in a lifetime and Ludendorff knew it. Within fifteen minutes he had packed, said his
farewells at von Bülow's headquarters and was driving back to
Coblenz in the staff car. On the journey he met the 31st Infantry
Regiment moving up to the front and stopped for a moment to
shake hands with his seventeen-year-old stepson, Heinz, who
was serving in the unit as an ensign. Later in the day he passed
through Wavre. Ludendorff commented: "Only the day before
it had been a peaceful town. Now it was in flames. Here, also,
the populace had fired on our troops. That was my farewell to
Belgium." [26]

CHAPTER IV

THE SUMMONS TO THE EAST

LUDENDORFF stared at the big map of East Prussia on the wall of the Operations Room at Coblenz while General von Moltke explained the strategic situation. There was little about the tall figure and sad countenance of the Chief of the General Staff to suggest the victorious commander. He looked worn, with haunted eyes and deeply etched lines on his face.[1] When Ludendorff had reached Supreme Headquarters at six o'clock that evening, Saturday, the 22nd of August, he had not been kept waiting, but nevertheless he already knew that the senior staff officers at Coblenz had not liked Moltke's reaction to von Prittwitz's panic-stricken telephone call two nights previously. When informed that the Eighth Army was abandoning East Prussia and retreating to the Vistula and that, because of the low water level of the river, even the Vistula line might not be held without reinforcements, Moltke had been "deeply shattered . . . but he did not think of giving a resolute counter-order." [2]

All the doubts and irresolutions that had troubled him when the Kaiser first wanted to make him Chief of the General Staff had returned with the outbreak of war. He was far too sensitive not to be tortured by the decisions he had to make and, disconcertingly, from time to time his eyes would fill with tears. Only the independent action of his Operations Section had forced him to deal firmly with Prittwitz. Colonel Max Bauer had telephoned each of the Eighth Army's four corps commanders to ask for an opinion of the situation. All had reported that retreat would be premature. With this evidence to support them, the staff had gone to Moltke and persuaded him to remove Prittwitz.[3]

Yet the 22nd of August had brought nothing but good news to Coblenz. When Moltke saw Ludendorff, he knew that Namur had fallen, that the French were retreating in the Ardennes and that Crown Prince Rupprecht of Bavaria had won a victory at Morhange, but he realized too that the decisive battle in the West had still to be fought and he evinced none of the "fabulous confidence" [4] that had briefly seized him on hearing of the fall of Liège.

As Ludendorff looked at the map on the wall, he thought about East Prussia. He knew it well, for it was his native province. If he still considered any particular place home, it was this country of wide flat spaces beside the gray waters of the Baltic. It was a land of brown clay and sand, innumerable still lakes and small streams, marshland, and stunted forests of birch, beech, and pine. Heaths overgrown with scrub were interspersed with neat farmlands, fields of rye and oats, and small white villages eloquent of German industry and frugality. More to the point, East Prussia was a tongue of land, some 160 miles long by 100 miles deep, projecting into Russian territory north of Poland.

In the days when Count Schlieffen had been planning his two-front war, Ludendorff had frequently gone on staff rides through East Prussia. He remembered the long straight roads that dwindled into rutty tracks as soon as they crossed the frontier, the excellent railway network that covered the whole province, and — most important of all — the 50-mile-wide barrier of the Masurian Lakes near the eastern border. Since the causeways between the lakes were held by small German forts and blockhouses, the Masurian Lakes would split any considerable body of Russian invaders in two. The Grand Duke Nicholas, the Russian Commander-in-Chief, could not concentrate the whole of his force on one side of the Lakes, for neither in the east nor south were the roads and railways adequate for a unified advance of the half million men he was prepared to use against Germany.

Moltke briefly told Ludendorff what had already happened. After concentrating at Vilna, General Rennenkampf's Russian

First Army of three corps and five cavalry divisions, some 246,000 men and 800 guns, had crossed into East Prussia on the 17th of August, moving north of the Masurian Lakes to turn the German left flank and cut off the German army from the fortress of Königsberg. Because General Jilinski, the commander of the Russian Northwest Front, hoped that Rennenkampf would draw the Germans eastwards to oppose him, he had deliberately held back his Second Army. Not until the 19th of August did General Samsonov march north from Warsaw with six corps and three cavalry divisions, some 289,000 men and 780 guns. Samsonov's Second Army was striking up well to the west of the Masurian Lakes to operate against the rear of the forces facing Rennenkampf and come between them and the Vistula.

To oppose this double invasion, Germany had only her Eighth Army, composed of four corps: the Ist (von François), the Ist Reserve (von Below), the XVIIth (von Mackensen), and the XXth (von Scholtz), plus a cavalry division, some Landwehr and Landsturm units and the fortress garrisons — in all, about 210,000 men and 600 guns. Thus the Germans were outnumbered by each Russian army. If Rennenkampf and Samsonov could concert their attack, they could certainly crush the Eighth Army, overrun East Prussia and drive on unopposed to Berlin. No victory in the West could compensate for the loss of the capital and all northern and eastern Germany.

Prittwitz had left the XXth Corps in the southwest to guard against Samsonov's advance and had concentrated the rest of his army in the northeast to oppose Rennenkampf. His plan had been to wait until Rennenkampf was well inside the frontier, then to attack and defeat him before turning back to deal with Samsonov. But as the Russian First Army advanced into East Prussia it had clashed sharply with German forces at Stallupönen on the 17th of August. This battle had been brought about by the aggressiveness of one of Prittwitz's corps commanders, General von François, who disobeyed his orders and attacked as soon as he saw a good opportunity. Hermann von François was a fiery, headstrong East Prussian who hated to yield a foot of German soil to the invader. Apparently Prittwitz had been unable to control him or impress on him the desirability of allowing Rennenkampf to thrust deeper into Germany. Stallupönen had been a tactical defeat for the Russians, but Eighth Army Headquarters had ordered von François to disengage. He had done so reluctantly, withdrawing towards Gumbinnen and taking with him a large number of prisoners. Rennenkampf's pursuit had been leisurely and on the 20th he had halted his army for a day's rest.[5]

Prittwitz had hoped that Rennenkampf would advance to attack the prepared German positions along the Angerapp River but the First Army's halt on the 20th upset this plan. Prittwitz did not know how long the Russians intended to remain stationary, and while he waited undecided, he learned that Samsonov was advancing in great strength against his rear.[6] He had had the choice of moving boldly forward from the prepared Angerapp line to attack Rennenkampf in the open field or of retreating to reunite his army behind the Vistula.

Once again the commander of the Ist Corps had taken the decision out of his hands. Von François had positioned his corps well forward in close contact with the enemy and had urged Prittwitz to attack. Weakly, Prittwitz had agreed. The result had been the battle of Gumbinnen on the 20th of August — and Gumbinnen had been a German defeat. On the left wing von François's Ist Corps smashed through the Russian positions, and Below's Ist Reserve Corps on the right did well, but in the center the XVIIth Corps, handled clumsily by the impetuous von Mackensen, attacked without adequate artillery support and suffered a bloody repulse. Many units of the XVIIth Corps fled in panic, and Prittwitz had decided to break off the action and run for the Vistula. Two days later he had been superseded.

This was the situation Moltke outlined to Ludendorff. The picture was black enough but perhaps not hopeless. Instinctively, Ludendorff found himself agreeing with the Eighth Army

corps commanders that a retreat to the Vistula would be premature. Although the evacuation of East Prussia had often been
practiced by Count Schlieffen in strategic war games, Ludendorff
felt that now "it did not allow for the realities of war, nor did it
take into account the immense responsibility of exposing part of
one's country to invasion . . . As events were shaping, retreat
behind the Vistula would have spelled ruin. We should not have
been able to hold the Vistula line against the numerically superior forces of the Russians." [7]

Ludendorff made up his mind quickly. With Moltke's concur-
rence, he telegraphed his initial orders direct to Prittwitz's corps
commanders. The retreat to the west was to be discontinued, at
least temporarily. The Ist Reserve Corps and the XVIIth Corps
were to halt where they were for one day. The Ist Corps was to
move south by rail to support von Scholtz's XXth Corps which
was standing alone in the path of Samsonov's advance. Von
François's troops were to detrain as near as possible to Scholtz's
position, somewhere east of Deutsch-Eylau. Army Headquarters
at Neidenburg was too far forward and in the path of Samsonov's
advance, so Ludendorff ordered it back to Marienburg and directed the staff to meet him there the next day.

These orders, and the promptitude with which they were
dispatched, are a measure of Ludendorff's military ability. As
it turned out, the one day's halt ordered for the Ist Reserve
Corps and the XVIIth Corps may have been a mistake, but it
was a mistake hardly avoidable under the circumstances. As
Ludendorff later said: "Of course an actual decision as to the
plan to be adopted could only be given on the spot. The Russians should not be let off without a battle. No staff officer
would miss such a chance of turning to good advantage the fact
that their two armies were separated from each other." [8]

For the moment there was no more to be done. Since the
Kaiser had expressed a wish to meet the hero of Liège, Ludendorff was ushered into the Imperial presence. Now that war had
actually come, Wilhelm seemed a different person. His bluster-
ing aggressiveness had quite disappeared and he was quiet and

subdued with a strange new dignity. Even his moustaches no longer bristled so fiercely. He seemed after all to be only a modest monarch with a withered arm who knew he was in the midst of events beyond his control. This evening he was calm and confident, although much concerned over the sufferings of the German population in East Prussia. He hung the *Pour le Mèrite* about Ludendorff's neck with his own hands and wished him Godspeed.

At nine o'clock, just three hours after his arrival at Coblenz, Ludendorff boarded the special train that was to take him to the Eastern Front. The train consisted only of an engine, a coal car and three coaches. One coach contained Ludendorff's sitting-room and bedroom; another was reserved for the Eighth Army's new commander, von Hindenburg; and a third coach had been fitted out as an operations room with desks and map tables.

That afternoon one of Moltke's staff had telephoned Margarethe Ludendorff at the Westens Hospice in Berlin. The conversation had been brief: Frau Ludendorff was to be at the Tiergarten Station the next morning at eight o'clock to meet her husband, who would be passing through the capital.[9]

In Hanover that day Paul von Hindenburg had gone shopping. Three years before the war he had retired at the age of 63 with the rank of General of Infantry. "There was no war in sight," he said, "and so I recognized it as my duty to make room for younger officers." [10] Now, however, he felt very much out of things and had almost given up hope of being recalled to active duty. It was a pity, because his massive, thick-set frame was as strong as ever and his will and character as firm. But so many younger men were available.

When he completed his purchases that morning, he was asked by the shopkeeper if they should be delivered.

"Give them to me," the old general said, a brooding look on his heavy face, "I've nothing else to do. They don't want me now."

He went home to lunch in his first-floor flat in the Holzgraben, and after eating settled down to read a book. At three o'clock in the afternoon his wife brought him the telegram from Coblenz. It asked if he was ready for immediate duty. Hindenburg replied: "I am ready," and began to pack. A second telegram arrived to tell him that Ludendorff would be his Chief of Staff and that he should meet the special train at Hanover Station at four o'clock the next morning. A little later a third telegram explained that he had been appointed to command the Eighth Army in East Prussia.[11]

Ludendorff's train made good time as it rattled through the night towards Hanover, Berlin, and Marienburg. Along the way, red and green signal lamps winked hastily in the blackness; switches were thrown; and troop trains and long lines of munitions wagons running westwards were sidetracked to let it roar by. Ludendorff sat in his private coach and stared out at the darkened countryside flashing past, his mind busy with the strategic possibilities in the East. Just seven hours after leaving Coblenz, the train pulled into Hanover station. Ludendorff rose, opened the carriage door and stepped onto the platform.

Under the glaring lights of the main waiting room Hindenburg stood, silent and solid. He was a big man with a large, flat forehead and thick hair cut *en brosse*. His square face and strong jaw showed character; his blue eyes were kindly and very placid; and he had an air of childlike simplicity about him that most people found instantly appealing. He had had no time to obtain one of the new field-gray uniforms, so he wore the old-fashioned one his wife had carefully laid away in mothballs three years before. He must have put on a little weight, for the tunic would no longer hook at the collar. Frau von Hindenburg stood beside him, quiet and nervous. After Ludendorff introduced himself, the old general said good-bye to his wife and the two officers went aboard the train, which started immediately.

Hindenburg had never met Ludendorff before and had not even heard of his exploits at Liège.[12] They went into the swaying operations coach and sat down at a map table. Ludendorff began to brief his superior on the situation.

Hindenburg's shrewd old eyes watched his Chief of Staff more intently than they regarded the map. After 45 years of service, he knew something of men. The new commander of the Eighth Army had no illusions as to what Supreme Headquarters expected of him. He had never been a brilliant soldier and although he knew East Prussia thoroughly — like Ludendorff, he had been born there and had commanded a corps at Königsberg and at Allenstein — he knew it no better than dozens of other general officers. No better, for instance, than his cousin, von Prittwitz, had done. No, he was certainly not the man chosen at the last moment to snatch victory from defeat by some startling combination.

Of course, he was very senior on the Army List. As a subaltern he had fought at Königgrätz, St. Privat, and Sedan, and had won the Order of Swords and the Iron Cross, but mere seniority counted for little when Germany was at war. He knew himself to be simple, modest, loyal, and patient — and his nerves were good. Yet it was obviously Ludendorff who had the confidence of von Moltke, who was expected to provide the magic formula that would save East Prussia. His own role, if not exactly that of figurehead, would be to clear the way, with the authority of his rank and years, for his younger Chief of Staff.

He listened closely to what Ludendorff said and agreed with all of it. The briefing lasted only half an hour, then both men went to bed.

In her anxiety to see her husband, Margarethe arrived at the Tiergarten station long before eight o'clock. Berlin was quiet that early on a Sunday morning, and although the sun was well up, the air was still pleasantly cool. She walked up and down the platform, a slim attractive figure in her long-skirted dress, wide-brimmed summer hat and gloves. Like Frau von Hindenburg, she was nervous, for she knew in general terms of her husband's appointment and realized how much depended on his success or failure.

Sharp on time the special train rolled into the station, with a squealing of brakes and hissing of white steam. Ludendorff was on the platform beside his wife almost as soon as the train stopped. He looked alert and vigorous, although he had had only three hours' sleep.

The special train lingered no longer in Berlin than in Hanover. As soon as Margarethe was settled in Ludendorff's private coach, it moved off again, running smoothly eastwards towards the climbing sun.

Margarethe spent an hour alone with her husband in his compartment. They talked, of course, of the war, and Ludendorff related how he had met Heinz on his way to the front. That was two of her three boys who were already in action, for little Franz, the eldest, who had been so proud of his lieutenant's uniform and so sensitive about his height, was somewhere west of the Rhine with his stepfather's old regiment, the 39th Fusiliers.

At nine they went in to breakfast with General von Hindenburg in his coach. Ludendorff was somewhat abstracted, but Hindenburg exerted himself to be charming to Margarethe, a task few men ever found difficult. He greeted her with real kindliness, and as they sat at the swaying little table with its white linen and gleaming silver, tried to divert her mind from her anxieties. While the farms and villages of West Prussia flickered by the window, he spoke of how he had waited impatiently in Hanover to be called back to the colors, and of how when the summons did arrive it was, of course, on a Saturday afternoon when there was not a tailor to be had.

"Look," he said, "my uniform and boots are not according to the regulations, and I have to go to the front with my old Litewka from the 3rd Guards Regiment." [13]

Several times that morning they passed crowded troop trains, decked with flowers and with grinning young soldiers at every window. The trains were all running west, for Schlieffen's master plan was still directing the course of the war and the Eastern Front would have to get along as best it could until the French were beaten.

Margarethe had to leave the train at Küstrin on the Elbe. She was handed over to the care of the station commandant, an elderly reserve officer who was as happy as a boy because he was in uniform again and doing his best for the Fatherland. Margarethe had a reserved compartment for her journey back to Berlin, but she had to wait several hours for the train and then the short trip took ten hours. Long before she reached the capital, her husband had arrived at Marienburg.

At two o'clock that afternoon Ludendorff looked out his carriage window and glimpsed the red-brick towers of the ancient Marienburg castle that had been built centuries before by the rapacious Teutonic Knights. Down below him in the town he could see a steady stream of refugees flowing westward across the bridge over the Nogat River. They looked much the same as the refugees he had seen in Belgium only the day before, the same as refugees looked all over Europe that August.

The Eighth Army staff, headed by General Grünert, the Quartermaster General, and Lieutenant Colonel Max Hoffmann, the First General Staff Officer, was waiting for Hindenburg and Ludendorff. Von Prittwitz and Count von Waldersee had already left East Prussia. Neither had uttered a word of complaint,[14] but they could not help feeling that they had been treated as scapegoats by Supreme Headquarters.

"Our reception in Marienburg was anything but cheerful," Ludendorff recalled. "It seemed like entering another world to come into this depressing atmosphere after Liège and the rapid advance in the West." [15]

One member of the Eighth Army staff was not in the least depressed. Behind his air of witty cynicism, Lieutenant Colonel Hoffmann possessed one of the most brilliant brains in Germany. Sooner or later his superiors — reluctantly or otherwise, depending on their broadmindedness and sense of humor — came to recognize this, and so Hoffmann had long exercised more influence than his rank would normally have entitled him to do. When he had been promoted to lieutenant colonel and posted to Eighth Army Headquarters on the outbreak of war, he had immediately begun to have doubts about the ability of his general and Chief of Staff. Prittwitz, he decided, was "a clever but harsh superior," who was apt to be weak. Count Waldersee, he noted in his diary, had recently undergone a serious operation that affected his nerves.[16]

From the outset Hoffmann had favored a bold strategy in East Prussia and had gone so far as to suggest to General Grünert that it might be best not to tell Prittwitz or Waldersee the news of Samsonov's advance against the Eighth Army's rear. Grünert agreed with Hoffmann's estimate of the command but had been scandalized by this suggestion, although he could never quite be sure whether Hoffmann was joking. When Prittwitz announced his decision to retreat to the Vistula, Hoffmann argued against it so strongly that Prittwitz and Waldersee actually changed their minds. His clinching argument had been that Samsonov's Second Army was already closer to the Vistula than the Eighth Army. At this Prittwitz had snapped that he was the commander-in-chief and responsible for making the decisions. Thereupon Hoffmann turned to Waldersee and said: "Very well then, we retreat to the Vistula. Tell me how to do it before Samsonov gets there ahead of us."

A few minutes' calculation with dividers and map had convinced Waldersee that his irritating subordinate was right. Samsonov's left wing was already eighty miles nearer the Vistula than the most easterly portion of the Eighth Army. The orders Hoffmann suggested were issued, but this reversal of plan came too late to save Prittwitz and Waldersee from Moltke's displeasure.

Hoffmann was not sorry to see a change in command, especially since the new Chief of Staff was Major General Ludendorff whom he had known for years in the Red House in Berlin. After Ludendorff was introduced to the staff, he dismissed them to their duties but told Hoffmann to remain behind to brief him on the situation. Ludendorff was surprised to learn that action had already been taken to implement his own tentative plan of campaign. Hoffmann, too, had glimpsed the possibility of a decisive stroke and had decided to concentrate the Eighth Army for this purpose.

The fact that both Ludendorff and Hoffmann, one in Coblenz and one 800 kilometers away in Neidenburg, had reached substantially the same solution to the strategic problem throws a fascinating sidelight on the training of the German General Staff. Ludendorff had telegraphed orders for the Ist Corps to move southwest by rail to reinforce the XXth Corps and had ordered it to detrain at Deutsch-Eylau; Hoffmann had previously issued exactly the same order except that he had specified detrainment at Gosslershausen, a little further west. Ludendorff had ordered Army Headquarters to move to Marienburg; Hoffmann had previously ordered it to Mühlhausen, a little further east. At the request of General von Scholtz, Hoffmann had ordered the 3rd Reserve Division to the XXth Corps' left instead of its right, where Ludendorff had decided it should go. The division had already marched from Gumbinnen to Nordenburg and entrained for Allenstein. While Hoffmann was briefing Ludendorff, the first trains were unloading at Allenstein, the men forming into columns and marching away to the front. The only slight difference in strategic thinking was that Hoffmann had thought to concentrate near Osterode for a blow at either Samsonov or Rennenkampf, while from the beginning Ludendorff had decided to concentrate further south to strike at Samsonov.[17] Possibly Ludendorff knew that Supreme Headquarters had already asked von François if he believed an attack on Rennenkampf feasible and that von François had replied that the moment had passed.

Hoffmann bent over the map as he pointed out the enemy's dispositions and made his comments on them. If Rennenkampf was moving too slowly, Samsonov, on the other hand, was advancing far too fast, urged on recklessly by General Jilinski from Army Group Headquarters at Bialystok. The Russian Second Army's front had been extended progressively to the west as

Samsonov hurried his troops forward. By now there was a distance of nearly sixty miles between its extreme left and its extreme right. On the southwest the Russian Ist Corps was moving towards Soldau, and far off on the other wing, two days' march from the rest of the army, the Russian VIth Corps and 4th Cavalry Division were advancing on Bischofsburg and Sensburg. In the center, the XXIIIrd, XVth, and XIIIth Corps were pushing on into a broken countryside of forests, swamps and lakes.

All the Russian commanders from Jilinski down seemed obsessed with the idea that the Germans were retreating to the Vistula. This accounted for Rennenkampf's tardiness and for Samsonov's desperate haste. Both foresaw a decisive, annihilating battle once the Russian Second Army had interposed itself between the Germans and the Vistula.

Every day for the past week Samsonov's men had marched sixteen or seventeen miles in blazing August weather. The long straggling columns in variegated khaki uniforms shaded from sage green to near yellow had toiled laboriously forward over poor sandy roads, and each day's march had further dislocated their administrative arrangements. Because the army had been set in motion before its mobilization was completed, there were not nearly enough horses, wagons or field bakeries to supply and feed the troops.[18] Since the country through which the Russians passed was sparsely settled, they were unable to obtain food locally. By now many units were actually hungry, for they had not received even their minimum ration of black bread, cabbage soup and tea. Nevertheless, Samsonov continued to urge them on, confidently believing that only a few more marches would see the Eighth Army cut off and a great victory won.

Hoffmann described Samsonov to Ludendorff — he was a man of fifty-five and his fighting qualities rather than his intellect had gained him his military reputation. Ludendorff knew that Hoffman was inclined to think most members of his own profession fools but it was not a judgment with which he entirely disagreed. In any case, he was willing to accept Hoffmann's assess-

ment of Samsonov as a simple, bluff, and kindly soldier, a courageous extrovert who was hail-fellow-well-met with his troops, but
a man who possessed more stubbornness and resolution than
brains. Moreover, Samsonov had been on sick leave in the Cau-
casus when war broke out and had reached his headquarters in
Warsaw only on the 12th of August. Therefore he could not be
familiar with either his staff or his subordinate commanders.

Rennenkampf was of quite a different character. Hoffmann
thought him cleverer than Samsonov but his little shrug as he
said so belittled the difference. The commander of the Russian
First Army was sixty-one, a man with a military bearing and a
carefully cultivated moustache. Hoffmann twinkled at Ludendorff as he described him. Probably a vain man and certainly an
indolent one.

Hoffmann doubted whether either Rennenkampf or Samsonov
had any clear idea where the Germans were or what they were
doing. Both Russian armies possessed great masses of Cossack
cavalry, but apart from terrorizing the East Prussian countryside, these horsemen had been singularly ineffective. They were
good at murdering civilians, raping women, and burning villages, but they seemed to have no idea of how to conduct reconnaissance and were habitually beaten by much smaller numbers
of German cavalry. As a consequence, Rennenkampf and Samsonov were, for all military purposes, blind.

Ludendorff made no definite plan on the 23rd. What Hoffmann had told him was encouraging, but it was still too early to
know whether the Ist Reserve Corps and the XVIIth Corps could
be used against Samsonov. He went to bed early, for he and
Hindenburg had arranged to be up at dawn on the 24th. Immediately after breakfast, they motored southwest to Tannenberg to meet the XXth Corps commander, von Scholtz, and his
Chief of Staff, Colonel Hell. Hoffmann came along in a second
car.

The XXth Corps was deployed between Frankenau and Or-
lau, a distance of some twelve miles, blocking the main

Neidenburg-Allenstein road. The Germans were in an excellent position, well dug in with good fields of fire to their front and flanks across flat acres of potato crops. When the Russian XVth Corps, advancing without adequate reconnaissance, blundered into the German line early in the morning, a sharp fire-fight developed in which Samsonov's troops lost heavily. They attacked with great courage and persistence but made no impression on the German position. Von Scholtz, discussing the situation with Ludendorff in Tannenberg, was quietly confident. His corps might have to bend beneath the weight of Russian attacks but it would not break.

Ludendorff and Scholtz decided that the XXth Corps would retire slightly during the night to a new line Gilgenburg-Mühlen-Hohenstein. This retirement was not absolutely essential, but the enemy pressure made it advisable, for time would thereby be gained while the Russians organized a new attack. Moreover, the new line would not run parallel with the old. As the XXth Corps retired, it would swing back its left flank like an opening door through which Samsonov would be beckoned to disaster. This refusal of a flank was a tactic the Germans used frequently in the East, often with great success.

One possible image of the battle to be fought was already forming in Ludendorff's mind. It was based on the concepts of Schlieffen but was more sternly realistic than the old field marshal's plans had been. Perhaps it would be possible to deceive Rennenkampf by leaving only a light cavalry screen in front of the Russian First Army and to mass almost all the German forces against Samsonov, using the XXth Corps as a framework for the new grouping. Perhaps as the three Russian corps in the center advanced against the XXth Corps, the two isolated Russian wings could be driven in and the Russian center enveloped. The XXth Corps' refused left flank would be the bait at the bottom of the sack.

But Ludendorff still did not accept these mental pictures as more than possibilities. The question was whether it would be possible to draw off most of the troops facing Rennenkampf for a concentrated blow against Samsonov. Part of the Ist Corps was already moving south, but its entrainment was delayed because the necessary rolling stock had to be brought from west of the Vistula.

Thanks to Hoffmann's far-sighted orders, von François's men had begun to march back from the battlefield of Gumbinnen on the 21st, their retirement covered by troops from the Königsberg garrison. They were now waiting at the long sidings east of Königsberg for engines and coaches to carry them southwest to the right flank of the XXth Corps. They bivouacked in the railway yards at Insterburg, Norkitten, Wehlau, Tapiau, and Königsberg itself, resting, cleaning their equipment, writing letters home. As the trains were made up, they filed aboard, quickly and in good order, the right number of men to each coach under their own NCOs. Unit vehicles and horses were loaded smartly and guns were lashed to flat-cars. Special coaches at the end of each train were reserved for officers. Within forty hours they would all detrain again at Neumark, Deutsch-Eylau, Osterode, and Biessellen, quickly and in good order under their own NCOs. German organization was at its superb best in such situations — and it certainly helped win battles, even though it was not enough to win wars.

Whether the Ist Reserve Corps and the XVIIth Corps could be brought south as well depended entirely on Rennenkampf. If the Russian commander advanced quickly and maintained contact with the forces opposing him, no concentration against Samsonov would be possible and the best that could be achieved would be a fighting retirement towards the Vistula. However, if Rennenkampf continued to move slowly, a great victory might be won.

For Eighth Army Headquarters the night of the 24th of August was the most nerve-wracking period of the entire battle.[19] Although Ludendorff believed that the Ist Reserve Corps and the XVIIth Corps might still be required to ward off a blow from

Rennenkampf, he nevertheless ordered these formations to begin their march south. The XXth Corps, destined to be the anvil against which Samsonov's Second Army was to be hammered, was ordered to hold its positions to the last man. Any further retirement here would ruin the entire German plan.

Even more important than these decisions were the orders Ludendorff drafted for his right wing. The question was where von François's Ist Corps should attack. If it moved to the south of Soldau, the Ist Russian Corps might be enveloped as well as the Russian center. The temptation was great, but Ludendorff, looking coldly at the forces at his disposal, firmly rejected it. The Ist Corps would attack towards Usdau, driving the Russian Ist Corps away from the main battlefield. "We had to confine ourselves to this plan if we wished to succeed," [20] Ludendorff later wrote, and Hoffmann, suddenly no longer cynical about his superiors, was of the opinion that this was "the decisive point of the whole battle of Tannenberg." [21]

Early on the morning of the 25th, Eighth Army Headquarters intercepted a wireless message sent in clear from Rennenkampf to his corps commanders, giving the dispositions and objectives of each corps for the next two days. The Russian First Army would not reach the line Gerdauen-Allenburg-Wehlau until the 26th. Obsessed with the idea that the Germans were in full retreat to the Vistula, Rennenkampf was in no hurry to press them. He felt that, since Samsonov was behind schedule, it would be a mistake to hurry the German retirement. It would be time enough to advance once the Russian Second Army had interposed itself between the Germans and the Vistula. Indeed, when Rennenkampf had heard that the Eighth Army was withdrawing after the battle of Gumbinnen, his only comment had been that the danger was over and his staff could now get some sleep.[22] For the next sixty hours Rennenkampf's army had made no move.

At first Ludendorff was inclined to be skeptical of the intercepted wireless message, but Hoffmann believed it without reservation, for he knew the Tsarist army well. For some time he had been a military attaché at St. Petersburg and no technical stupidity the Russians committed could surprise him. For an army commander to radio his corps commanders their objectives and orders of march in clear was exactly the sort of thing he expected from the Russians. He also assured Ludendorff that Rennenkampf would be in no hurry to support Samsonov. There was bad blood between the two. Hoffmann had heard the story when he had been military attaché with the Japanese Army at the time of the Russo-Japanese War. At the battle of Liauyang, Samsonov's Siberian Cossack Division had had to evacuate the Yentai coal-mines because Rennenkampf refused to reinforce him. Later the two generals met and quarrelled on the Mukden station platform; blows had been struck; and a duel was prevented only by the intervention of the Tsar. Since then Samsonov and Rennenkampf had not been on speaking terms.[23]

Hoffmann at last convinced Ludendorff that the Russian message was genuine and that Rennenkampf would not be in time to interfere with the battle shaping up in the southwest against Samsonov. His doubts thus resolved, Ludendorff ordered the Ist Reserve Corps, the XVIIth Corps, and the 6th Landwehr Brigade to hurry south by "enormous forced marches"[24] in order to attack the Russian VIth Corps and turn the Second Army's right flank.

When the troops were told what they were to do, they stepped out eagerly, resolute to come to grips with the enemy. The pitiful streams of refugees fleeing westward along all the main roads were a constant incentive, and as Below's and Mackensen's men marched hard to the southwest there was almost no straggling.

At eight o'clock on the morning of the 25th, Hindenburg, Ludendorff and Hoffmann met General von François on a hill southeast of Montovo. Thus within 36 hours of assuming his appointment Ludendorff personally visited two of his four corps commanders near their own headquarters. However, this trip had a more important purpose than the acquisition of first-hand tactical information. Ludendorff was determined to impress on von François that the new command of the Eighth Army intended to exact obedience. Von François's independence of mind, which had already approached downright insubordination more than once in the campaign, would no longer be tolerated. Hindenburg came along, impassive and dignified, to lend his prestige to Ludendorff's orders, but as the little group of officers stood on the windy hilltop near Montovo the real clash of wills was between Major General Ludendorff and General of Infantry von François.

Ludendorff ordered the Ist Corps to capture the Heights of Seeben and go on to take Usdau on the morning of the 26th. He anticipated that by then the XXth Corps would be under heavy attack from greatly superior Russian forces and that the Ist Corps' assault would be necessary to relieve Scholtz's hard-pressed men. Moreover, the attack on Usdau would turn the Russian Second Army's left flank, just as the attack of the Ist Reserve Corps and the XVIIth Corps on Bischofsburg would turn its right flank. The vision of a classic double development was already before Ludendorff's eyes, a new Cannae that might utterly destroy Samsonov's army. The maneuver would be the more deadly because the countryside through which the Russian center would have to retreat was largely wild heath and rough forest land where units would lose all cohesion and direction.

Von François protested that the attack on Usdau would be a frontal one and that not all his artillery and ammunition columns had arrived. Having heard him out, Ludendorff coldly reiterated that the timing and direction of the attack would be unchanged. Hindenburg stood like a massive figure carved in wood and said nothing at all, but his very silence was all the support Ludendorff required. Resentfully von François bowed to the direct order, but with mental reservations.

On the way back to Marienburg from this interview Hindenburg and Ludendorff stopped at the Montovo railway station to telephone headquarters for the latest news. While they were there the telegraph instrument began to clack away frantically. Colonel Hoffmann remained behind to take the message. It proved to be a report of another Russian wireless intercept, again sent in clear, but this time from Second Army Headquarters. Samsonov, apparently believing that the XXth Corps' retirement the day before had been a full-scale retreat, ordered his center to pursue in the direction of Osterode. This meant that the greater part of the Russian Second Army was shambling blindly forward into the open mouth of the sack being held ready to enfold it.

As Hoffmann read the report, his eyes glinted behind his *pince-nez*. He shouted for his chauffeur, jumped into his car and went roaring down the road after Hindenburg and Ludendorff. He caught up with them a few miles further on and handed the message over while the two cars ran side by side. East of Löbau, Ludendorff stopped while he and Hoffmann studied the map. There was no need to change the orders already issued, but copies of the Russian message were sent to Generals Scholtz and von François. The trap was set to spring. As Samsonov's center groped forward to find the new front of the XXth Corps, the 3rd Reserve Division waited to take the attackers in flank; the Ist Corps was poised to strike fiercely at the Russian left; and down from the northeast, column after column of grimly determined men belonging to the Ist Reserve Corps and the XVIIth Corps were pounding along the dusty roads to fall upon the isolated Russian right at Bischofsburg.

Hindenburg had found it a long day. Early that evening he turned to Ludendorff and Hoffmann and said: "Gentlemen, our preparations are so well in hand that we can sleep soundly tonight." Then he went unconcernedly off to bed, leaving Ludendorff to stare after him with a mixture of awe, envy and incredulity. In the background, Hoffmann looked on with a speculative smile.

CHAPTER V

TANNENBERG

LUDENDORFF thrust halfway across the desk as though lunging at an adversary. His big face was crimson and the curved ebonite telephone receiver shook in his hand. That morning after an early breakfast he had motored to Löbau where Army Headquarters had moved during the night. When he telephoned Ist Corps at half-past ten he had expected to hear that the Heights of Seeben had been captured six hours previously and that Usdau had already fallen, but General von François had had the colossal impudence to tell him that so far the Heights of Seeben had not even been attacked. Ludendorff spoke very plain words into the telephone, and although he represented everything he said as coming from Hindenburg, this polite pretense, which was not intended to deceive, was the only polite part of what he had to say.[1]

This time von François had some cause for his insubordination. Since only four of the Ist Corps' batteries had detrained, an attack might well have failed,[2] and the wireless message intercepted the previous afternoon indicated that Samsonov did not intend to press the German right wing on the 26th. Anyone else would probably have accepted this reasoning, but Ludendorff had refused to begin his relationship with a difficult corps commander by countermanding an order. Shortly after midnight, Ist Corps had received written confirmation of the verbal instructions Ludendorff had issued on the hilltop of Montovo.

Von François, his bright eyes snapping fiercely in his tanned face, had at once telephoned XXth Corps to ask whether its situation was really so serious as to justify a premature attack. General von Scholtz had been calmly reassuring: his position was by no means desperate. Thereupon von François, with a certain grim satisfaction, had told his staff there would be no attack until all the guns and ammunition arrived.

Ludendorff's call changed his mind. Obviously he could not treat the new Chief of Staff as cavalierly as he had old Prittwitz and Waldersee. Von François did not like it, but he obeyed.

His infantry went forward at noon, keeping close to the few black shell-bursts of the bombardment. The Russians put up surprisingly little resistance and by one o'clock General von Conta reported his division on the Heights of Seeben. He added, however, that his troops were too tired to go on to Usdau that afternoon and that in any case he could not complete his artillery preparation before evening. Von François, who had had enough of obedience for one day, readily agreed and postponed the attack on Usdau until the next morning.[3]

On the German left wing nearly sixty miles farther east, von Below's Ist Reserve Corps and von Mackensen's XVIIth Corps had been marching from sunup till sundown for eight sweltering days, covering twenty miles each day. For the past three days they had had to use sandy by-ways because the main roads were choked with refugees. When at sunset on the 25th their vanguards bivouacked near Seeburg and Bischofstein, the exhausted soldiers scarcely had the strength to eat a hot dinner from their field kitchens before falling asleep on the ground.

A few miles to the south, near Bischofsburg, the advance guard of the Russian VIth Corps slept as soundly as the Germans. General Blagovestchensky, who still believed he was pursuing a retreating enemy, had pressed on, heedless of the widening gap between his corps and General Kliouev's XIIIth Corps at Allenstein twenty-five miles to the southwest. Since Russian corps had only enough telephone cable to connect with their divisions, they had to use wireless to communicate with other corps and army headquarters, and because the VIth and XIIIth Corps had thoughtfully been provided with different cyphers,

Blagovestchensky could communicate with Kliouev only in clear.[4]

Shortly after dawn on the 26th, Mackensen's men were on the march again, moving south towards Bischofsburg to find and attack the Russian flank. By the roadside the 65-year-old commander, slim and straight as a subaltern in his frogged hussar tunic, sat motionless on his big white mare and watched the dusty battalions swing by. Under his Death's Head Hussars shako the General's blue eyes were keen as a falcon's in his sharp ruddy face. He might not be a great military thinker, but like all the aristocratic corps commanders of the Eighth Army, he was spirited and active and had the instincts of the hunter.

Farther west General von Below, who felt that his reservists needed additional rest, waited until ten o'clock before advancing on a broad front to cut the Russians off from Allenstein. Although both corps used every available road, the long columns stretched out for miles. Ahead of them and on the flanks Uhlan patrols walked their horses along forest paths, searching for any sign of a Russian soldier.

Originally Samsonov had instructed the VIth Corps to remain near Bischofsburg to protect the right flank of his army, but then had changed his mind and ordered it southwest to Allenstein. One of Blagovestchensky's divisions was already on the road when a third message arrived from Samsonov, ordering the VIth Corps to stay where it was.[5]

By mid-morning 120,000 sweating, thirsty men in field-gray and earth-brown uniforms were converging on a few square miles of desolate countryside. Under the blazing August sun, forests and swamps shimmered in the breathless air, white roads writhed across the landscape, and the little lakes north of Bischofsburg glinted like pools of light. A Taube reconnaissance plane droned high in the bright sky, the black Maltese crosses on its wings looking like markings on a big beetle.

Just before eleven o'clock, patrols from Blagovestchensky's remaining division, the 4th, sighted Mackensen's vanguard mov-

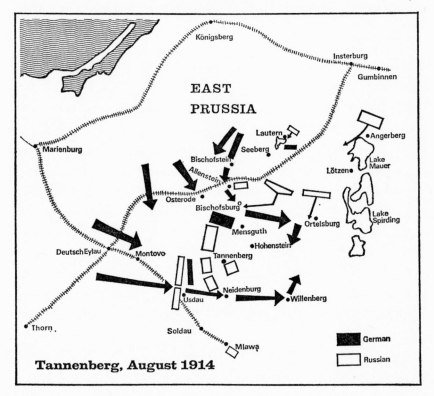

Tannenberg, August 1914

ing down toward Bischofsburg. Assuming that this was a German column in headlong retreat from Rennenkampf, the Russian division commander ordered an attack. The first clash occurred on the road that skirted the eastern shore of Gross-Lautern Lake near the village of Lautern. Russians and Germans deployed in the fields, firing at each other from a few hundred yards' distance and both sending back urgent calls for reinforcements. Along the line of march Mackensen's gunners dropped their trails by the roadsides and went immediately into action. At first the Germans were hard pressed, but as more and more of their battalions came up and worked continually around the left flank, the Russians began to fall back.

Some Russians who were pinned against the shore of Lake Bössau were overrun after a desperate defense, and a few drowned attempting to escape. From this minor incident grew the legend that tens of thousands of Samsonov's soldiers perished in the lakes and swamps of East Prussia. Eyewitnesses later told with circumstantial detail how the Russians sank until only their heads showed above the morass, like thousands of footballs on a field, and how out of pity the Germans finally turned machine-guns on them. "I will hear their cries to my dying day!" one lecturer delared to credulous audiences in Berlin.[6]

Inevitably, old Hindenburg became the hero of the legend. He was said to have spent his years of retirement walking through the lake district, noting the causeways and plumbing the quicksands, planning the perfect battle which — thanks to the Kaiser's royal perspicacity — he was summoned from obscurity to fight.

The defeat of the Russian VIth Corps, if less spectacular than claimed, was nevertheless complete enough. Blagovest-chensky hurriedly recalled his 16th Division that had already marched eight miles along the road to Allenstein, but by now the Russian 4th Division, which had lost 5000 soldiers and 16 guns, was in full retreat. The 16th Division hastened southward in its wake.

As the slow summer dusk crept across lakes and heaths, the roar of gunfire faded. The VIth Corps began to disintegrate; units became intermingled on the roads; and flurries of panic swept the disorganized mass of Russians streaming back through Bischofsburg. Samsonov's right flank had been turned.

By nightfall the trap had more than half closed. Mackensen and Below had only to drive forward on the left and von Fran-çois had only to break through at Usdau on the right to complete the doom of Samsonov's army. In the center "a gaping chasm" remained between the Russians at Usdau and those facing the XXth Corps' right wing, and von Scholtz had penetrated some way into this gap. However, the 3rd Reserve Division had not obeyed Ludendorff's order to advance towards Hohenstein be-cause General von Morgen had decided this would be a mere frontal attack. "The training of our generals to make independent decisions has, as can be seen, its disadvantages," Hoffmann commented ironically.[7]

At dinner that evening in the command mess at Löbau, Ludendorff sat silent at the table, the corners of his small mouth pulled down and a scowl on his face, while he compulsively rolled bread crumbs with both hands. (His staff were later to recognize this as a sign of nerves. When he rolled crumbs slowly with one hand, he was meditating; when he rolled them quickly with one hand, he was worried; when he rolled them with both hands, he was savage with tension.)

Now that the Eighth Army was committed to battle, Ludendorff saw all that could go wrong. Before his eyes rose the terrible consequences of defeat. It would mean nothing less than the loss of the war. And the responsibility was his alone. He glanced across the table at Hindenburg, impassive and stolid, eating an enormous dinner as calmly as though he were home in Hanover. Hoffmann too seemed perfectly serene. He had not had an unbroken night's sleep for nearly a month, but his smooth face was as rosy and boyish as ever. He was drinking a bottle of Moselle in respectful silence, but Ludendorff imagined he saw a mocking light in the pale blue eyes that darted quick little glances at him from time to time.

Didn't these people realize how disastrously everything might still turn out? God alone knew, for instance, what von François might next take it into his head to do. And was old Mackensen to be relied on? He had not shown up brilliantly at Gumbinnen. Worst of all, what about Rennenkampf? Just before dinner Ludendorff had seen another intercepted message which revealed that Rennenkampf's IInd Corps was moving south and west through Angerburg to link up with Samsonov's VIth Corps. Perhaps Blagovestchensky had not been as decisively defeated as Mackensen and Below believed. If the VIth Corps stood and fought the next day and if Rennenkampf hurried, it might be the Eighth Army that was caught in a trap.

Ludendorff rose abruptly from the table and made a sign to

Hindenburg that he would like to see him privately when he had finished his dinner. Hoffmann's slanting eyebrows rose a little quizzically as he watched the Chief of Staff stalk out of the room. Then he began to talk in a quiet voice to the old Commander-in-Chief.

Even Hoffmann had to guess what passed in the interview between Ludendorff and Hindenburg, but his guess was that Ludendorff "lost his nerve a little." [8] Hindenburg later wrote:

> Is it surprising that grave thoughts filled every heart: if the strongest wills showed signs of weakening, and doubts found their way into the clearest heads? Should we not strengthen our forces against Rennenkampf, and not make a serious effort against Samsonov? Were it not better not to try to destroy [Samsonov's] army, but make sure of avoiding destruction ourselves? We overcame the inner crisis, held by the decisions we had taken, and tried to find a solution by an attack with all our forces.[9]

After his talk with Hindenburg, Ludendorff confirmed that Mackensen and Below were to pursue the Russian VIth Corps the next morning. Mackensen would attack frontally while Below enveloped the Russian left. Hoffmann smiled in relief once these orders had gone out, for he had all along been certain that the bold course was the right one and that "the slightest delay could only have made things worse." [10]

Just then the telephone rang. Colonel Gerhard Tappen, the Chief of Operations at Supreme Headquarters in Coblenz, wanted to talk to General Ludendorff.

Ludendorff may still have been resentful that Tappen, an unimaginative man of mediocre intelligence, had replaced him as head of the Second Section, or he may merely have wanted a witness of any instructions from the Supreme Command. At all events, he gestured to Hoffmann: "Take the second receiver, so you can hear what Colonel Tappen wants and my answer."

Obediently Hoffmann picked up the telephone. As Tappen's voice crackled out cheerfully from the Rhine, Hoffmann's expressive eyebrows went up and up. Von Moltke had decided to reinforce the Eighth Army with three corps and a cavalry division from the Western Front. Where should these troops detrain?

Ludendorff knew exactly where they should detrain and gave the necessary instructions without hesitation, but he could scarcely believe what Tappen was telling him. The Schlieffen Plan called for every available man on the right wing and Schlieffen had always worried lest there be too few. This was why Ludendorff had fought the War Department over the army increases. And now Moltke was sending three whole corps to the East!

Without giving too optimistic an account of the situation in East Prussia, Ludendorff clearly told Tappen that the Eighth Army did not desperately need reinforcements. In any case, they would arrive too late for the decisive battle about to be fought. If there was any doubt at all about victory in the West, the corps should remain there. Tappen cheerily said that the troops could be spared and would be sent. He wished Ludendorff good night and good luck and hung up.[11]

That same afternoon General Samsonov had established his headquarters in Neidenburg, twelve miles behind the front. A few days previously Neidenburg had been a neat little town of white frame houses nestling among black fir forests and tall pine woods, but the Cossacks had wantonly set it on fire and now most of it was a smoldering ruin. The odor of charred wood was strong as Samsonov sat waiting for word from the front.

Outside in the cobbled square, a Cossack sotnia rested beside their horses, their carbines piled and their long lances leaning against the metal posts of the street lamps. Some of them, more fortunate then their comrades in the infantry, were sprinkling salt on coarse black bread and carving off chunks with big knives. The Cossacks looked very fierce and warlike with their waved forelocks sticking out from under their round caps, but they had not been of much use to Samsonov, who was still not certain what enemy formations faced him.

He believed that the Germans were retreating to the Vistula, and although his troops were dead tired and his supply columns *versts* away, straggling along the earth roads of Poland, he was determined to drive his divisions forward at least until they occupied the line Allenstein-Osterode. Then perhaps he could permit a day's rest while he waited for Rennenkampf to close in from the northeast.

Late in the afternoon he learned that his XIIIth Corps had occupied Allenstein and that the Germans were attacking the 2nd Division of his XXIIIrd Corps south of Mühlen. Unperturbed by this, he issued orders for the XIIIth, XVth, and half of the XXIIIrd Corps to advance in the morning. Some time later his meditations were disturbed by a sudden uproar outside. He heard the sound of galloping horses, the rumble of wheels and cries of "The Uhlans are coming!" Going out, he found the street filled with panic-stricken soldiers, many of them wounded and some without their rifles. They streamed by, their blouses stained with sweat and their high boots white with dust. Samsonov stopped a few, who said that they were members of the 2nd Division that had been broken by the enemy near Mühlen.[12]

When order had been restored, Samsonov decided to go to dinner. General Postovsky, his nervous-looking Chief of Staff, Major Alfred Knox, a British military attaché, and one or two other officers set out with him for the house that served as a mess. Halfway across the square, Samsonov suddenly stopped and turned to an aide-de-camp.

"I've forgotten my sword," he said with a hearty laugh. "I'm now in the enemy's country and must go armed."

When the aide returned with the sword, Samsonov buckled it on and the party went in to dinner. Halfway through the meal an officer interrupted them to say that the Ist Corps Commander, General Artamanov, urgently wanted to speak to Samsonov on the telephone. The Army Commander and his Chief of Staff at once excused themselves and left the room.[13]

When Samsonov finally returned to his dinner he was looking thoughtful. Later that evening his forebodings deepened when he heard that his left flank had been driven from the Heights of Seeben by German units identified as belonging to the Ist Corps, which was supposed to be retreating from Rennenkampf. Before midnight a report came in that Blagovestchensky's VIth Corps had been flung back from Bischofsburg by greatly superior forces.

For the first time it began to dawn on Samsonov that he, and not the Germans, might be in danger of envelopment, but he did not cancel the attack his center was to make in the morning. After all, his army by itself was larger than the German army, and Rennenkampf was surely hurrying down to strike the enemy rear. Samsonov ordered General Artamanov to protect the left flank of the army at all costs, adding that "not even a greatly superior enemy can break the resistance of the famous Ist Corps" and pointing out that the outcome of the battle depended on Usdau's being held.[14]

In the Operations Room at Löbau the hard glare of electric light reflected blankly from the big map on the wall. A shiver passed through Lieutenant Colonel Hoffmann's giant frame as he turned away to stare at the pre-dawn darkness outside the window. This was the worst time in the whole twenty-four hours, the time for suicides, for wounded men to die, the time for doubts. The August morning felt as chill as November and the forests around Löbau were as still as death.

Hoffmann had not had two consecutive hours' sleep all night. And it had been the same since the beginning of the campaign. He had the constitution of an ox and no nerves at all, but he was terribly tired. Whenever he stretched out on his camp bed, someone was sure to come in with a problem — Grünert, or Kersten, the Director of Railways, or Ludendorff himself — and he would shake himself awake, sit up, sip a little neat cognac from the tumbler he kept beside him, and say: "Very well, let me see the map." [15] All of which was flattering, no doubt, but exhausting.

His orderly entered the Operations Room and handed him a

steaming mug of strong Turkish coffee. Taking a silver flask
from his pocket, Hoffmann poured brandy into the coffee, then
tasted it. His bristling eyebrows went up and his huge shaven
head cocked to one side. These were the difficult decisions. One
couldn't take too long over them either. He made up his mind,
reached down and flung open the window. Carefully he poured
an inch of liquid from the mug and replaced it with brandy from
the flask. Then he turned back to the map on the wall.

Later that morning Mackensen's XVIIth Corps, finding
Bischofsburg abandoned, moved through the town and advanced towards Mensguth and Passenheim. When Ludendorff
heard that the Russians had evacuated Bischofsburg, he ordered
the Ist Reserve Corps to deflect to the west, but did not yet decide its ultimate destination. The German left wing was no
longer meeting organized resistance, for Blagovestchensky had
completely lost control of his troops. Once that afternoon when
he drove up to a column of retreating infantry in his motorcar,
accompanied by his sotnia of Cossacks, someone raised a cry of
"Uhlans!" and the soldiers opened fire.[16] This further demoralized Blagovestchensky, who did not call a halt until nightfall
when his disorganized rabble had passed through the burning
town of Ortelsburg.[17]

However, the action that made the 27th of August the decisive day of the battle was fought on the other German flank. At
five o'clock in the morning von François's Ist Corps opened a
shattering bombardment on the Russian positions in front of Usdau. When the infantry advanced they found the shallow Russian trenches filled with the dead and the dying, but otherwise
undefended. Usdau was occupied by 11 o'clock, but by early
afternoon von François halted his weary troops. By then the
Ist Corps was east of Usdau and west of the town of Soldau.

With the Russian VIth Corps fleeing south from Ortelsburg
and the Russian Ist Corps driven from Usdau, Samsonov's center was all but surrounded. No matter what the XIIIth, XVth,
and XXIIIrd Corps now did, they were destined to thresh help-

lessly about in the forests and swamps, increasingly hungry and short of ammunition. All that Ludendorff required was time for his two wings to close the ring. Typically, he decided to gain that time by ordering his XXth Corps to attack.

The fighting in the center on the 27th, however, was inconclusive, and in the afternoon Hindenburg, Ludendorff, and Hoffmann, who had been watching the battle from an observation platform in a fir tree north of Usdau, returned to headquarters at Löbau "not altogether satisfied." [18] Here they were greeted with the appalling news that the routed remnants of von François's corps were fleeing through Montovo. It would have been utterly unbelievable except that the main street of Löbau was certainly jammed with Ist Corps supply columns all heading north. Hoffmann at once got on the telephone and after an agonizing interval learned that only one battalion had given way. His stern orders soon had the unit turned about again and marching toward the enemy.[19]

In St. Petersburg on the 27th, aristocratic ladies held a fête and by the sale of flags raised £20,000 to be presented to the first Russian soldier to enter Berlin.

Early on the morning of the 28th, Ludendorff set up a small command post near XXth Corps Headquarters at Frögenau. Gray wraiths of mist swirled among the trees, preventing any observation of the battlefield and muffling the sound of gunfire. Ludendorff spent a frustrating morning. None of the wireless sets worked properly, although the operators labored at them frantically, their peakless round caps set aside and earphones clamped over their heads. An erratic telephone connection was maintained with Ist Corps, but Ludendorff was out of touch with his other formations.[20] Even liaison officers in their fast gray staff cars found it difficult to reach Mackensen's and Below's headquarters because of Cossack patrols on the roads.

In the forests in the center the Russians fought valiantly, and as the battle ebbed and flowed among the trees, great flocks of angry rooks circled in the air, their clangor plainly heard between the sounds of firing. The Germans gained no ground here until afternoon.

On the left the XVIIth Corps, owing to a misunderstanding of orders which had been passed to it through the Ist Reserve Corps, had given up its southerly pursuit and moved northwards toward Allenstein, leaving only a small force to follow Blagovestchensky through Ortelsburg. General von Below then learned that there were only weak Russian detachments at Allenstein and suggested that Mackensen should turn south again and march through Passenheim. The fiery old hussar, who had had more than enough of countermanded orders, rejected the proposal out of hand. He declared he would continue in the direction he was going and demanded that, since he was senior to von Below, the Ist Reserve Corps leave the roads free for him. He sent a staff captain to Frögenau by airplane to inform Army Headquarters of his intentions and ask for orders.

The staff captain landed at Frögenau to "a far from friendly welcome," [21] for Ludendorff, already nervous about his center, now discovered that both his left-hand corps were confused, behind schedule, and might not be able to attack that day. He sent the staff officer back with peremptory orders for the XVIIth Corps to turn about and march south with every available man. The Ist Reserve Corps was ordered to attack the Russian XIIIth Corps about Grieslienen that day without fail. Shortly after the staff officer took off on his return flight, Ludendorff was able to repeat these instructions to the XVIIth and Ist Reserve Corps by telephone.

Only on the right wing where von François was attacking did the 28th go as Ludendorff had planned, and even here a full measure of success was achieved only because von François again disobeyed orders. After another whirlwind artillery bombardment, the Ist Corps drove east from Usdau toward Neidenburg, cutting across the rear of the three Russian corps in the center. At noon Ludendorff, worried lest von Scholtz's XXth Corps might not withstand the Russian pressure, ordered von François to swerve north towards Lahna. After five days' experience of von François's personality, Ludendorff ended his order almost pleadingly: "The [Ist] Corps would render the greatest possible service to the army if these intentions were duly carried out. All depends on the Ist Army Corps." [22]

Von François was "surprised" [23] at the order but never for a moment considered obeying it. The change of direction would have allowed the XVth, XXIIIrd, and XIIIth Russian Corps to escape southward. Moreover, it would have entangled the Ist Corps in difficult forest country and slowed its advance. Von François smiled his grim little smile and pressed on due east.

His advance guard was already through Neidenburg and well on the way to Willenberg, and once Willenberg was reached every Russian north of the road was as good as dead or captured. Along his line of march von François dropped off picquets and machine-gun posts at regular intervals. The cordon was thin — only one battalion to every two kilometers — but in general there was a clear 400-yard field of fire between the road and the dark mass of forest to the north. By the time darkness fell, elements of the Ist Corps were in Willenberg and Mackensen's advance guard was not far away. Von François had not bothered to tell Ludendorff what he was doing, but as it happened, it made no difference. Early in the afternoon Ludendorff had recovered from his loss of nerve and issued fresh orders for the Ist Corps to resume its original line of march.

The day's fighting had not gone entirely as Ludendorff had intended, but by late afternoon there was no doubt that the battle had been won. There was, Hoffmann said, "a very cheerful feeling about." [24] Ludendorff, too tense to rejoice, was already planning his regrouping for a blow at Rennenkampf. By 5:30 he was ready to dictate a preliminary order, which he began by saying: "Frögenau — leave the exact time open."

Hoffmann interrupted to suggest that, instead of heading the order "Frögenau," he might choose the historic name of Tannenberg, a hamlet some two miles away, where in 1410 A.D. a

Polish and Lithuanian army had broken the power of the Teutonic Knights. Ludendorff at once saw the force of this proposal and was later to claim he had thought of it himself.[25]

All this while Hindenburg had been a silent onlooker but now he made a suggestion of his own. In his deep rumbling voice he said that he would like to go to the front to visit the victorious troops. The somewhat startled staff saw no reason to disagree, so the old general, Ludendorff, Hoffmann, and Grünert set out in two staff cars. Halfway between Tannenberg and Mühlen they had to stop, for coming toward them down the road were dozens of ambulance wagons, commissariat carts, and supply vehicles, all mixed up together in panic-stricken flight. Ludendorff quickly took control and ordered the officers to spread out across the road with drawn pistols. The fleeing drivers, seeing a line of determined staff officers prepared to shoot them, reined in their horses, but the road to Mühlen was blocked by so many overturned wagons that Hindenburg did not get to the front that day.

The way the panic started was a good illustration of how unused all these troops were to war. A column of Russian prisoners, escorted by a detachment of Landwehr with fixed bayonets, had been passing through Mühlen when they met a supply convoy going in the opposite direction. A transport driver had shouted back a warning to clear the road — "They're coming!" Someone passed the cry along as: "The Russians are coming!" A nervous driver who heard this and caught a distant glimpse of marching men in khaki wheeled his wagon around. A moment later the entire supply convoy was in wild flight.

While the senior army staff had spent the day at Frögenau, the headquarters had moved to the village of Osterode, and Hindenburg was pleased to find himself quartered in the same inn where he had stayed as a subaltern during a staff ride in 1881.[26] That evening Ludendorff learned that Rennenkampf was at last marching south to support Samsonov but this no longer worried him. Nothing now could save the Russian Second Army.

That night Colonel Tappen again telephoned from Coblenz, and again Hoffmann listened on the second receiver. Tappen told Ludendorff that only two corps, not three, were now being sent East. The Guard Reserve and XIth Corps could be spared, but the Vth Corps was needed in the West. Ludendorff repeated that if the reinforcements were required in France they had much better be kept there. Tappen, as optimistic as before, promised that the two corps would shortly be on their way.

Thus on the 28th of August there was elation in German headquarters on both the Western and Eastern fronts. Ironically, the self-congratulation was noticeably less in Osterode where it was more thoroughly justified. Ludendorff was still feeling the effects of the previous days' anxiety. "I could not," he said, "rejoice wholeheartedly at our mighty victory, for the strain imposed on my nerves by the uncertainty about Rennenkampf's army had been too great." [27]

Meanwhile, Samsonov had at last realized that disaster threatened his command. When he had ordered his center corps to advance, he had entangled them inextricably in the German net. The only hope of saving even a portion of the army would have been for the flank corps to have attacked on the 27th while the center retreated as rapidly as possible. Now it was too late. Only a miracle could save the Second Army, and Samsonov did not believe in miracles, or at least not when they depended on Rennenkampf. In his heart he knew that Rennenkampf would not come, just as he had not come long ago at the Yentai coal mines in Manchuria.

Samsonov faced the truth quietly, with gentle resignation. His joviality had gone but it was replaced with the fatalism of Old Russia. At Neidenburg, he could hear von François's guns booming away across the forests, coming nearer and nearer. He informed Jilinski that he was leaving for the front, then broke up his headquarters. He sent the baggage and wireless sets back to Russia, severing communication with Army Group Headquarters. In any case, those communications had brought him nothing but trouble. With General Postovsky and six other staff officers, he set out by motorcar for the front, as submissive to fate as some lost wanderer on the winter steppes who at last lies down to accept a drowsy death from frost.

Later in the morning Major Knox found Samsonov by the roadside with his little staff around him and his Cossack escort nearby. Maps were spread out on the ground beneath the trees and the Russian commander was studying them. Knox waited a little way off until Samsonov rose to his feet and waved for an officer to fold up the maps. Since motorcars could not go forward over the broken country ahead, Samsonov ordered the Cossacks to provide horses for himself and his staff, announcing that he would make his way to General Martos and the headquarters of the XVth Corps.

Before mounting, Samsonov drew Major Knox aside.

"The position here is very critical," he said. "My own duty lies with the fighting troops, but you have a duty to report to your own government. You had better go back now while you still can. But remember that even if the worst happens here, it will not effect the ultimate result of the war."

He swung himself into the saddle and looked back at Knox for the last time, his face gentle and sad.

"The enemy has luck one day," he said. "We will have luck another."

Then he rode slowly away across country toward the sound of the guns. Major Knox joined a long column of wagons going back to Neidenburg. In the cobbled square of the town, outside the house where he had dined with Samsonov two nights previously, Knox saw a screaming Russian soldier being flogged by Cossacks. He carried the sight away with him as his last memory of the invasion of East Prussia. That night he slipped across the Russian border before the German cordon closed.[28]

Samsonov rode forward until he came on General Martos still trying to direct his battle from a hilltop. The little gray-bearded commander of the XVth Corps was astonished to see the army

commander ride slowly up the hill toward him. He had not realized how critical was the situation, but one look at Samsonov's
face told him it was hopeless. Samsonov reined in his horse close
beside Martos and reaching down put an arm around his shoulder.

"You alone will save us," he said quietly. But Martos, looking
him in the eyes, knew that his corps was lost.[29]

That night Samsonov finally ordered a general retreat. General Kondratovitch, the commander of the XXIIIrd Corps, had
already made the same decision for himself. Disguised in a German cloak, he fled incontinently back to Russia, leaving his
troops to fend for themselves. For this he was court-martialed
and dismissed from the service.

On the 29th the three corps of the Russian center fell back
into the forests. Units became mixed up, guns had to be abandoned, officers had difficulty reading their maps printed in the
Roman alphabet, columns lost their way, and by now every
man could hear the German guns firing behind them, in front,
and on both flanks. The ominous sound drew steadily nearer
as the noose tightened. By now, too, the Russians were literally
starving. The XVth Corps had received no rations for four
days, and the XIIIth Corps had marched 42 miles in 40 hours
and fought a battle, without food or water for men or horses.

The road between Neidenburg and Willenberg was held by
25 German battalions. It was not a strong force, but von François had rightly estimated the fighting power of his enemy. During the night of the 29th a few Russians slipped through the
cordon unseen, but far more frequently they were detected and
shot down.

On the 30th, Russian columns tried to fight their way out of
the trap at Saddek, Muschaken and Wallendorf. The left-hand
column at Wallendorf surprised a force of Germans in the forest and by a violent charge captured twenty guns, some complete with their teams. However, the cordon still lay ahead, and
that night, when the Russians tried to crash through, they were

caught in the beams of searchlights and cut down by machine gun fire and shrapnel. One of those taken prisoner here was General Kliouev, commander of the XIIIth Corps. The column at Saddek met a similar fate.[30] At Muschaken, east of Neidenburg, the Russians attempted to break out by daylight. As they emerged from the trees, a bearded Orthodox priest in a long black cassock walked in front of them, holding aloft a crucifix. They came on fearlessly, accompanied by horse-drawn wagons and carts.

In the ditch beside the highway lay two German battalions, their spiked helmets in gray linen covers almost invisible in the dusty grass. The Germans watched incredulously as the Russians approached, then a few excited soldiers opened fire. Within a second two thousand rifles were spitting flame and six machineguns had begun their peculiar halting stutter. The column melted away; those not killed or wounded fled back to the forest; and out in the open, wounded horses whinnied high in fear as they pulled overturned wagons wildly about behind them.

A few brave Russians returned a desultory fire from the rim of the forest, but this soon died down and long poles were poked out with white blouses and cloths tied to them. Then the Russians began to emerge with their hands above their heads.

Meanwhile, Samsonov and his staff had left the headquarters of the XVth Corps. By the night of the 29th, the army commander, his seven staff officers, and an NCO had made their way through the swamps and forests, skirting the railway line as far as the outskirts of Willenberg, only seven miles from the Russian frontier. Here, however, they found the Germans ahead of them. They waited another hour for the darkness to thicken, then moved off again, leading their horses, since it was unsafe to ride through the treacherous undergrowth.

One officer had a compass, and they tried to keep direction by this, pausing every few minutes to take a bearing by the light of a spluttering sulphur match. When the matches ran out, they joined hands to avoid becoming separated and went on in the blackness. Samsonov, who suffered from asthma, was noticeably weakening and had to be supported by two of his officers. Again and again he wheezed out to General Postovsky: "The Tsar trusted me. How can I face him after such a disaster?"

At about one o'clock they paused to rest, sinking down gratefully on the thick carpet of pine needles beneath the tall black trees. It was a moment or two before the others noticed that General Samsonov had slipped away. Suddenly, from the patch of deeper shadow farther inside the forest, a single revolver shot rang out. General Postovsky jumped to his feet, knowing at once what the sound meant. Earlier in the day Samsonov had told him he intended to commit suicide, but Postovsky had believed he had changed his mind.

The officers searched for Samsonov's body, but the night was too dark and the trees too thick. At last when they heard a German patrol approaching, they abandoned their search and moved off. Later, accompanied by a small group of Cossacks they met in the forest, they managed to re-enter Russia.[31] A day or two later the Germans found General Samsonov's corpse with a single bullet-hole through the head. They buried him in Willenberg, but in 1916 his widow was allowed to transport his body back to Russia.

When General Martos had done all he could for his shattered corps, he also tried to escape with his staff and five of his Cossack escort. On the afternoon of the 29th they met two Polish peasants in the forest who directed them straight into a German ambush. General Machugovsky, Martos' Chief of Staff, was killed by machine-gun fire and the rest of the party scattered, so that by evening only Martos himself, an officer and two Cossacks were left. None of them had had anything to eat or drink since early morning. Their horses were exhausted, and when one lay down and died, the others had to be led. Having no compass, the little party tried to take their bearings from the stars, but before midnight the sky clouded over and they were soon lost.

Suddenly the blackness was cut by a searchlight beam. As it

swept over them, there came a shout in German, followed by a fusilade of shots. Martos mounted and galloped off, but before he had gone a hundred yards his horse was shot from under him. He fell heavily and the next moment was seized by rough hands.

The following morning Martos was being escorted to Neidenburg when General von François himself appeared by the roadside and called on the vehicle to halt. Looking down the road, Martos saw with surging hope that Neidenburg had actually been occupied by Russian cavalry. However, if von François was perturbed by this he did not show it. His hard blue eyes twinkled as brightly as ever as he drew the captured general over to his staff car and offered him wine and chocolate.[32]

Martos did not know it, but General Sirelius, who had replaced Artamanov as commander of the Russian Ist Corps, had made a final belated attempt to break the German cordon. Early on the 30th he had massed his troops at Mlawa and begun marching on Neidenburg. A German airman who sighted Sirelius' column reported to Ludendorff that it stretched for 23 miles. Ludendorff hastily scraped together what troops he could spare to deal with this new threat, but von François already had the situation in hand. He did not withdraw his line of picquets between Neidenburg and Willenberg, but launched a delaying attack on the flank of the advancing Russians. Before daybreak on the 31st, Sirelius had retreated back to Mlawa.[33]

On the evening of the 30th General Martos was brought to Eighth Army Headquarters at Osterode. He sat for awhile alone in the dining room of the ancient inn, huddling disconsolately on a plain chair beside the empty white-tile stove. Two sentries with fixed bayonets stood by the door. Martos was no longer a young man, and in the previous twenty-four hours he had suffered a terrible defeat, had lost his corps, and had seen friends and comrades killed. He had had no sleep for several days and very little to eat. He had not even had a cigarette since the morning of the 29th. Try as he would, he could not prevent a few tears trickling down his cheeks onto his iron-gray beard.

At that moment General Ludendorff strode into the room on his short legs and stood over him. After a few seconds Ludendorff abruptly demanded in good Russian:

"Tell me, what was the strategy of your famous General Samsonov when he invaded East Prussia?"

Martos replied that as a corps commander he had nothing to do with strategy but had had only tactical tasks.

"Yes," Ludendorff said, "but now you are all defeated and have laid down your arms. Now the Russian frontier is open to our invasion from Grodno to Warsaw."

Martos straightened in his chair. "I was surrounded by superior forces," he said. "But before that I had considerable success against your troops when my strength was equal to yours. I had trophies: field guns, machine-guns, and prisoners — staff officers and many men."

Ludendorff's expression changed and a cold glint came into his eyes.

"Have you any money?" he asked abruptly.

Martos replied that he had some Russian paper money with him.

"But that money will be worth nothing now," Ludendorff said.

Just then the door opened again and Hindenburg came in. Seeing the signs of agitation on Martos' face, the massive old man crossed the room and with a characteristic gesture took the prisoner's hand in both his own. In halting Russian he begged Martos to calm himself, promised that his sword would be returned to him, and told him that he and his troops had fought well. Only when Martos had smiled and thanked him did Hindenburg drop his hands. He straightened, bowed formally, and departed with Ludendorff. At the door Hindenburg turned and said quietly: "I wish you happier days." [34]

Now that the battle was over, the victors could scarcely believe the extent of their success. Great crowds of prisoners, apathetic and weak from starvation, sat dumbly about on the ground, unwinding from bleeding feet the homespun cloths they wore instead of socks or merely looking dejectedly at nothing. Many of the Cossacks, fearful of retribution for their treatment of civilians, busily tried to pick off their distinctive red trouser stripes. When Hoffmann, driving over the battlefield with the cavalry general, Count Dohna, came on a railway station packed with prisoners, the two Germans began to argue about the probable number of captives.

Count Dohna asked: "Well, how many prisoners do you think there will be?"

"We have no exact reports," Hoffmann replied, "but I should estimate at least 30,000 to 40,000."

Count Dohna disagreed, saying that the total could not possibly exceed 20,000. Hoffmann promptly offered him a wager — the Count to pay one mark for every prisoner over 20,000 and Hoffmann to pay one mark for every prisoner short of that total. Very wisely Dohna refused to bet.[35]

A single battalion of the 43rd Regiment of von François's Ist Corps captured 17,000 Russians, and when the final count was made the Germans found they had 95,000 unwounded and 30,000 wounded prisoners.[36] Only one officer of Martos' XVth Corps had escaped back to Russia. The number of Russian dead, never accurately computed, was also very high. Nearly a week was required to collect the 500 captured guns and the abandoned horses and transport.

On the 31st Hindenburg telegraphed the Kaiser:

I beg most humbly to report to Your Majesty that the ring round the larger part of the Russian Army was closed yesterday. The XIIIth, XVth, and XVIIIth [sic] Army Corps have been destroyed. We have already taken more than 60,000 prisoners, among them the Corps Commanders of the XIIIth and XVth Corps. The guns are still in the forests and are now being brought in. The booty is immense though it cannot yet be assessed in detail. The Corps outside our ring, the Ist and VIth, have also suffered severely and are now retreating in hot haste through Mlawa and Myszaniec.[37]

That evening in Allenstein, Hindenburg and Ludendorff attended a service of thanksgiving in the Protestant Church that stood near the old castle of the Teutonic Knights. The plain bare building was filled with worshipers in field-gray, and Hindenburg at least was overcome with emotion at the scene. What more fitting end for a great victory? The ancient Teutonic god of battles had been kind to the German people. The old general's warrior heart swelled with pride and thankfulness as he heard strong German voices raised in Luther's hymn: *"Eine feste Burg ist unser Gott . . ."* [38]

Dutifully Ludendorff knelt beside the army commander, but when he gave thanks, it was Count von Schlieffen and his teaching rather than the Almighty who had first call on his gratitude.[39] In any case, Ludendorff had little time to spare for emotion. The army had to be regrouped to strike at Rennenkampf.

CHAPTER VI

THE MASURIAN LAKES

T HE OLD INN at Osterode throbbed with activity; staff cars were parked three deep in the cobbled courtyard; officers hurried in and out; and the big signal switchboard on the ground floor clicked busily day and night. General Ludendorff had a thousand things he wanted done, and he worked his staff practically round the clock.

General von Gallwitz's Guard Reserve Corps and General von Plüskow's XIth Corps were on their way by rail from Namur, and the 8th Cavalry Division was also arriving from the West. Ludendorff had ordered them to detrain on the Allenstein-Elbing line[1] so as to be ready to advance northeast against Rennenkampf's First Army. Meanwhile, every available man was put to work repairing the railways in the territory the Russians had occupied. Rennenkampf might outnumber even the reinforced Eighth Army, but as long as the East Prussian railroads worked efficiently the strategic advantage would rest with the Germans.

Ludendorff was surprised that the Russians had not destroyed the railway lines as thoroughly as he had anticipated. The Germans had done better in their retreat from Gumbinnen, but even their demolitions were soon repaired. Typically, Ludendorff showed no pleasure at this; instead, he made a mental note to tell the German engineers their faults and give them extra training as soon as time permitted.[2]

From his new headquarters in a little red-brick schoolhouse in Luxembourg, von Moltke had sent Hindenburg a telegram on the 31st of August:

. . . The first task of the Eighth Army will be to clear East Prussia of Rennenkampf's Army.

It is desired that with such troops as you can spare you should follow up the enemy you have just beaten in the direction of Warsaw, bearing in mind the Russian movements from Warsaw towards Silesia.

When the situation in East Prussia permits, you are to contemplate employing the Eighth Army in the direction of Warsaw.[3]

Ludendorff was very well pleased with this order, for it gave him a clear objective and left him to get on with the job in his own way. He was at his brilliant best during the early days of September, ardent, energetic, and exacting, the master of every detail, his mind working with the accuracy of a computing machine.

Eighth Army Headquarters had no definite information of what was happening farther south where huge Austrian and Russian forces struggled in a titanic battle about Lemberg, but Ludendorff suspected that Conrad was not doing well. Ludendorff had always felt that Austria's armaments were inadequate and her strategic railways insufficiently developed. Moreover, there had been scarcely any military co-operation between Austria and Germany before the war and a joint plan had been decided on only in the "roughest outlines." [4] But there was no sense now in bewailing lost opportunities. First he would drive the invader from East Prussia, then consider future moves. As for the situation in the West, he could only hope that Colonel Tappen's optimism was justified. Presumably it was, or Moltke would never have sent him two army corps.

In fact, however, Germany was already well on the way to losing the war. On the last day of August General von Kluck, commander of the German First Army on the extreme right of the wheeling wing, had turned southeast to march across the front of Paris instead of behind it as the Schlieffen Plan had specified. Two days later Moltke gave his official sanction in a telegram to the First and Second Armies:

> It is the intention of the High Command to drive the French back
> in a southeasterly direction, cutting them off from Paris. The First
> Army will follow the Second in echelon and will also cover the right
> flank of the armies.[5]

This meant that the Schlieffen Plan had definitely been abandoned. Von Kluck's army became no more than a flank guard,
whereas in all pre-war planning it was to have been the swinging
hammerhead of the German offensive. Although Kluck and
Moltke both believed the French had been decisively beaten, the
Prussian Minister of War, General Erich von Falkenhayn, had
doubts about the completeness of the victory. After studying the
master map in the Operations Room in Luxembourg, he turned
to Moltke and said: "This isn't a battle won, it's an orderly retreat. Show me your trophies and your prisoners."

Happily unaware of any of this, Hoffmann was writing up his
diary in his room in Osterode: "The battle [of Tannenberg]
was a huge success — greater than we could have supposed . . .
One entire Russian army is disposed of: now for the other." [6]
He had good reason to be pleased, for Ludendorff was far
readier to listen to his ideas than Prittwitz or Waldersee had
been. In another diary entry Hoffmann wrote: "Ludendorff is
a first-class fellow to work with. He is the right man for this
business — ruthless and hard. We get on admirably, and I am
proud that some of my ideas have been considered for his new
plan of operations." [7]

Germany hailed the victory of Tannenberg with hysterial de-
light, and the popular imagination seized on the figure of the
Commander-in-Chief. Hindenburg's calm face, his huge square
head — "like a woodcut" — and his inner strength and repose
all gave the German people confidence. With such a Siegfried
who could doubt that Hagen would be slain? Overnight the unknown general became a symbol of certitude to millions. His
portrait looked down with unbelievable benevolence of countenance from billboards all across the Fatherland. During Sep-

tember, as the strategic situation darkened, as Austria suffered a calamitous defeat and the German armies fell back baffled from the Marne, the Germans clung desperately to the image of Hindenburg. And in order to belittle the failure in the West, the authorities deliberately encouraged this hero-worship and exaggerated the victories in East Prussia.

Hindenburg himself had no illusions. He knew that Tannenberg had been won by Ludendorff, Hoffmann and von François, but he did nothing to stop his idolization. Perhaps there was nothing he could have done. Gifts and congratulations showered on him from all over Germany. People from all walks of life wrote asking his advice about their problems; women sent him jellies and homemade nostrums for illness; young girls sent him pillows stuffed with their hair. He took it all calmly, although at about this time he developed an irritating habit of referring to Ludendorff as "my loyal assistant."

Ludendorff and Hoffmann were not entirely gratified by the adulation accorded their commander. Ludendorff soon began to speak of: "When *I* won the Battle of Tannenberg . . ." And Hoffmann, more modest and more sardonic, poked quiet fun at the legend. "Since I heard that Hindenburg won the Battle of Tannenberg," he remarked, "I have ceased to believe in Hannibal and Caesar." And once when he was showing visitors over the battlefield, he pointed out the building in Marienburg which had housed Eighth Army Headquarters. "That," he said, "is where Hindenburg slept before the Battle of Tannenberg." Later at Osterode he indicated the old Gasthaus: "That is where Hindenburg slept after the Battle of Tannenberg." He had arranged the tour so that Löbau was visited last, and there, with a perfectly straight face, as bland and innocent as a baby's, he pointed to a house and remarked: "And that, gentlemen, is where Hindenburg slept all *during* the Battle of Tannenberg."

In the first days of September, however, Ludendorff and Hoffmann were in no mood for criticism. Both were awarded the Iron Cross and both were delighted. Even after the war Ludendorff wrote that his heart still swelled with pardonable satisfaction at the thought of it. He added, it is true, that "the value of the Iron Cross, 2nd Class, dwindled in the course of the war," but pointed out that anyone who had won it honorably as he had done should nevertheless wear it with pride.[8] Hoffmann's comment was also typical. "I had never thought," he confided to his diary, "that this finest of all military decorations could be won by sitting at the end of a telephone line." [9]

By the 4th of September Ludendorff had completed his regrouping and was ready to advance against Rennenkampf. The Russian general had made no offensive move and had actually withdrawn his advanced troops several kilometers. Jilinski was partly responsible for this lack of initiative, for on the 30th of August he had instructed Rennenkampf:

> General Samsonov has suffered a complete defeat and the enemy now has full liberty to turn against you. Keep this in view. You must take every measure to interrupt the railway lines by which the enemy may move troops against you. Be careful that the enemy does not operate against you through Lötzen.[10]

From this it might have been thought that the Germans greatly outnumbered Rennenkampf, yet by the end of the first week of September the Russian First Army consisted of 14½ infantry divisions and 5½ cavalry divisions to Ludendorff's 9 active and 4 reserve divisions and 2 cavalry divisions.* [11] Another four to six Russian divisions were massing at Osowiec and Augustovo. Moreover, each Russian division was composed of 16 battalions to the German 12. Nevertheless, on the 2nd of September, Rennenkampf ordered his army to entrench a defensive position from the Baltic to the northern end of the Masurian Lakes. Mindful of Jilinski's advice, he left an entire corps to watch the exits of the Lötzen Gap.

During the fighting in August the Germans had never relin-

* In East Prussia the Germans also had about 5½ equivalent divisions of fortress troops, Landwehr and Landsturm, not fully suited to field service.

quished their control of the Masurian Lakes. The causeways between the lakes had been strongly fortified in peacetime, for the
whole defense of East Prussia had been based on the idea that
the 50-mile chain of lakes would divide the invading forces.
The most important fortification was at Lötzen, 30 miles from
the southern end of the lakes. Here Fort Boyen guarded the
mile-wide gap between the northern and southern lakes.
Through the Lötzen Gap ran the railroad to Lyck and a metal-
surfaced military road. Jilinski was right to be nervous of this
gap, for if any considerable German force could sortie from it,
Rennenkampf's position in the north would be turned.

On the 27th of August, while he had been marching down to
Samsonov's aid, Rennenkampf had sent a staff officer, accompanied by a trumpeter, to Fort Boyen. The trumpeter had blown
a fanfare, just as in the days of medieval warfare, and the officer
had bellowed out a demand for surrender, ending with the
words: "You are given four hours to decide. If the fort is not
surrendered in that time, not one stone will be left upon another." [12]

Colonel Busse, the commandant of Fort Boyen, was not living in the days of chivalry. He had curtly ordered his Landwehr to open fire; the staff officer and trumpeter were wounded
and captured; and Rennenkampf was left to contemplate how
best to put his threat into execution.

Unlike Ludendorff at Liège, Rennenkampf had made no plans
for the reduction of Fort Boyen. In all his army there was not a
single howitzer large enough to smash the fortifications and so
the vital Lötzen Gap remained firmly in German hands.

In his plan of campaign Ludendorff took full advantage of
this. He intended to grip the Russian First Army by a frontal
attack delivered with four corps — the Guard Reserve, the Ist
Reserve, the XIth and the XXth — while the XVIIth and Ist
Corps, together with the 1st and 8th Cavalry Divisions, wheeled
wide to the south to strike Rennenkampf's left rear, roll up his
line and pin him against the seacoast. It would be another Tan-

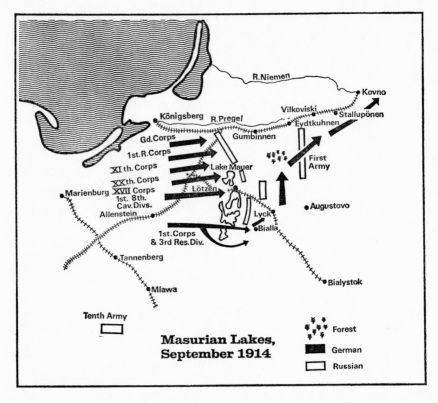

**Masurian Lakes,
September 1914**

Forest

German

Russian

nenberg, except that a double envelopment would be unnecessary. Since the enveloping German right wing might itself be
exposed to a flank attack, Ludendorff detached three divisions
under General von der Goltz to act as right flank guard.

The Russians may have had a dearth of good generals, but
they certainly had no shortage of men. When Japan had joined
the Allies on the 15th of August, the IIIrd Siberian Corps had
been packed into large shed-like railway wagons and sent on the
long journey across Russia to Poland where they were joined
about Mlawa by the XXIInd and Ist Turkestan Corps. These
corps, which were later formed into a new Tenth Army under
General Flug, might have posed a serious threat to Ludendorff's
encircling southern wing had not von der Goltz been imbued
with the General Staff's doctrine that attack is often the best defense. Although he did not have sufficient strength to threaten

the Russians seriously, von der Goltz advanced boldly towards Mlawa, brushing aside light opposition.

His move had important psychological results. Far away in his office in Bialystok, Jilinski at once became convinced that the entire Eighth Army was about to attack Warsaw. Conrad, in fact, had suggested this as a means of relieving his forces fighting in front of Lemberg, but both Moltke and Ludendorff had rejected the plan as too dangerous while Rennenkampf remained undefeated.

Now Jilinski fancied that the opportunity lost at Tannenberg was again presenting itself. Here, surely, was another chance for a great concentric offensive to crush the Eighth Army. He began to prepare for a major battle which he thought would develop in Poland on or about the 14th of September and he ordered Rennenkampf to descend upon the rear of the German invaders. None of this had any basis in reality. Jilinski played with his colored pins and little flags on the map on his office wall but the movements he imagined and the forces with which he dealt were phantoms. Rennenkampf paid no attention whatsoever to the orders emanating from Bialystok.

On the 5th of September Ludendorff began his advance. The four corps that were to make the frontal assault closed by easy marches on Rennenkampf's line between the Pregel River and Lake Mauer, while von Mackensen prepared to break out from the Lötzen Gap and von François marched south of the lakes. Von François, always inclined to be critical of Ludendorff, complained that the enveloping wing was too weak and demanded an extra corps, but Ludendorff, while recognizing the advantages this might bring, decided that for a frontal attack on a 50-kilometer front even four corps were no more than enough and firmly refused the request.

The battle that flared up on the 8th of September was unlike any so far fought on the Eastern Front. The Germans assaulted all along the line but their attack nowhere had sufficient weight to succeed. The Russians, in good deep trenches and relatively safe from artillery fire, everywhere maintained their positions, and after a long day's fighting the Germans were shaken by their failure.

In the Lötzen Gap the XVIIth Corps marched past Fort Boyen and took up rather cramped positions on the perimeter of the defenses. Mackensen attacked at five in the morning, at noon and at eight in the evening, but the Russian IInd Corps, which was reinforced during the day by two divisions, held firm. Even worse, the narrow bottleneck of the gap became choked with administrative units, as supply wagons, ammunition columns, and ambulances formed a solid mass that could move neither forward nor backward. The 1st and 8th Cavalry Divisions, which should by now have been many miles in the enemy's rear, still waited behind Lötzen, unable to advance.

Farther south, von François with the Ist Corps and 3rd Reserve Division made better progress on both sides of Lake Spirding. He captured the village of Bialla on the 7th, and the next day, after a sharp little battle with eight Finnish battalions, took the town of Arys to the north. The Ist Division had an interesting advantage in this day's fighting, for it attacked on its old peacetime maneuver ground which all the officers and NCOs knew as well as their own gardens at home. After breaking the resistance at Arys and capturing 1000 prisoners, von François wheeled north with the Ist Corps and sent the 3rd Reserve Division toward Lyck.

Von François's northern wheel marked the decisive break in the battle. At first light on the 9th of September, his 2nd Division, advancing through the wooded broken country east of Lake Kruglinnen, fell on the left rear of the Russian IInd Corps opposite Mackensen. The Russians fought well, but as more and more German battalions deployed, lapping farther and farther around them, four divisions finally broke and fled, leaving behind 5000 prisoners and 60 guns. The road was now open to the north. The XVIIth and Ist Corps had only to strike through Gumbinnen to Stallupönen and Vilkoviski to cut off Rennenkampf's retreat and encircle his army.

Although on the 9th of September Ludendorff received reports
from airmen that the Russian positions opposite Mackensen
were weakly occupied or abandoned,[13] he did not give full
credence to this until the next morning when infantry patrols
confirmed it.[14] By then von François was already in full cry to
the northwest and Mackensen was advancing in the same direction.

Samsonov had reacted to disaster with fatalistic courage; Rennenkampf now reacted with panic. And the panic proved more
effective.

As soon as he learned that his left flank had been turned, the
First Army Commander had only one thought — to escape from
the terrible foe who was closing in on him. Without bothering to
inform Jilinski at Bialystok, Rennenkampf ordered an immediate retreat of the entire army, except for the 40th Division of the
IVth Corps and the 26th Division of the IInd Corps which he ordered to counter-attack. The rest of the Army streamed back
the way it had come three weeks previously. Divisions moved
parallel to each other on both sides of roads that were packed
with wheeled transport. They marched along all day on the 10th
under the hot sun. They marched all that night, and all the next
day. In the first fifty hours of the retreat Rennenkampf's army
covered 55 miles. Such a pace could not be maintained without
serious deterioration in fighting power and organization. Units
were thinned as stragglers fell out; units became mixed together;
infantry were separated from their guns; and formation headquarters soon ceased to exercise control. Still the army fled, in
mounting confusion and disorder and with increasing discour-
agement and fear.

Rennenkampf himself was infected by the panic. He moved
his own headquarters with suspicious haste, sometimes three or
four times each day. Finally he gave up all pretense of con-
trolling the retreat and scurried across the Russian frontier by
motorcar,[15] not stopping until he reached Kovno, a hundred
miles from the Masurian Lakes.

The two divisions left behind to counter-attack carried out

their suicidal mission with the greatest gallantry on the 10th of September. The 40th Division's attack surprised the XIth Corps north of Gerdauen, and although the German lines held, the XIth Corps could make no advance that day. To the southeast, where the 26th Division struck at Scholtz's XXth Corps, the Germans suffered even more heavily.

On the morning of the 11th, when XIth Corps Headquarters reported that the Russians were counter-attacking in great strength, Ludendorff, who already knew of the attacks from intercepted wireless messages, suggested to von Plüskow that the XIth Corps was opposed by only three regiments of the 40th Division. Plüskow, however, insisted that the Russians were in greatly superior numbers. The more Ludendorff thought about it, the less he liked it. Rennenkampf's force was larger than the Eighth Army. Perhaps the Russians were concentrating for a single heavy blow at the thin German line between Lake Mauer and the River Pregel. If so, the enveloping wing would be needed on that battlefield. Against his own better judgment, Ludendorff ordered the XVIIth and Ist Corps to deflect north to the aid of the XIth and XXth Corps.

Von François and von Mackensen were thus drawn closer towards the German main body and further away from the vital junctions of Stallupönen and Vilkoviski where they could have stood astride the Russian line of flight. Late in the afternoon the XIth Corps reported that the Russian attacks were not, after all, of very great strength. Ludendorff at once countermanded the orders deflecting the XVIIth and Ist Corps to the north, but by then it was too late. Half a day had been lost.[16] If the chaotic masses of fleeing Russian soldiers had found themselves suddenly faced by hard lines of German infantry deployed between them and their home, little of Rennenkampf's army could have escaped. Instead, the broken remnants streamed on through Stallupönen and Vilkoviski unopposed. The envelopment had become merely a stern chase.

By the evening of the 11th Ludendorff realized that the great opportunity had gone. His face was stern and scowling as he spoke to his corps commanders over the telephone. Never one to admit that the fault could be his, he vented his spleen on his subordinates. Now that it was too late, he angrily ordered the XIth and XXth Corps to press ahead and blamed von François for holding up the advance of the XVIIth Corps.[17] In a desperate attempt to regain the strategical advantage, he ordered his two cavalry divisions to sweep wide to the south of the Forest of Rominten.

However, nothing could compensate now for the fatal loss of nerve earlier in the day. On the 12th von François's 1st Division skirted the northern edge of the Forest of Mehlkehmen as it advanced toward Pillupönen. When, in an attempt to break south into the forest, several Russian columns attacked the division's rearguard, a portion of the main body had to turn back. The Russians were driven north again with the loss of over 1000 prisoners, and the 1st Division entered Pillupönen.

Von François's 2nd Division advanced by the road that ran through the center of the forest to Wisztyniec. They passed the Kaiser's hunting lodge, which looked as ruined and romantic as the Sleeping Beauty's castle. In the forest the trees grew tall and straight and close together, and between them the undergrowth was so thick that bodies of troops could not move in formation. Every few hundred yards the forest was cut by long straight rides, like backdrops for a pantomime production of Grimm's fairy tales.

Before the 2nd Division had advanced far, it discovered that the Forest of Mehlkehmen was swarming with Russian soldiers. Most of them had no other idea than to escape and, as the division pushed on, droves of khaki-clad men could be seen running between the trees and crashing through the undergrowth in every direction. A few Russians showed fight. At one point the 1st Corps Headquarters column was suddenly attacked by Cossacks who sabered down the guards and captured all von François's personal baggage, but when a troop of divisional cavalry galloped up, the Cossacks fled. The Corps Commander spent a pleasant day, riding about the forest hunting down Russians. It was not unlike a pheasant shoot on his East Elbian estates.

By sunset on the 13th, the fighting was virtually over. A Russian rearguard, left behind at Vilkoviski and never ordered to withdraw, resisted valiantly until it was overwhelmed, but Ludendorff had no intention of pressing the pursuit beyond the Niemen River.[18]

General Jilinski was beside himself when he heard what had happened to the First Army. For the second time in a fortnight one of his army commanders had deliberately severed all communication with Bialystok while his army disintegrated around him. Jilinski telegraphed the Grand Duke Nicholas:

> General Rennenkampf has thought more about the safety of his Staff than of directing the movements of his army, which he has not in actual fact commanded for several days. He reports that he is moving personally to Vilkoviski and that he is withdrawing the IIIrd and XXVIth Corps eastwards, leaving the remaining corps of his army to their fate. His Staff has gone with him. The behavior of the Army Commander has made all direction of operations impossible. He has altered the position of his headquarters four times in the last 24 hours, each time completely breaking off communication.[19]

The Grand Duke, however, was no longer willing to believe any explanation from Jilinski, whom he already intended to replace as commander of the Northwest Army Group by General Ruszki. Jilinski received only a cold reply which suggested that it was "quite in the nature of General Rennenkampf to wish to direct his troops personally." [20]

The battle was over, and miraculously the Russian First Army, although utterly disorganized and terribly depleted, had made good its escape. On the 14th Rennenkampf reported by telegram to the Grand Duke Nicholas: "All corps have now broken off the battle."

They had indeed. And it is a measure of the control exercised by the Stavka that Nicholas should have sent Rennenkampf the incredible reply: "With all my heart I thank you for your successful leadership. Convey my thanks to the heroic First Army for its efforts. For the future we place our faith in your energy and in God's help." [21]

Things were in a bad way in Holy Russia.

The Russian First Army had spent exactly 28 days in East Prussia. During that time it had lost 145,000 men — 45,000 prisoners and 100,000 casualties — 200 guns, and virtually all its transport. The remnants that recrossed the Niemen River would take weeks to reorganize and re-equip. Even worse than this was the blow that had been struck at Russian morale. A significant portion of the Tsar's forces was now convinced that the war was lost and that nothing the Russians could do could compensate for German organization, equipment, training, and leadership.

This view was well founded. Between the 15th of August and the 13th of September the Russian First and Second Armies had deployed 410 battalions, 232 cavalry squadrons and 1392 guns on German territory. This huge force had been cut to pieces by a single German army containing, at the maximum, only 224 battalions, 128 cavalry squadrons, and 1130 guns.[22] Samsonov and Rennenkampf between them had lost 310,000 men and 650 guns, a force equal to seven and a half army corps at full field establishment. Moreover, this appalling loss had been inflicted upon the flower of the Russian regular army, and although the vast empire of the Tsar had men aplenty, it could never replace the trained officers and NCOs who had been squandered among the forests and swamps of East Prussia.

CHAPTER VII

THE ADVANCE TO THE VISTULA

G ENERAL VON HINDENBURG wrinkled his nose as he went from room to room of the Hotel Dessauer in Insterburg where Rennenkampf had had his headquarters. Even allowing for the Russians' hasty departure, the place was far from clean by German standards. "This first evacuation had left behind remarkable traces of Russian semi-civilization," Hindenburg recalled later. "The heady odors of scent, leather, and cigarettes were not able to cover the odor of other things." [1] After his tour of the building, the old general was glad to get out into the fresh air. He decided to go for a walk across the nearby Heide. Perhaps he would find some wild flowers he could send to his wife in Hanover.

While Hindenburg walked on the heath, Ludendorff was on the telephone to Freiherr Conrad von Hötzendorff at Neu Sandec, the Austro-Hungarian Supreme Headquarters. Until Rennenkampf had been driven back across the Niemen, Ludendorff had been too busy to spare much thought to other fronts. Now, on the 14th of September, he received his first accurate report of the fighting around Lemberg. Conrad's voice over the wire was calm and matter-of-fact, but his news was very bad indeed.

Between the 23rd of August and the 12th of September, three Austrian and four Russian armies had clashed in a series of bloody battles along a 200-mile front between the Vistula and the Dniester Rivers. At first the Austrians had done well, but as each side was reinforced with an additional army early in September, the Russians began to prevail. The Austrian Third Army had been defeated and Conrad had reluctantly ordered a general retreat on the 11th.

Listening to Conrad's cautious phrases, Ludendorff could sense that the Austrians were in grave difficulties. For the past 60 hours, they had been streaming rearward through heavy rain, with the Russians in full pursuit. Conrad did not believe that he would be able to re-form his front behind the San River, but spoke of continuing the retreat as far as the Dunajec, more than 130 miles west of Lemberg.

After his conversation with Conrad, Ludendorff was put through to von Moltke in Luxembourg. What Moltke had to say was even more alarming than Conrad's report had been. As he listened, Ludendorff felt a chill creep into the bright September air. Schlieffen's master plan had failed.

As their vast wheel had taken the invaders ever deeper into France and as von Kluck had moved across the front of the Paris defenses instead of passing west of them, a gap had appeared between Kluck's First and Bülow's Second Armies. There had been no German reserves to throw into this gap because the right wing had been weakened by the detachment of five corps — two to invest Antwerp, two sent to the Eighth Army, and one to invest Givet and Maubeuge. The French Government had hastily abandoned the capital on the 2nd of September, but the French Army, after twelve terrible days of retreat, had turned to fight on the Marne. A force hurriedly assembled under Gallieni, the military governor of Paris, had moved out to strike von Kluck's exposed flank, and British and French formations had penetrated into the gap between the First and Second Armies. As this threat developed, Moltke sent a staff officer, Lieutenant Colonel Hentsch, to assess the situation at Kluck's and Bülow's headquarters. On his own initiative Hentsch had ordered a retirement, and on the 9th of September Bülow and Kluck had begun the retreat which ended all hopes of quick victory in the West. By evening on the 12th of September the German First Army was back across the Aisne and the other four German armies west of Verdun had retired to conform.

Even over the telephone Ludendorff could tell that Moltke was deeply moved.[2] In fact, *der traurige Julius* was a broken man who felt, with every reason, that his inadequacies had lost Germany the war. However, he went on to say that Ludendorff was being appointed Chief of Staff of a new Southern Army to be created under General von Schubert at Breslau. The Eighth Army was to send two corps to form the nucleus of the new force. To Ludendorff this appeared a half-measure, and he suggested instead that the entire Eighth Army go to Upper Silesia under Hindenburg's command. For the time being at least, East Prussia could be defended with one, or at the most two corps, together with the fortress troops. Moltke did not commit himself but promised to consider the suggestion.

This was the last official conversation the two men ever had, for the next day Moltke was superseded by General Erich von Falkenhayn, the Prussian Minister of War.

When he put down the telephone, Ludendorff was looking very worried. His splendid victories in East Prussia seemed suddenly to have shrunk in importance. But however much he might curse Moltke's weakness or Austria's inefficiency, he knew what he himself had to do. The "troth of the Nibelungs" had to be honored and Austria saved, if only because Germany had no other ally.

Early the next morning Ludendorff set out by motor-car for Breslau and the Austrian front. He traveled across a rainy landscape under lowering pewter-colored skies, passing the blackened ruins of farms and groups of refugees returning to their villages. In the afternoon the weather grew worse and a high wind dashed sheets of rain against the windscreen and mica side-curtains of the staff car. The day matched Ludendorff's mood, for he was oppressed by the thought that the war must now be a long one which would require the utmost sacrifice from the German people.[3] Reaching Posen after nightfall, he found lodging at an inn. Ten years ago he had been stationed in this city as a staff officer with the Vth Corps. Now, unless he could perform a military miracle, Posen and much of Upper Silesia would soon be as ravaged as the burnt-out battle-zone in East Prussia.

A few minutes after Ludendorff arrived in Breslau on the morning of the 16th, he received a telegram from Supreme Headquarters informing him that most of the Eighth Army would be transferred under Hindenburg to Upper Silesia to form a new Ninth Army, consisting of four corps, the XIth, XVIIth, XXth, and Guard Reserve, as well as the 8th Cavalry Division, the 35th Reserve Division, and Count von Bredow's Cavalry Division. Hoffmann would join the new formation as Chief of Operations. The reduced Eighth Army would be commanded by von Schubert.

Another official telegram, containing painful personal news, was delivered to Ludendorff in Breslau. His eldest stepson, Franz Pernet, had been seriously wounded in the head by a grenade splinter while fighting with the 39th Fusilier Regiment near Bouconville in France. For the next few weeks, while Franz lay near death, Margarethe Ludendorff spent her days by his bedside, watching for the least change in the unconscious bandage-swathed figure. But little Franz was tough. In time he regained consciousness, and his mother was able to surprise him by placing on his counterpane the Iron Cross he had won. Thereafter his recovery was rapid, but the doctors refused to certify him fit to return to the infantry. Franz began to write his step-father, begging that he might be transferred to the flying corps, and Ludendorff agreed.[4]

On the evening of the 19th of September, Hindenburg and Hoffmann arrived at Breslau. Ludendorff was not there to greet them, for the previous day he had motored to Neu Sandec to confer with the Austrian Commander-in-Chief, the Archduke Frederick, and with Conrad, his Chief of Staff. The Archduke was a pleasant man and a competent enough soldier, but the real power at Austrian Supreme Headquarters lay with Conrad. Although his armies had just suffered a more disastrous defeat than the Russians at Tannenberg, Conrad was by no means downcast. His seamed old face still looked as though it were made from durable leather and his eyes sparkled as brightly as ever.

He was delighted to hear that a new German Army would co-operate with him, and he and Ludendorff found themselves in complete agreement on strategic possibilities.[5]

Although he was quick to recognize the clarity and sweep of Conrad's strategic thinking, Ludendorff took a gloomy view of Austrian fighting capabilities. By now he realized that the Austrian Army had suffered a disaster from which it might never recover. It had retreated back and back from Lemberg, harried by Cossacks and Russian shell-fire. In spite of some fine rear-guard actions, it had found no place where it could turn and give battle. When the San had been reached on the 16th, Conrad had left a corps to guard the first-class fortress of Przemysl and had continued the retreat. Day and night in the steady rain, long columns of Austrian infantry had trudged along with bowed heads behind their transport wagons. Guns sank up to their axles in the muddy roads, and cavalry regiments, "in molten confusion, like horsemen of the Apocalypse," struggled on amid the penetrating odor emanating from the festering galls of hundreds of led horses.[6]

In three weeks' fighting the Austrians had suffered 250,000 casualties and lost over 100,000 prisoners — nearly one-third their total force. Even more serious was the very high percentage of German-speaking officers that had been killed. In the future their place would have to be taken by men of the Empire's subject nationalities, many of whom were inadequately trained and of doubtful loyalty.

Ludendorff found more than 40 Austrian divisions crowded together on the west bank of the Wisloka River between the Carpathians and the Vistula, and he judged they would be unable to launch an offensive against serious opposition for some considerable time. Rather tactlessly, he criticized the Austrian peacetime training program, contrasting it unfavorably with the German. Conrad politely agreed but promised that he would take the offensive again early in October, even if in the meantime his army had to retire further.

Neither Conrad nor Ludendorff had more than the vaguest idea of the Russian dispositions but both believed there might still be a gap between the armies opposite East Prussia and those further south opposing Conrad. Only a few divisions of Cossacks and one or two rifle brigades were in the Vistula Salient west of the river, and the Russian forces investing Przemysl and deployed west of the San were also weak. No immediate Russian advance was to be feared because it would be some time before sufficient food, fodder, ammunition, and supplies could be brought forward.

Ludendorff and Conrad agreed to take advantage of the enforced Russian pause. The German Ninth Army would attack in the Vistula Salient where the enemy was weakest, seize the river crossings, and drive on to Warsaw itself. If the Russians concentrated to oppose this advance, the Austrians should at least be able to regain the ground they had just lost. When Ludendorff returned to Breslau he grouped the Ninth Army in three localities: the XIth Corps northeast of Cracow; the Guard Reserve, XXth and XVIIth Corps and the 35th Reserve Division between Kattowitz and Kreuzburg; and the 8th Cavalry Division and Count von Bredow's Landwehr Division between Kempen and Kalisz.

One important difference between the campaign in southern Poland and the previous fighting in East Prussia was to be that the Russian forces were now under the direct command of the Grand Duke Nicholas, an immensely tall, silent and somber man who had devoted his life to the army. On the 22nd of September, at a conference in Kholm, Nicholas and General Ivanov, the Commander of the Russian Southwest Front, decided to regroup their armies in the salient behind the Vistula as a prelude to a second invasion of German territory.[7] During the first two weeks of October three Russian armies moved by road and rail to take up positions along the Vistula between Warsaw and the confluence of the San. The Russian Ninth Army marched to the southernmost position next to the San; the Fourth Army concentrated in the center about Ivangorod; and the Fifth Army joined the Second in the vicinity of Warsaw. Between them these four armies totalled about one and a quarter million men. In addition, the reorganized First and Tenth Armies were grouped between the Niemen and Narev Rivers. At the end of September Rennenkampf again attacked East Prussia and gradually began to drive the weakened Eighth Army back to, and in some places over, the German frontier.

The German Ninth Army began its advance on the 28th of September, moving forward toward the Vistula against light opposition. On its right flank the Austrian First Army under General von Dankl kept pace. Once again the German troops demonstrated their marching ability, for despite muddy roads and wet weather, they pushed forward as much as 30 kilometers a day. In six long marches they reached the Vistula.

By now the Grand Duke Nicholas had discovered, from papers found on the body of a dead German officer, that only two German corps remained in East Prussia. The news did not perturb him, for although he guessed that the other corps had moved south to Poland, he had already made his preparations. As the Germans advanced they would be gripped by the encircling arms of Russian armies which outnumbered them by more than four to one.

Summer had faded into a miserable Polish autumn; disconsolate leaves whirled down from shivering trees; most birds had migrated; and at night the earth often hardened with frost. In the early morning the soldiers could see their breath white in the damp air and could feel the thin ice in the ruts of the road star and crackle under their boots. The Ninth Army marched across a flat dreary landscape sodden with rain and through the tortuous streets of ramshackle wooden towns. Billets were verminous and bivouacs wet, and everywhere the advancing columns went, black-clad Jews with side-curls, sullen peasants and stolid women with shawls over their heads gazed at them silently and without hope.

The Army's rapid progress was possible only because Ludendorff paid the closest attention to prosaic administrative details. Even the high road between Cracow and Warsaw was knee-deep in mud and the minor roads were often completely impassable. The road-mending companies worked frantically. Railways were repaired; broad gauge Russian lines were changed to the narrower German gauge; branch lines were constructed; and bridges rebuilt. Because in their pursuit of the Austrians the Russians had rather unreasonably destroyed all telegraph lines and cut down the poles, Ludendorff had to rely largely on liaison officers in motorcars and despatch riders on motorcycles to maintain communications with his corps and divisions. In view of his uncertainty about enemy dispositions and strength Ludendorff made thorough preparations for retreat at the same time as he drove his army forward. Railway lines and bridges were mined when they were repaired and fighting units were given strict orders to leave behind all unessential equipment.

On the 9th of October, near the little Polish town of Grojece, Mackensen's XVIIth Corps brushed against some Siberian units and heavy fighting developed before the Siberians were thrown back. Except to the participants, it was an unimportant engagement, but what was significant was that the Russian order of battle was discovered on the dead body of a Russian officer. For the first time Ludendorff learned that between the confluence of the San and Warsaw he faced four Russian armies — 60 strong divisions against his 18 — and even this was not an accurate comparison, for most German units were seriously below strength because of recent heavy fighting in East Prussia or France.

Nevertheless, Ludendorff unhesitatingly chose the bold course, deliberately pushing on into the trap the Russians believed they were setting for him. If only the Austrians acted with vigor, the gamble would be worthwhile. Conrad's First, Third and Fourth Armies had begun their advance on the 4th of October, and the next day crossed the Wisloka River without meeting anything except Cossack sotnias and small cavalry detachments.

On the 9th they reached the San and relieved Przemysl. Ludendorff believed that, if the Austrians attacked vigorously while the Russians concentrated against the Ninth Army, it might be possible to win back more than had been lost at the Battle of Lemberg.

However, the Austrian idea of hurry was very different from the German. As early as the 23rd of September Hoffmann noted in his diary: "Yesterday we had our first row with the Austrians. They aren't out for business as we are." As the days went by, Hoffmann's comments grew more caustic. On the 2nd of October he wrote: "I do not believe we shall fail, but we might. In the first place we must reckon with the Austrians, and we have also left our best corps and leaders in East Prussia." * Six days later in Kielce he wrote: "Here everything is in excellent order except for the Austrians! If only the brutes would move!" [8]

That indeed was the trouble. By now Mackensen's XVIIth Corps, strengthened by three divisions under General von Frommel, was advancing directly on Warsaw. The XXth Corps was watching Ivangorod and preventing the Russians from crossing the Vistula to the north. South of Ivangorod the Guard Reserve Corps held the Vistula as far as Novo Alexandria. South of that again the river line was guarded by Landwehr troops. The XIth Corps, which had been incorporated into von Dankl's Austrian First Army, was holding the Vistula line south as far as Annopol. But the Austrians had not as yet crossed the San or gained any ground east of Przemysl.

Less serious, but still annoying, was the fact that a Caucasian corps had established a bridgehead on the west bank of the Vistula at Kosjenice, ten miles north of Ivangorod. Throughout days of incessant rain which made it impossible to entrench in the flooded Vistula lowlands, the Caucasians successfully re-

---

* The best of the corps commanders was no longer even in the theater. Von François had again disobeyed orders and refused to construct some field fortifications because he "did not believe in them." This final provocation had led to his being allowed to resign his command "for personal reasons." Later in the war he commanded a corps on the Western Front.

sisted every attempt to dislodge them. The Russians actually fought with the trails of their gun-carriages in the Vistula,[9] and even attempted to gain more ground. German artillery and machine-guns smashed all these attacks with heavy loss but could not prevent the Caucasians from building a bridge across the half-mile-wide river.

Ludendorff began to fear that the four German brigades deployed around the bridgehead might be taken in flank. When an airman reported that strong Russian forces had crossed the Vistula south of Ivangorod, the whole headquarters underwent a nervous crisis, for the Ninth Army had no reserves left. Ludendorff "could not sleep a wink" that night,[10] and even Hoffmann noted in his diary: ". . . the hardest time of the campaign in my experience: the strain goes on day and night — endless panics and alarms . . . Ludendorff and I stand by and support each other, and the Chief says: 'God be with us, I can do no more!' " Hindenburg's simple nature was something of a trial during this period, for he could never understand why they did not win another victory like those in East Prussia.[11]

Fortunately, the report of a second Russian bridgehead was erroneous. The aviator had mistaken south for north, and the bridgehead he had seen was the one at Kosjenice.

Meanwhile the Grand Duke Nicholas was throwing more than 14 divisions against Mackensen's five divisions on the left wing. As the danger in the north grew more menacing hour by hour, Ludendorff petitioned Supreme Headquarters for reinforcements, but von Falkenhayn refused. The new corps raised that autumn were earmarked for the Western Front where Falkenhayn was about to launch a desperate assault on the British lines at Ypres. The XVth Reserve Corps, which might have reinforced the Ninth Army, was sent instead to East Prussia. Conrad refused Ludendorff's request for Austrian troops to reinforce the German left, and when the Kaiser was induced to appeal to the Austrian emperor, old Franz Joseph declined to interfere in the military conduct of the war. The most Conrad would agree to was

that Austrian forces should relieve the Guard Reserve, the Landwehr and the XIth Corps, so that these could be sent north. The
Austrians moved so slowly, however, that it soon became evident
the relief could not be completed before the 20th of October at
the earliest. This would be too late, for by then the German left
wing might be completely turned.

On the evening of the 17th, Ludendorff reluctantly decided
to refuse his left flank by withdrawing it to a position some fifty
kilometers west-southwest of Warsaw. The retirement took place
the next night, so smoothly that the Russians were slow to realize they had lost contact with the enemy.[12] By now, however,
the Russians, not the Austrians, had crossed the San River, and
Hoffmann noted in his diary: "I still count on victory; Ludendorff does so no longer." [13]

Certainly, if the Austrians were unable to profit by the Russian weakness on their front, it would be pointless to prolong
the campaign. No sooner had Conrad taken over a stretch of
the Vistula line north of Ivangorod than he decided deliberately
to leave the river undefended so that he could attack the Russian
columns in the act of crossing. This bold maneuver had been
practiced often enough at war games and peacetime maneuvers,
but Ludendorff or Hoffmann would have hesitated in war to attempt with German troops what Conrad was now attempting
with Austrian. All protests went unheeded; large Russian forces
were allowed to cross the river; the Austrian counterattacks failed;
and the Austrians, not the Russians, were forced to retreat.[14]

As the situation worsened, Hoffmann's diary struck an interesting new note: "Ludendorff has become frightfully nervous,
and the chief burden lies on me . . . if we had been given only
two or three more corps here I could have guaranteed a decision . . . I am full of admirable schemes . . ." [15]

When Mackensen was sharply attacked on the 25th and 26th
of October, his left wing had to swing farther back towards
Lodz, and the next day the Austrian retreat from Ivangorod
forced Ninth Army Headquarters to move from Radom to Kon-

skie. There, at one o'clock on the afternoon of the 27th, Hoffmann was called to the telephone. A German lance corporal in
the signals section with the rear party at Radom wanted to speak
personally to the Chief of Operations. When Hoffmann came
on the line, the corporal said: "I have just intercepted an Austrian Army order that I think will interest you. The Austrian
First Army is to begin a retirement at once, but the German
Guard Reserve Corps is not to be informed of this till six o'clock
this evening."

For once Hoffmann lost his mocking detachment and was
frankly furious, the more so since the Guard Reserve Corps was
even then preparing an attack to relieve the pressure on the Austrian First Army. When he got Colonel von Waldstatten, Dankl's
Chief of Staff, on the telephone, he told him exactly what he
thought of such conduct and obtained a promise that at least
the left wing of the First Army would remain in position until
the Guard Reserve Corps could be withdrawn.[16]

There could be no doubt now that the time had come for a
general retirement, and Ludendorff issued the necessary orders
that evening. By forced marches, through vile autumn weather,
the Ninth Army retreated towards Silesia, devastating the countryside as it went. Only the Guard Reserve Corps had any hard
fighting, because the Austrian First Army on its right crumbled
under every Russian attack. The Austrians fell back until they
were level with Cracow, and some of their forces did not halt
until they were actually in the Carpathians southwest of Przemysl.

So thorough had been the German demolitions that the Ninth
Army was never in any danger. The German General Staff had
always believed that a German pursuit would have to stop 100
kilometers beyond railhead, and a similar calculation, modified
for the Russians' lesser administrative requirements, led Ludendorff and Hoffmann to believe that the Russians would have to
halt when they were 120 kilometers away from their nearest railways. On the 1st of November an intercepted Russian wireless

message was brought to Ludendorff: "Having followed up the enemy more than 120 *versts,* it is time to hand over the pursuit to the cavalry. The infantry is tired and surprise difficult."

In truth, the Russians could pursue no farther, for they were overextended and off balance. As Ludendorff sat at his desk, considering these facts with half-veiled eyes, a look of grim satisfaction settled on his face. Even after his retreat he had retained the initiative.

Very well then, where should he strike his next blow?

CHAPTER VIII

THE BATTLE OF LODZ

GENERAL VON FALKENHAYN and Ludendorff sat facing one another in the Red House on the Königsplatz, in the same office that Moltke had used and that had been Schlieffen's before him. It was only the end of October, but already between the two men, unmentioned but persistently intrusive, lay thoughts of Tannenberg and the Marne, of victory in the East and defeat in the West, creating antipathy and latent rivalry.

At 53 Falkenhayn was a strikingly handsome West Prussian, vigorous, courteous, and suave, but with a somewhat ambiguous military reputation. In common with many German officers, Ludendorff probably suspected that he was half politician and felt that he owed his appointment to the Kaiser's favor. He had graduated from the *Kriegsakademie* with distinction, but in 1896 had left the army because of debt and become a military instructor in China. After serving on the staff of the German Expeditionary Force during the Boxer Rebellion, he had returned to Germany and in 1913 had been made Minister of War. General Stürgkh, the Austrian representative at Supreme Headquarters, described him as "tall, slim, with a particularly youthful face in which were a pair of very sharp and clever but sarcastic eyes, with the striking contrast of a very gray, but very thick, head of hair." [1]

While Moltke ruined the campaign in the west, Falkenhayn had watched, outraged but helpless. On the 5th of September, just before the Battle of the Marne, he had written: "Only one thing is certain: our General Staff has completely lost its head.

Schlieffen's notes do not help any further, and so Moltke's wits come to an end." [2] Now that he was Chief of the General Staff, it was his thankless duty to repair the mistakes of his predecessor. At the Marne the German Army had suffered a strategic but not a tactical defeat, and Falkenhayn, who believed he could still win victory in the West, was attempting to revive the Schlieffen Plan by breaking through on the right wing. For the past ten days he had been throwing his new corps against the British positions about Ypres. With the utmost gallantry the young German troops had marched straight down the Menin Road in fours, singing the patriotic songs they had learned at school, but they had been met by the withering rifle-fire of the best-trained infantry in the world, and the British line had held. So appalling were the German losses that the battle soon came to be known as the *Kindermord*, the German biblical term for Herod's Massacre of the Innocents. But there was a fatality about the Western Front that made many generals accept such casualties as commonplace. At the end of October, in spite of repeated failures, Falkenhayn was still determined to break the deadlock at Ypres, restore mobile warfare, and end the war in 1914.

Therefore he was not much interested in Ludendorff's suggestion that reinforcements be sent to the East. Conrad had already made the same proposal and received the same answer. Ludendorff could not argue his case strongly, for he had only a sketchy idea of the overall military situation, but when additional troops were refused him, he suggested that at least unity of command be established on the Eastern Front, with Hindenburg becoming responsible for all German forces there. Falkenhayn did not commit himself and Ludendorff went away dissatisfied.

His mood was angry and embittered, much the same as it had been during his last months in the Red House prior to the war, for once again he sensed the approach of terrible danger but found his proposed countermeasures frustrated by bland men who were his military superiors. Sometimes he wondered whether most of his countrymen were not completely blind. He found that in the autumn of 1914 Berlin was a depressing place for dedicated soldiers. Life seemed to be going on much as it had before the war. In the evening, theater crowds filled the streets; bars and dance-halls were packed; and the strains of the latest tangos were heard everywhere. Ludendorff was shocked by "the passion for amusement and pleasure" he saw around him,[3] and noted with disapproval that many able-bodied young men were still in civilian clothes. With Margarethe away, he felt like a stranger in Berlin and was glad to return to the front.

Once back at Ninth Army Headquarters in Czestochova, he immediately began to consider possible courses of action. As he and Hoffmann studied the maps and Hindenburg stood impassively behind them, a plan gradually emerged. Although the Russians would be immobilized in their present positions for some time while they repaired railways and bridges, the Germans were by no means immobilized. Moreover, the Russian armies in the north, facing East Prussia, and those in the center, facing Hindenburg, were separated by many miles of almost empty country, for this theater of war was too vast to be filled even by the Tsar's huge forces. To Ludendorff and Hoffmann this virtual gap in the Russian line glittered with tactical opportunity. Surely there was an opportunity here for a flank attack on a grand scale. If the entire Ninth Army suddenly disappeared from its present front and moved by rail through Germany to the vicinity of Thorn, it would be poised above the exposed right wing of the central group of Russian armies. An attack along the Vistula towards Lodz might gain another great victory.

After debating the question for several days, Ludendorff finally made up his mind. When the staff gathered in the Operations Room for their morning briefing on the 3rd of November, Hindenburg walked heavily over to stand before the large-scale map on the wall. For a moment he looked at the assembled officers without speaking, then slowly raised his left hand. Everyone knew what the gesture meant. The next blow would be launched from Thorn.[4]

The control of the new offensive would be the easier because on the 1st of November Hindenburg had been appointed Commander-in-Chief East with Ludendorff as his Chief of Staff. Mackensen became commander of the Ninth Army with Grünert as his Chief of Staff, but most of the Ninth Army's operations staff, including Hoffmann, was transferred to the new *Ober-Ost* headquarters. In addition to the Eighth and Ninth Armies, Hindenburg and Ludendorff now commanded the corps in East and West Prussia, Pomerania, Posen and Silesia, as well as the garrisons of all the frontier fortresses. Headquarters was established in Posen, an ancient town at the confluence of the Cybana and Warthe Rivers, 150 miles east of Berlin and 130 miles north of Breslau. The staff moved into luxurious quarters in the Royal Castle, a pretentious Romanesque building that had been opened by the Kaiser in August 1910.

Ludendorff, who already foresaw a grim and protracted war, greatly upset the Silesians by immediately issuing a series of decrees for the removal of all youths of military age from the frontier provinces and the destruction of the railways and coal mines in the area that might be invaded. Some coal mines in Upper Silesia were actually put out of operation, but in general the local inhabitants managed to procrastinate until the danger was past.

As Ludendorff pondered his problems and perils, he slowly determined to turn the coming attack into "an overwhelming and annihilating blow."[5] A prolonged two-front war meant slow death for the Fatherland; only a victory that would completely destroy Russia's offensive power could save Germany. He therefore assembled every available man between Wreschen and Thorn. The Eighth Army was forced to give up the XXVth Reserve and Ist Reserve Corps and the 1st and 36th Reserve Divisions, but even so the German left wing, which would deliver the decisive flank attack, could muster only five and a half corps. Ludendorff again begged for reinforcements from the West, but Falkenhayn, still unwilling to admit failure at Ypres, again refused.

During this time, Colonel Tappen, who had stayed on as Chief of Operations under Falkenhayn, passed through Posen. Hoffmann went to the railway station to meet him and there, amid the garish red plush and mirrors of Tappen's first-class carriage, explained the tremendous possibilities of an offensive in northern Poland. He spoke passionately and with conviction, imploring Tappen, "almost on his knees," to persuade Falkenhayn to send at least two corps from the West. Tappen, whose chief military virtue was an obstinate loyalty to whoever was his immediate superior of the moment, listened superciliously and refused.[6]

Ludendorff believed that his flanking blow could be decisive only if it were a surprise. He envisaged the Russian armies being gripped by a strong frontal attack and then struck violently on their right rear by the heavy hammerhead of fast-moving German forces swinging down from Thorn. Agonizing decisions had to be made. Should the attack be launched at once or would it be better to wait until the Ninth Army was stronger? Falkenhayn was at last sending reinforcements, but these were arriving in driblets and most of the troops were exhausted by their recent experiences in the Ypres fighting. Moreover, the troops that came East were those Falkenhayn did not want in the West. Von Richthofen's Cavalry Corps, von Hollen's Cavalry Corps, and the 2nd and the 4th Cavalry Divisions arrived. They were better than nothing, but they could not take the place of good infantry formations, and their horses were not shod for a winter campaign.

Ludendorff's plan for an offensive from Thorn at once appealed to Conrad's fine strategic imagination, and he readily agreed to transfer Böhm-Ermolli's Austrian Army from the Carpathians to replace the Ninth Army north of Czestochova. Meanwhile the Eighth Army was again attacked and slowly driven back into East Prussia, reaching the Angerapp Line about the middle of November. The frontier of West Prussia, between the Eighth and Ninth Armies, could be only weakly defended, and grave risks, which were ultimately justified by the result, had to be faced in this sector.

On the 11th of November, Mackensen advanced toward Lodz, his open left flank covered by von Morgen's Ist Reserve Corps. The main weight of the attack struck first at the thinly held joint between Rennenkampf's First and Scheidemann's Second Armies. On the 12th, Rennenkampf's Vth Siberian Corps, which was covering the gap, was heavily defeated with the loss of 12,000 prisoners. In the next four days Rennenkampf's left-hand and Scheidemann's right-hand corps were driven asunder, with a loss of over 25,000 prisoners and many casualties.[7]

The Ist Reserve Corps, reinforced by a cavalry division, cut its way through into open country, then turned north to take the First Russian Army in flank, driving it northeastward towards Lowicz and away from the Russian Second Army. The other four corps, the XXVth Reserve, the XXth, the XVIIth, and the XIth, wheeled right and marched south toward Lodz to encircle it on three sides like the gripping fingers of a giant hand. By the 18th of November the XXth and XVIIth Corps were pressing in on Lodz from the north, the XIth Corps had lapped around to the west, and the XXVth Corps, with the 3rd Guards Division and the 19th Cavalry Division attached, was driving down to the east of the city. On this day Ludendorff was briefly encouraged by an intercepted wireless message announcing Scheidemann's intention of abandoning Lodz, but he was soon shown a second message in which the Grand Duke Nicholas personally countermanded the order for retreat and instructed the Second Army to stand and fight it out.[8]

Meanwhile, Scheidemann's Army, already much reduced by casualties, threshed helplessly in the German grasp, with its four corps crowded into an area sixteen miles long by eight miles wide. Although the 150,000 Russians about Lodz fought desperately, their position seemed hopeless as the iron ring steadily closed.

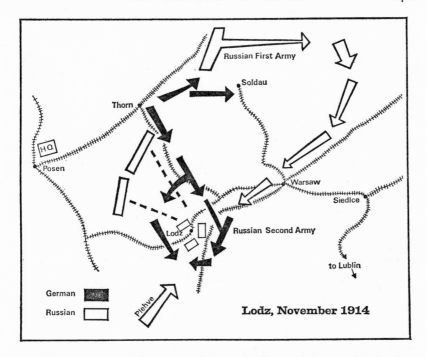

German
Russian

Lodz, November 1914

Russian First Army
Soldau
Thorn
HQ
Posen
Warsaw
Siedlce
Lodz
Russian Second Army
to Lublin
Plehve

Scheidemann sent out desperate appeals for help. Rennen-kampf's First Army could do little, for it had been driven far-ther up the left bank of the Vistula and the Ist Reserve Corps stood between it and the Second Army. Back in the Royal Castle at Posen, under the antlers and stuffed elks' heads that decorated the panelled walls of the Operations Room, Ludendorff and Hoff-mann scanned the map hopefully. Already it was beginning to look at though their daring plan had succeeded. Hour by hour, as the reports came in and the pins were moved to repre-sent the constricting battle-fronts, the map indicated more and more clearly that the German forces were on the brink of a sec-ond Tannenberg.

South of the beleaguered Second Army, and separated from it by two days' march, stood Plehve's Fifth Army. On the night of the 17th of November the Grand Duke Nicholas had ordered Plehve to turn about and counter-attack north to drive back the

right wing of the German envelopment. General Plehve was
small, old, wizened, and ill, but he had the heart of a soldier.⁹
As soon as he received the Grand Duke's order he turned his
army about and marched it north across the frozen countryside.
On the 18th a staff officer sent from Scheidemann's headquarters
found the Fifth Army's vanguard on the road and was conducted to General Plehve, who was riding along on horseback
in the center of his troops. The staff officer drew rein and reported breathlessly: "Your High Excellency, the Second Army is
surrounded and will be forced to surrender!" Plehve glared at
him fiercely from under his bushy eyebrows: "Have you come,
little father, to play a tragedy or to make a report?" he asked. "If
you have a report to make, make it to the Chief of Staff, but
remember, no tragedy playing or I'll place you under arrest." ¹⁰

Throughout the 18th, 19th, and 20th of November, as Mackensen's four corps tightened their grip on Lodz, Plehve's infantry pressed north by long forced marches. On the night of
the 18th/19th November Plehve's Ist Siberian Corps in the van
relieved Scheidemann's left wing by driving back a division of the
XIth Corps with the bayonet. On the eastern side of Lodz, however, General Freiherr von Scheffer-Boyadel's XXVth Reserve
Corps had completely turned Scheidemann's other flank and was
now due south of Lodz.

The next day Plehve's men struck at the XXth Corps, forcing
von Scholtz to retire some distance. The Russian Second Army
fought on with half its guns turned north and half south. The
weather was bitterly cold; the temperature dropped nearly to
zero each night; snow lay deep on the ground; and many of the
wounded froze to death before they could be evacuated.¹¹ Scheidemann continued to send out frantic appeals for aid, but also
continued to defend himself ferociously.¹² On the night of the
19th of November the Stavka received a wireless report from him,
saying that the Second Army's right wing had been completely
enveloped, that he had committed all his reserves, and that the
Germans were south and southwest of Lodz. Communications

then failed, and the Grand Duke Nicholas was left to contemplate an awful silence from the encircled city.

Meanwhile Rennenkampf had ordered three and a half divisions from the First Army to march south to the aid of Scheidemann. This force moved slowly, and although the Grand Duke impatiently replaced its commander twice in the first 36 hours, it was not until late afternoon of the 21st that it began to press on the rear of von Scheffer's XXVth Reserve Corps.

However, as the early November twilight closed in that evening, the German left wing east and south of Lodz found itself in a desperate position. After Plehve's Siberians had forced back the German right west of Lodz, all chance of closing the trap had disappeared. The clutching fingers of the German attack had been prized open, and now one of them was about to be gripped in its turn. Von Scheffer's group, consisting of the XXVth Reserve Corps, von Richthofen's Cavalry Corps, and the 3rd Guards Division under General Litzmann, now discovered that the Russians had driven a wedge between their right flank and von Scholtz's XXth Corps. The Russian Fifth Army was attacking them from the west, and the three and a half divisions from the First Army were attacking them from the east. That night anyone who traveled 25 miles south from the Vistula would have passed through eight successive lines of Russians and Germans fighting each other back to back. The war map in the Operations Room at Posen was colored in layers "like a Neapolitan ice." [13]

Scheffer's 60,000 men were now themselves completely surrounded by greatly superior forces of Russians. Ludendorff and Hoffmann passed nerve-racking hours listening to the terrible reports that came in. On the 22nd they learned from a Russian wireless message that the Grand Duke Nicholas was having 60 trains shunted onto sidings in preparation for the shipment of German prisoners of war.[14]

In the broken forest country south of Lodz, Scheffer's Germans fought on as though they had never heard the word "surrender." All night on the 21st of November they hurled back repeated attacks. Morning came, dismal and cold, and with it the Russians poured forward again in seemingly inexhaustible numbers, but the field-gray firing line held fast. Assault after surging assault broke against that line during the daylight hours and receded again, each leaving behind its debris of khaki-clad dead as a high-water mark. It was already dark at seven o'clock on the evening of the 22nd when Mackensen finally ordered Scheffer's group to retire as best it could. The order had been late in coming, but within five hours all the German troops were in column and moving along the roads to the northeast.[15] Nevertheless, it seemed impossible that any other fate awaited them but humiliating surrender, for Scheffer's men were much more completely surrounded than Samsonov's had been at Tannenberg.

At dawn the 6th Siberian Division northeast of Lodz was suddenly struck by German infantry coming fiercely out of the darkness that still clung about the west. The flat-faced, sturdy little Siberians defended themselves well, but as the pale day brightened, column after column of desperate Germans closed in on them. The Russian divisional commander repeatedly sent out appeals for help, but although several Russian formations were within easy marching distance, no help arrived. Nor did the Fifth Army, which should have been treading hard on Scheffer's heels, come up in time to take part in the battle. By five o'clock in the afternoon Scheffer had three divisions attacking the 6th Siberian Division.

The unequal struggle could not continue indefinitely. During the night, the Germans, as was their custom, worked around both flanks, and early the next morning a half-hearted relief attempt by the Russian 63rd Division, only four miles away, was beaten back. At eleven o'clock on the morning of the 24th the surviving Siberians began to retire. Almost immediately the Germans burst triumphantly through and the retirement became a rout as the broken defenders fled wildly in all directions. Only some

1500 exhausted Siberians finally made their way west to find shelter with the Second Army. Scheffer's force promptly veered northwest and by hard marching soon rejoined the rest of the Ninth Army, going into the line between the Ist Reserve and the XXth Corps.

Scheffer's 60,000 men had marched and fought continuously for ten days. For nearly 72 hours they had been completely surrounded by half a million Russians, but by discipline, intelligence, and courage had cut their way through cleanly and decisively. Not only had they escaped, but they also took with them behind the German lines the 10,000 prisoners they had captured and 64 Russian guns.

With this heroic little epic the Battle of Lodz drew to a close. Ludendorff had gambled against heavy odds in sending 250,000 Germans to attack 600,000 Russians, but few campaigns in the entire history of warfare present so brilliant an aspect. In two months the Germans had dashed from Cracow to the Vistula to relieve their Austrian allies; they had been forced to retreat on Czestochova; then within a space of fifteen days they had loaded their trains and transferred their entire army to Thorn, vanishing from their former front as silently and swiftly as ghosts at daybreak; finally they had struck boldly at an enemy nearly three times their numbers, pierced his front clean as a lance, and sent a steel claw groping around one of his armies. When their attack had failed, they had extricated their forces magnificently and established a firm line well in advance of their starting place. Hoffmann was almost certainly right when he characterized the campaign in southern Poland as the finest operation of the whole war, to be classed much higher than the more spectacular victories of Tannenberg or the Masurian Lakes.[16]

The nation thrilled to these events, which were in such sharp contrast to the bloody, inconclusive fighting in Belgium, and the legend of the Great Twin Brethren of the East took deeper root. On the 27th of November Hindenburg was promoted to field marshal and Ludendorff to lieutenant general. Two days later when the Kaiser arrived at Posen to congratulate them both, Ludendorff was grimly complacent and Hindenburg was "the personification of calm." [17]

The Russians remained in Lodz until the 6th of December, then retired to a new line south of Warsaw. By now winter had closed down on Europe, making further major operations impracticable, and both sides took stock. In the East as in the West, 1914 ended in apparent stalemate. The French Plan XVII for the invasion of Alsace-Lorraine and the Schlieffen Plan for the rapid defeat of France had both failed. In the East the Russians stood helpless before the barrier of the Masurian Lakes and had abandoned their hopes of invading Silesia. Yet in spite of enormous losses, both the Allies and the Central Powers remained strong. All the death and suffering of the previous five months had only steeled their intransigent wills. Ludendorff had better reason than ever to believe that it would be a long war.

In the Royal Castle at Posen the staff of *Ober-Ost* slipped into the pleasant habit of sitting around the table for an hour or two after dinner to discuss military problems. The table was a great round one of polished wood, adorned in the center with a potted palm, the gift of the Kaiserin, and that winter it was graced with many distinguished guests. One dark December night when the snow lay deep and crisp in the royal park and the wood fires in the castle crackled brightly, Chancellor Bethmann-Hollweg was seated on Hindenburg's right at dinner. During the meal the conversation had been about the war, but when coffee and brandy were served, the talk turned to peace and how it could be obtained.

Bethmann-Hollweg had always wanted peace: peace with victory if possible, but failing that a peace based on a return to the status quo. This evening, as he sat at the table, tall, awkward, and sorrowful of countenance, he listened to what the Generals of the East had to say. Hindenburg's opinions were hardly worth hearing, for he had a simple conventional mind, as predictable as the patriotic press. Ludendorff, already growing savage from frustration, was dreaming of a greater Fatherland and of territorial acquisitions that would compensate the German people for their sacrifices. His view was that "if Germany makes peace without profit, Germany has lost the war." Hoffmann sat silent as he smoked his cigarette and sipped his cognac, his glance veiled behind his pince-nez. At last Bethmann-Hollweg turned and fixed him with his bright blue eyes.

"And what is your opinion?" he asked.

Hoffmann hesitated a moment before answering, then spoke in a steady voice. "In my opinion," he replied, "the first condition before peace can even be talked of is for Germany to declare publicly by the mouth of the Chancellor that it does not want to keep a single square yard of Belgian territory." His sudden smile flashed out, but he went on with quiet seriousness. "I say this because England will never tolerate a German Belgium, and will fight to the bitter end to prevent it. Besides, I do not think that an addition of Belgian subjects to the Empire is at all desirable for Germany."

The Chancellor looked at Hoffmann in surprise. There was nothing about his appearance to indicate that he might hold such views. His field-gray tunic with its little black and white ribbon of the Iron Cross was stretched tight across his chest in the approved military style. His close-cropped bullet-head, just turning gray, looked typically Prussian. Only the mocking eyes behind the pince-nez gave any clue that this might be a man who thought for himself.

Bethmann-Hollweg said very slowly: "You are the first soldier from whom I have heard this opinion. I quite agree with your point of view." He paused, a brooding far-away look in his eyes, then went on: "But if I tried to express it in Berlin at the Reichstag, a storm of public protest would sweep me from my post." [18]

The dinner party broke up shortly afterwards. Both Ludendorff and Hoffmann looked pensive when they rose from the table, but they were thinking very different thoughts about the future of Germany.

CHAPTER IX

THE WINTER BATTLE OF MASURIA

LUDENDORFF had explained it all very clearly in his hard nasal voice. And Hindenburg could plainly see that his Chief of Staff was right too. Of course the Austrians were no good by themselves. Never had been. Why in 1866 . . . But they were allies now and would have to be supported. Still . . .

The old man let his placid gaze wander from the map to the window. Outside he could see the gabled rooftops of Posen's Old Town, the Gothic spire of the Marienkirche, and a line of snow-covered hills beyond. A shadow of doubt lingered on his large square face. After all, no matter what Ludendorff said, Falkenhayn was the Chief of the General Staff. And old habits of obedience stayed with a man even after he had been made a field marshal. But he was uneasily aware of Ludendorff watching him, so he looked back from the window, hesitated a second more, then picked up the pen and signed the letter.

✠

In the first week of January 1915, while the long zigzag of the Western Front was congealed into quiescence from Switzerland to the sea like an ice-bound river, the Grand Duke Nicholas was preparing an offensive which he hoped would carry his armies over the Carpathians into the plains of Hungary. The first five months of the war that Austria had so light-heartedly provoked had shaken the Empire to its foundations. Russia was threatening invasion; the Serbians were still stubbornly defending their frontiers; and Italy, the former ally, bribed by Allied promises of territory, was about to hurl 600,000 soldiers at Austria's southern border. To meet this triple threat Conrad had asked for four or five German divisions to help him make a forestalling attack against Austria's principal enemy, the Russians.

Ludendorff had foreseen the need to reinforce the Carpathian front and had already thinned his line in Poland to obtain troops. Since the Germans had no liking for positional warfare or the construction of field entrenchments, it had taken all his energy to get his armies satisfactorily below ground,[1] but once this was accomplished, he was able to promise Conrad several divisions.[2]

However, Falkenhayn, with shrewd political insight, no longer believed a clear-cut victory possible and now aimed only at a satisfactory peace. To achieve this, Germany would have to convince the Allies to accept stalemate. In Falkenhayn's opinion, a precondition for this would be the closing down of one of Germany's two fronts. But which? This was the basic German dilemma of the war. East or West? The problem was so simple that the toss of a coin could have resolved it, were it not that so many sound arguments clamored to be heard on both sides. Britain and France were democracies who could only fight at all by stirring up their peoples to implacable moral anger, but they were angered now and would not readily settle for anything less than victory. Russia, on the other hand, might be easier to convince, but Russia, with her great reserves of manpower and almost limitless space, could not be knocked out of the war while most of the German Army was held on the Western Front.

After long thought, Falkenhayn reached a decision. France would have to be brought to see reason. The coin had come down with its western side uppermost, and German troops could therefore not be spared to help Conrad.

Ludendorff flatly refused to accept this decision, which would have made the Eastern Front no more than a secondary theater and reduced his own role correspondingly. He had weighty — and probably conclusive — strategic arguments to support him, and he did not pause to consider what evils might result from divided counsels, indiscipline, and enforced compromises. In this he was not different from most men, although as a general in time of war his willfulness touched the fate of Germany and the lives of three million soldiers. In the letter Hindenburg had just signed, *Ober-Ost* announced that it intended to support Conrad and that the headquarters staff of the IInd Corps, the 1st Infantry Division, the 48th Reserve Division, a special brigade of three regiments, and the 5th Cavalry Division were already earmarked for the Carpathians.[3]

This flinging down of the gauntlet put the whole German system of government to the test. And the system failed. The Kaiser, who alone could arbitrate such a direct challenge to Falkenhayn's authority, would have liked to support his Chief of the General Staff, but it was unthinkable for him to dismiss the victors of Tannenberg. On the 8th of January he announced that a new German *"Südarmee,"* would be formed under General von Linsingen to bolster Conrad's forces in the Carpathians.

Falkenhayn, humiliated and angry, had no difficulty in obtaining the Kaiser's consent to the obvious counter. The Great Twin Brethren of the East, whose fame allowed Falkenhayn no rest,[4] would be far less formidable if they were separated, for Ludendorff depended on Hindenburg's popularity, and Hindenburg without his Chief of Staff was only a man of straw. While Ludendorff was discussing the coming operation with Conrad, he was surprised to receive a telegram appointing him Chief of Staff to Linsingen. At *Ober-Ost* no one had any doubt as to the reason for the posting, especially since the *Südarmee* already had a highly competent Chief of Staff.

Ludendorff said his good-byes and left Posen for the headquarters of the Southern Army at Munkacs. He was not unduly worried, for before he left he had helped Hindenburg compose a second letter, this time to the Kaiser:

Your Imperial and Royal Majesty has been graciously pleased to command that General Ludendorff, my Chief of Staff, should be

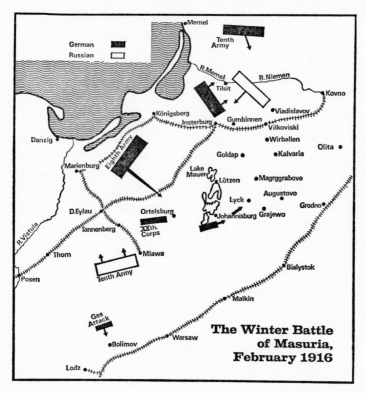

German ▨
Russian ☐

Memel

Tenth
Army

R. Memel

R. Niemen

Tilsit

Kovno

Königsberg

Insterburg

Gumbinnen

Viadislavov

Vilkoviski

Danzig

Eighth Army

Wirballen

Olita

Marienburg

Goldap

Kalvaria

Lake
Mauer

Lötzen

Magrggrabove

Augustovo

Lyck

Grodno

D. Eylau

Ortelsburg

Johannisburg

Grajewo

Tannenberg

XXth.
Corps

R. Vistula

Thorn

Mlawa

Posen

Tenth Army

Bialystok

Malkin

Gas
Attack

Warsaw

**The Winter Battle
of Masuria,
February 1916**

Bolimov

Lodz

transferred from me to the Southern Army . . . During the days
of Tannenberg and the Masurian Lakes, the operations against
Ivangorod and Warsaw, and the advance to the Wreschen-Thorn
Line, I have grown into close union with my Chief of Staff; he has
become to me a true helper and friend, irreplaceable by any other,
one on whom I bestow my fullest confidence. Your Majesty knows
from the history of war how important such a happy relationship is
for the conduct of affairs and the well-being of the troops. In addition, his new and so much smaller sphere of action does not do
justice to the General's comprehensive ability and great capacity
. . . On these grounds I venture most respectfully to beg that my
war comrade may graciously be restored to me as soon as the operations in the south are under way. No personal ambition leads me
to lay this petition at the feet of your Imperial and Royal Majesty.

That lies far from me! Your Majesty has overwhelmed me with favors beyond my desserts and after the war has ended I shall retire again into the background with a thankful and joyful heart. Far rather do I believe that I am fulfilling a duty in expressing with all submission this request.[5]

While the Kaiser pondered this obsequiously insolent letter, Ludendorff and Conrad planned their joint offensive. The main Austrian attack would be towards Przemysl, while a subsidiary German-Austrian attack would be launched to the east. Closer contact did not increase Ludendorff's confidence in the fighting capabilities of the Austrian Army, which was of a distressingly polyglot composition. One day when he was walking with a group of Austrian officers in the wooded hills behind the lines, he met a sentry who spoke to him in some foreign language. He was forcibly struck by the fact that none of the officers with him were able to understand the man.[6]

The war was already leaving its mark on Ludendorff. His complexion had grown sallower and the deep wrinkles on either side of his nose were more pronounced. His share of Hindenburg's reflected fame irritated rather than gratified him. At about this time he had to make several trips to Berlin, and often when Margarethe met him at the Friedrichstrasse station they could scarcely make their way to the waiting staff car for the cheering crowds. Once Margarethe, looking at her husband's face, asked with a smile: "Aren't you pleased by the gratitude and admiration of the people?"

Ludendorff growled: "Believe me, the people's favor is as changeable as their rulers'. You'll see that they stone me before they've done." [7]

On the 11th of January Falkenhayn talked with Conrad, Linsingen, and Ludendorff at Breslau and the next day he met again with Hindenburg, Ludendorff and Hoffmann at Posen. Falkenhayn's suave arguments and cool courtesy made no impression. "It was," Ludendorff said, "all unsatisfactory and unmeaning, a contest of opinions settled beforehand." He and

Hoffmann now persuaded Hindenburg to demand that the Kaiser dismiss Falkenhayn, that four corps be sent to help Conrad, and that Ludendorff be returned to *Ober-Ost*. Once again the Kaiser weakly ruled against his own nominee, agreeing that Conrad would get his four corps, that Ludendorff would return to Hindenburg and that Falkenhayn would resign as Minister of War, although he still remained Chief of the General Staff.

By the end of January, Ludendorff was back in Posen, and although Falkenhayn toyed for a time with the idea that he might assume personal command in the East, he was overruled here as well. He records that he continued as Chief of the General Staff "with a heavy heart," [8] but his sorrow did not prevent him from sharply criticizing the plans that emerged from *Ober-Ost*. The gist of his comments was that only "fairly large local successes" could be anticipated against Russia during 1915. Under the circumstances, it was a safe prediction, for Germany's strategy had fallen between two stools.

For several weeks the intelligence staff at *Ober-Ost* had been piecing together scraps of information from the reports of secret agents and intercepted wireless messages. The Russians were more careful now about broadcasting in clear, but this made little difference, since Ludendorff had two cryptographers, one of them a former mathematics professor, who were "geniuses at deciphering" and who soon mastered the enemy codes.[9] Gradually a fairly accurate picture was built up of the Grand Duke Nicholas' new "gigantic plan." [10] He would seek a definite decision in the East in the spring of 1915. Simultaneously with an advance in the Carpathians, he would attack between the Niemen River and the Gumbinnen-Insterburg road to throw the Eighth Army back across the Vistula, while other Russian armies, especially strong in cavalry, would break through between Mlawa and the Vistula to invade West Prussia.

Ludendorff knew that such concentric attacks against East and West Prussia would be dangerous. Moreover, he had no liking for defensive battles. If the Grand Duke intended to strike in the spring, he would forestall him by striking in mid-winter.

By now *Ober-Ost* disposed of three armies: the Eighth on the Angerapp Line and along the frozen Masurian Lakes; the Ninth, 200 kilometers to the south, deployed some forty miles from Warsaw; and the Tenth, under General von Eichhorn (Chief of Staff, Colonel Hell), just in the process of formation. Ludendorff and Hoffmann looked long and hard at the maps, then began to shift their forces for one of their deadly indirect blows.

They had seen that General Sievers' Russian Tenth Army, poised for the invasion of East Prussia, was somewhat weak on both flanks, and they set about exploiting this weakness with all the sureness and skill of a chess master who detects a flaw in his opponent's pawn formation. To isolate and overwhelm Sievers' force, the German Tenth Army would be assembled secretly northeast of Tilsit whence it could strike south toward Grodno. The Eighth Army would advance simultaneously from Johannisburg toward Lyck, and, while enemy reserves were pinned down elsewhere by strong frontal attacks, the Russian Tenth Army would be caught between two gigantic claws. The XXth Corps of the Ninth Army would move from Poland to Ortelsburg and Tannenberg to strengthen the southern flank of the offensive.[11]

Ludendorff issued preliminary orders to his army commanders on the 28th of January.[12] As a distraction, the Ninth Army was to launch an attack at Bolimov supported with 18,000 gas-shells. This was then considered an incredible amount of ammunition for a single operation, and surprise was counted on, since this would be the first time gas had been used in the war. However, when Hoffmann watched the attack from a church spire in Bolimov, he found it disappointing. Although tactical success was achieved, the gas did not function successfully because of the freezing cold.*

By the end of January German troop trains were again rat-

---

* The gas did achieve surprise. Less understandably, it was to do so again, two and a half months later, when the Germans employed it for the second time, on the 22nd of April in the Ypres Salient.

tling across the empty Baltic grasslands, forty trains for each of
the three assembling corps. In the long winter nights they
flashed by bare white fields and sped with lonely, long-drawn
whistling through the darkened little towns east of Königsberg.
Inside them, crammed together on the hard wooden seats of the
3rd-class carriages, the soldiers dozed under the dim electric
lights or turned the warm air blue with pipefuls of cheap can-
teen tobacco. Interspersed between the troop trains, long lines
of reddish-brown and gray-green goods wagons, drawn by two
engines, swayed and rumbled to the same inexorable timeable
as they rushed north with equipment, horses, guns, ammunition,
field kitchens, and ordnance stores.

Entirely unsuspected by the Grand Duke Nicholas, Ludendorff's northern concentration was completed early in February.
North of the line of lakes, the three corps of Eichhorn's Tenth
Army, the XXIst, XXXIXth Reserve, and XXXVIIIth Reserve,
covered by the 1st Cavalry Division and the 5th Guard Infantry
Brigade, stood between the Niemen River and the Gumbinnen-
Insterburg road. South of the lakes, between Lake Spirding and
the frontier, the XLth Reserve Corps, the 2nd Infantry Division
and the 4th Cavalry Division were massed for the southerly
attack.

On the 5th of February, *Ober-Ost* moved to Insterburg, and on
the same day the weather broke. For the next 48 hours a terrible
blizzard swept across East Prussia. A biting east wind piled the
snowdrifts as high as a man along the roads and in the railway
cuttings. The forests seethed and tossed in the storm, the trees
creaking and groaning like old ships in a heavy sea. Movement
across country was impossible and the temperature dropped to
more than 40 degrees below zero. In the Dessauer Hotel in Insterburg, Hindenburg, Ludendorff and Hoffmann watched the
snowflakes beat ineffectually against the darkened windowpanes
and wondered whether they could possibly order their men to
attack in such bitter weather. But time was short, the moment
of opportunity might pass, and it was, after all, snowing on the

Russians too. Steeling their hearts, they decided to persevere. On the 7th of February, the right-hand German thrust began with General Litzmann's XLth Reserve Corps and the 2nd Division advancing toward Lyck.[13]

The Russians were taken completely by surprise. For the last two days, they had been too busy shoveling the snow out of their trenches to anticipate any attack. The next day Ludendorff's left-hand assault went in between the Gumbinnen-Königsberg railway and the Memel River.

In spite of appalling conditions, the Germans pressed determinedly forward. Burial parties, moving behind the fighting troops, piled the grotesquely frozen dead like cordwood on their sleighs, and few of the seriously wounded survived the icy journey back to the nearest aid post. By the night of the 9th/10th February, General Fritz von Below's XXIst Corps, which had marched steadily for over 29 hours, reached Schirwindt and Vladislavov. At the same time the XXXIXth Corps captured Pilkallen, then turned south. During the 10th, the XXIst Corps passed through Vilkoviski, cut the Kovno railway, captured Wirballen and defeated a Russian division, capturing 10,000 prisoners and six guns. Two days later the front ran from Kalvaria to Goldap, and farther south the Tenth Army was well around the Russian right.

General Sievers could now retreat only in one of two ways — east to the Niemen by way of Olita or south through the forest of Augustovo. Farther south the XLth Reserve Corps was on the outskirts of Lyck which was defended by the 3rd Siberian Corps. The Siberians fought bravely, withdrawing from their positions in good order, although when the Germans entered the town on the 14th, they captured about 5000 stragglers. The following day the Kaiser visited Lyck to congratulate his troops whose vanguards had now pushed on nearly to Gravejo. Meanwhile, the Eighth Army, advancing from the Angerapp positions, had reached Sievers' old headquarters at Marggrabova.

By now General Sievers had only one thought — to get away

as rapidly as possible from the terrible steel claws closing in on him from the north and the south. As he fled, he devastated the countryside behind him, burned farmhouses, blew up bridges, and hanged dozens of Polish Jews who were suspected of being spies. The 350,000 retreating Russians who choked the roads were continually attacked on their right flank and driven steadily south toward the Forest of Augustovo. The infantry floundered in the snowdrifts and often had to leave their guns and transport behind.

On the afternoon of the 14th of February the dark sky lightened, a mild breeze came up from the south, and a sudden thaw set in. Overnight the snow melted, the roads turned to mud, and the pursuers, who had to use twelve to eighteen horses to move each field gun, were at last checked. As the Germans struggled on, their columns grew longer and longer, and infantry units had to squeeze past lines of wagons stuck fast in the mud. There was some closing up at night whenever there was fighting at the head of a column, and, fortunately for the attackers, the Russians had left behind their supply depots and many unloaded railway trains filled with food and provisions.[14] By nightfall on the 15th, the Russian IIIrd and XXVIth Corps, although depleted and disordered, lay about Grodno in comparative safety, but the XXth Corps, together with great masses of stragglers from the other two corps, many artillery units, and a great deal of transport still floundered in the Forest of Augustovo.

With almost reckless boldness, General Eichhorn ordered his left-hand corps, the XXIst, south around the forest, completely ignoring the danger of a Russian thrust from Grodno. On the 16th of February, the advance-guard of Eichhorn's XXIst Corps, as it penetrated far into the forest along the Seiny-Augustovo chaussée, was overrun by desperate Russian columns striving to break out to the east. However, the XXIst Corps continued its advance throughout the 15th, 16th, and 17th of February, and by the 18th had the forest completely surrounded.

For the next four days the Russians fought frantically to loosen the German grip. They formed up their columns in the depth of the forest, where it was dim and shadowy even at noontime, then plodded grimly southeast toward the lighter skyline that marked the beginning of open country. Sometimes fierce hand-to-hand clashes occurred at the edge of the forest, but more often the Russian attacks would break under German fire, and the survivors, hampered by their long greatcoats that came down to their ankles, would turn and stumble blindly back to the shelter of the trees. At night, when the firing died down and the forest was quiet except for the sighing of the tall pines, wolves could be heard howling as they hovered as close as they dared to the fighting and the dead.

On the 20th and 21st of February, the two Russian corps about the fortress of Grodno launched violent attacks to free their comrades trapped in the forest, but in spite of heavy losses the German ring did not break. On the 21st of February the surrounded Russians could endure no more; 30,000 of them surrendered, including eleven generals; and the Germans captured 200 guns and rescued large numbers of their comrades who had been taken prisoner. With this, one half of the Grand Duke's gigantic plan for the spring of 1915 lay in ruins.

The Kaiser, who had an ear for the dramatic, decided to call the great offensive that had just closed "The Winter Battle of Masuria." It had, in truth, been a terrible and heroic fortnight for the German armies. Field Marshal von Hindenburg, writing of it later (perhaps with some literary assistance), said:

> The Winter Battle in Masuria . . . the name charms like an icy wind or the stillness of death. As men look back on the course of this battle, they will only stand and ask themselves: "Have earthly beings really done these things, or is it all but a fable and a phantom? Are not those marches in the winter nights, that camp in the icy snow-storm, and that last phase of the battle in the forest of Augustovo, so terrible for the enemy, but the creations of an inspired human fantasy?" [15]

Ludendorff's plan had resulted in the capture of 110,000 prisoners and the death of another 100,000 Russians. The Russian Tenth Army had been completely broken, but as Hindenburg himself confessed:

> In spite of the great tactical success of the winter battle, we failed to exploit it strategically. We had once more managed practically to destroy one of the Russian armies, but fresh enemy forces had immediately come up to take its place, drawn from other fronts to which they had not been pinned down. In such circumstances, with the resources at our disposal in the East, we could not achieve a decisive result. The superiority of the Russians was too great.[16]

As spring crept across the Polish heaths, turning the wild junipers green and bringing the gorse to pale leaf, the sober-minded soldiers at *Ober-Ost* realized with heavy hearts that, in spite of their epic victories, it was all to do again.

CHAPTER X

THE GORLICE–TARNOW OFFENSIVE

O BER-OST now moved to the fortress town of Lötzen, a tiny neat place which had the bare scrubbed look of a Prussian recruit but which was surrounded by beautiful woods, undulating fertile fields and little lakes that flashed like opals in the evening light.[1] The inhabitants were delighted to have such famous people among them, and Hindenburg spent a good deal of time visiting neighboring estates "for hours of relaxation, recreation and good sport . . . and a certain amount of hunting." He had particularly happy memories of a fine elk he killed near the Kurisches Haff in the royal shoot at Niemonien.[2] When artists and sculptors, commissioned to portray the heroes of Tannenberg, came to Lötzen, they found that Hindenburg posed complacently and Ludendorff reluctantly. The latter once growled at Vogel, the well-known painter: "I'd rather wait until this job is finished. Popular favor and the fortunes of war are extremely fickle. The goddess of battle is a sorry baggage."

Intense little gusts of fighting flared all along the front from the middle of February until the beginning of April, as the Grand Duke Nicholas tried to implement the second half of his plan for the invasion of West Prussia and the southernmost portion of East Prussia. Between the Pissa and Orsritz Rivers, in a bogland broken only by patches of forest and scrub pine, the Germans had to reinforce their lines again and again. More than once the country-bred Russian infantry, holding their rifles high over their heads, waded neck-deep through swamps the Germans had considered impassable and burst suddenly into the defenses with the bayonet. But when the fighting died down at the beginning of April the Germans still stood everywhere on enemy territory.[3]

One small corner of East Prussia northeast of Tilsit had remained in Russian hands until the Governor of Königsberg, General von Pappritz, recaptured it with a scratch force on the 18th of February. Ludendorff and Hoffmann later heard reports of Russian concentrations near Memel, which might have given them forewarning of renewed attacks, but, preoccupied with larger designs, they disregarded them.[4]

During a lull in the fighting, Ludendorff telegraphed Margarethe, who was then in Strasbourg, to meet him in Thorn. She found him waiting on the platform in a black temper because his car had broken down on the way. "I should have had that chauffeur hanged if he had not got here in time to meet you at the station," he said grimly. Before returning to Strasbourg, Margarethe spent a few days at headquarters, but she saw her husband only at meal hours and after the long day's work was done. At this time Franz, who was with the Air Division at Posen, often visited Lötzen, although Hindenburg had more time to spend with him than his stepfather.[5]

On the night of the 17th of March an *Ober-Ost* signalman, taking a call on the civilian line from Memel, was surprised to hear a female voice urgently demanding to speak to a senior officer. When Hoffmann was summoned, the girl identified herself as Fräulein Erika Röstel, in charge of the telephone switchboard at Memel Post Office. She informed Hoffmann that a force of Russian frontier guards and militia had suddenly counter-attacked and taken the town. Although all her male co-workers had fled, she calmly proceeded to give Hoffmann an eye-witness account of the fighting going on in the street outside. At last she announced that she would have to leave. "They're coming up the stairs," she explained just before the line went dead.

The unexpected Russian attack drove on past Taurogeen towards Tilsit before the Germans rallied and pushed the invaders back again. Ludendorff later attempted to obtain the Iron Cross,

2nd Class, for Fräulein Röstel, but since the Kaiser's Military Cabinet stiffly refused to consider so unorthodox an award, she was presented with a gold watch instead.[6]

The Austrians meanwhile suffered another reverse when their attempt to relieve Przemysl failed. The fortress capitulated to famine, with the loss of 100,000 men and 100 guns, and Falkenhayn, who knew that his own position was strengthened by every set-back in the East, was quick to point out that he had predicted the disaster. In mid-March, the British Navy tried halfheartedly to force its way past the invisible portcullis that had clashed down across the Dardenelles when Turkey had entered the war on Germany's side.[7] The naval demonstration, unsuccessful as it was, decided Falkenhayn that an overland route to Turkey would have to be opened, an aim which could be achieved only after Serbia was crushed. He resolved to postpone for the time being the heavy blow he intended to strike at France and to shift the German offensive potential temporarily to the East. He had, however, no intention of seeking a decision there, but merely wished to strengthen his position and relieve his allies before turning finally to the West.

But strategy is necessarily a thing of makeshifts and expedients. Before Falkenhayn could strike at Serbia, Conrad had become seriously worried about his ability to hold the Carpathians. The Russians had actually occupied some of the forest-clad heights that overlooked the rich Hungarian plain, and every day Captain von Fleischmann, Conrad's liaison officer at *Ober-Ost*, reported more gravely on the Carpathian fighting and the condition of the Austrian Army. During April, Ludendorff, without consulting Falkenhayn, sent three divisions to Conrad's assistance.

By reducing the number of battalions in a division from 12 to 9, the War Ministry had been able to raise 14 new divisions by the end of April. These Falkenhayn formed into a new Eleventh Army, but although he appointed Colonel Hans von Seeckt its Chief of Staff, for the time being no commander was named and no decision made as to where it would be employed.

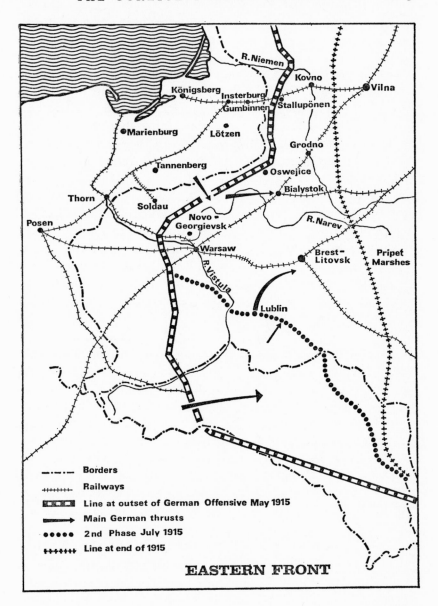

Borders
Railways
Line at outset of German Offensive May 1915
Main German thrusts
2nd Phase July 1915
Line at end of 1915

EASTERN FRONT

As usual, Conrad had a plan, and as usual it was a good one. The only trouble was that the Austrian Army was no longer capable of carrying out his bold designs. Conrad knew this and asked for German help to pierce the Russian front between Gorlice and Tarnow. Falkenhayn recognized the merits of the plan and wisely decided against half-measures. He promised Conrad the four corps of the Eleventh Army rather than the four divisions which had been all the Austrian had dared suggest. Von Mackensen was given the new command, probably on the calculation that Seeckt's cool brain would control the old man's fiery impetuosity. Mackensen was placed nominally under Conrad, although Conrad agreed to issue him no orders without Falkenhayn's approval. The elderly Field Marshal Prince Leopold of Bavaria, who willingly waived his seniority to serve under Hindenburg, was appointed to command the Ninth Army in Mackensen's place. *Ober-Ost* was given no part in the coming offensive, except that Ludendorff was requested to stage three small diversionary attacks in the north.

By the 28th of April the Eleventh Army, reinforced by an Austrian corps and a Hungarian cavalry division, had assembled secretly behind the 30-mile stretch of front between Gorlice and Tarnow. Conrad's plan called for a clean penetration of the enemy line in the low foothills between the Vistula and the mountains, followed by a wheel to the east which would roll up a large segment of the Russian armies. Falkenhayn could afford to let his handsome face relax into a cool little smile of satisfaction. For once there would be a victory in the East not associated with the Great Twin Brethren, and the fact that Mackensen had never got on easily with *Ober-Ost* would make this all the more galling to Ludendorff.

The attack, which was launched on the 2nd of May, was immediately successful. Only where the Russian front had run through thick forest or dead ground out of reach of the German artillery did any fighting occur; elsewhere the Russians abandoned their weapons and fled. The amazed Germans watched thousands of awkward running figures in gray fur caps and fluttering unbuttoned greatcoats stream rearward in panic, like rabbits flushed from a spinney.[8] Within two days Mackensen was clean through into open country. Behind his advancing columns, three lines of trenches were choked with Russian dead and 140,000 prisoners shuffled wearily toward the west. The Grand Duke Nicholas ordered a general withdrawal from the Carpathians, and by the middle of May Mackensen had reached the San.

Hindenburg, Ludendorff and Hoffmann watched all this in disgruntled silence, their patriotic hopes struggling unhappily with their personal emotions. Mackensen was not the man they would have chosen to direct the offensive, and although they recognized Seeckt's ability, they had no confidence in Falkenhayn. However, their command had been stripped of so many troops that they could do nothing but grumble and plan for a brighter future.

Falkenhayn was concerned with more than the Eastern Front. On the 25th of April an Allied landing at the Dardenelles placed Turkey in mortal danger, and on the 23rd of May the Italian Government, cautious even in treachery, declared war on Austria, although not on Germany. Because of these new threats, Falkenhayn wanted to halt Mackensen on the San, and when Przemysl was retaken at the end of May only Conrad's eloquent arguments persuaded him to continue the offensive.

In the Neue Schloss at Pless on the 3rd of June the reluctant Kaiser again had to arbitrate between his quarreling generals. In peacetime Wilhelm had much enjoyed being Supreme War Lord, but now the post no longer seemed so attractive. Falkenhayn, Hindenburg, Ludendorff, Mackensen and Conrad all had their say. Falkenhayn, who expected a major Allied attack in the West in the autumn, wanted to withdraw at least four divisions from the East; Conrad was burning to hit Italy; and Ludendorff argued that a gigantic enveloping move from the north could sweep across the rear of the retreating Russian armies and annihilate them. The conference achieved neither unanimity nor a

definite strategy. Wilhelm ruled that Mackensen would be reinforced from the troops under *Ober-Ost* and it was agreed that the
Austrian Second and Fourth Armies, advancing on either side
of Mackensen, would be placed under his command.

With the fall of Lemberg on the 22nd of June, Colonel von
Seeckt proposed that the Eleventh Army wheel north between the
Vistula and the Bug toward Syedlets and Brest-Litovsk. Falken-
hayn agreed and asked *Ober-Ost* to co-operate by employing the
Ninth Army in an attack across the Narev River toward Osovets.

By now, however, Ludendorff had another plan. At first he
and Hoffmann had disagreed on the correct strategy, and Ludendorff had been inclined to listen to a proposal from Major von
Bockelberg, his operations officer, whom he had known long ago
in the Red House in Berlin. Bockelberg urged an attack across
the Bohr River on both sides of Oswejice, while Hoffmann favored a much bolder and more sweeping movement across the
Niemen towards Vilna. All agreed that Mackensen's offensive
was a wasting asset, since it was restricted to frontal attacks and
since the Grand Duke Nicholas would suffer no grave disadvan-
tage by continuing to fall back. What was needed was some
way of catching and killing the Grand Duke's armies.

Hoffmann was sure his plan had a good chance of eliminating
Russia from the war. An attack by the Tenth Army from the
west, combined with a simultaneous envelopment by the Niemen
Army from the north, would capture Kovno. Then the road to
Vilna and the Russian rear would be open. Smoking endless
cigarettes and sipping from his glass of cognac the while, Hoffmann argued with a sort of cool desperation that this was perhaps the last opportunity that would be offered of striking Russia a crushing blow. He would point at the map, his gold signet
ring gleaming dully as his small, well-kept hand hovered over the
area of northern Poland where the Russian right flank petered
out before it reached the Baltic shore. "This is the only enemy
wing still open to our attack on the whole of the Continent," he
emphasized again and again.[9]

Ludendorff and Hoffmann debated the matter for several days, without making the least pretense of consulting Hindenburg. Finally, on the evening of the 29th of June, they met with the four army commanders in Lötzen Fortress. The argument continued until the small hours of the morning, but when all the army commanders supported Hoffmann, Ludendorff at last gracefully accepted the majority opinion.[10]

Once he did so, he embraced it with the enthusiasm of a convert. He began his preliminary dispositions immediately, reinforcing with one cavalry and two infantry divisions General von Below's Niemen Army which had been formed north of the river in May. All that remained to do was to obtain Falkenhayn's consent, and Ludendorff was sure that the Supreme Command would be unable to resist the strategic logic of the plan.

On the evening of the last day of June, Ludendorff left Lötzen in his special train for a Kaiser's conference at Posen. At the railway station the air was heavy with the fragrance of lilacs, for the cold northern spring had softened into a lovely summer; the blackthorn hedges were in blossom; and the storks were nesting again about the nearby lakes. For once Ludendorff's mood was in keeping with the hopeful world around him. He had prepared all the necessary orders for the Niemen Army. It would advance between Kovno and Grodno, cutting the Vilna-Petrograd railway before turning south to march between Brest-Litovsk and the Pripet Marshes. The nightmare war on two fronts might soon be over. He had arranged to telephone Hoffmann immediately after the conference, and as soon as the Kaiser's formal sanction was obtained, Hoffmann would issue the final orders. As his train steamed out of Lötzen, Ludendorff was reasonably content.

All the next afternoon Hoffmann sat anxiously by the telephone, but no call came from Posen. Twilight had crept into his office, filling the corners of the room with gray shadow, before the phone rang and Ludendorff's voice came over the wire. Hoffmann listened to the vicious snarl in shocked disbelief. He was to stop everything. No orders would be going out. The Kaiser had once again ruled in favor of Falkenhayn, who, with his eyes still fixed upon France, had unhesitatingly rejected the possibility of seeking a decision in the East and had insisted that the next attack be launched across the Narev, not the Niemen.

Ludendorff returned to Lötzen in a savage temper, a mood fully shared by Hoffmann. Falkenhayn's cautious offensive might force the Russians to evacuate Warsaw but could never be decisive, and what might be the last hope of victory would trickle away and be lost on the broad Polish plains. From now on there was implacable, undeclared war between Falkenhayn and *Ober-Ost*.

On the 10th of July Colonel Tappen arrived unexpectedly in a special train. He smiled as cheerfully as ever and made some tactful excuse for his visit, but everyone at Lötzen was furiously aware that Falkenhayn had sent him to see whether *Ober-Ost* was carrying out instructions properly. Hoffmann noted in his diary: "I am sick of Headquarters. The fellow [Falkenhayn] is not satisfied unless he can abuse us every day," [11] and Margarethe Ludendorff recalled that her husband's letters were now "nothing but one long complaint against Falkenhayn." [12]

On the 13th of July General von Gallwitz's new Twelfth Army of 12 divisions began its frontal attack southeast across the Narev. The Grand Duke Nicholas retired in good order, evacuating Warsaw on the 5th of August and abandoning the line of the Vistula. Strangely enough, he decided to defend the fortress of Novo-Georgievsk — which was a mistake, for when it fell on the 20th the Germans captured 30 Russian generals and 90,000 soldiers, as well as 700 guns.[13]

When the Kaiser, elated by this success, suddenly decided to review his victorious soldiers in Novo-Georgievsk, Supreme Headquarters duly notified *Ober-Ost* but made no mention of Hindenburg's being invited. Ludendorff and Hoffmann were immediately on their dignity. This would never do. If the Kaiser was to inspect Hindenburg's troops, the old gentleman would certainly have to be there. A special train was hurriedly prepared and Hindenburg, Ludendorff, and Major von Bockelberg steamed off to Novo-Georgievsk. They found the smoldering town filled with prisoners and the streets littered with dead horses the Russians had shot rather than give them up to the Germans.[14] Hoffmann was left behind to command the armies and speculate on how His Majesty and Falkenhayn would look when they found Hindenburg and Ludendorff awaiting them on the station platform.

The next day Hoffmann's curiosity was satisfied. Ludendorff returned to report that the meeting had been courteous but cool. At one stage Falkenhayn had turned to him and said: "Now are you convinced that my operation was correct?" And Ludendorff had coldly answered: "On the contrary!" The Kaiser, uncomfortably placed between his two glowering paladins, had smoothed matters over with a few hasty, noncommital remarks. "Then," Hoffmann noted, "decorations were distributed — to the wrong people, of course — the troops were reviewed, speeches delivered, and so on." [15]

Ludendorff could relieve his feelings by exchanging offensive telegrams with the Supreme Command, but Hoffmann — who would have been better at it — was denied this privilege. He turned to his diary instead, revealing there an entirely unPrussian sensitivity. Perhaps this, like his brilliance, was due to the French blood on his mother's side of the family; at all events, he recorded, rather sadly: "His Majesty is entirely under Falkenhayn's influence and does not love us . . . So long as I can remember only half my acquaintances have liked me. The less gifted have no use for me at all." [16]

Superficially at least, the Kaiser had good reason to place his confidence in Falkenhayn. More than ten divisions had been withdrawn from *Ober-Ost* for other theaters, in spite of insubordinate letters of protest drafted by Ludendorff and signed by Hindenburg.[17] Nevertheless, by the end of September the front ran almost due north and south from Dvinsk along the Dvina River to the Pripet Marshes and Roumania; the Russians had suf-

fered a million casualties and lost three quarters of a million prisoners; and the Tsar had dismissed the Grand Duke Nicholas and
assumed personal command of his forces. Ludendorff and Hoffmann were glad to see the Grand Duke go. He had been a ruthless, iron-willed opponent who had held his armies together admirably and whose strategic ideas had often been daring and
brilliant. There was little reason to fear that the Tsar would do
as well.

By now, too, the British had failed at the Dardanelles; on the
Western Front the French offensive in Champagne and the British offensive at Loos had alike broken down disastrously with
more than 300,000 Allied casualties; and Bulgaria had agreed
to join Germany and Austria in an attack on Serbia. The news
that the Serbian expedition was to be commanded by von Mackensen was received without enthusiasm at *Ober-Ost*. Hoffmann
wrote spitefully: "Now that all available honors, titles, and orders have been showered in so short a time on this one devoted
head, there will be nothing left for him after the capture of Belgrade but to be rechristened 'Prince Eugen'." [18]

All spring and summer Colonel Hentsch, who had been forgiven for whatever miscalculation he had made at the Marne,
had been studying the passages of the Danube and the Save. On
the 7th of October four armies, German, Austrian and Bulgarian, crossed these rivers and advanced into Serbia. Within
three weeks the country was overrun, and what was left of the
Serbian Army conducted a fighting retreat to the south and west,
fleeing in terrible winter weather across the Albanian mountains to the Adriatic coast. The Germans and Austrians were
content to let them go, but their hereditary enemies, the Bulgarians, pursued as fiercely as wolves. Only 125,000 Serbs survived
out of 450,000. The Allies later transported this remnant to the
Greek island of Corfu.

The long and bitter year was now drawing to a close. The
Eastern Front had become static, and at the end of October
Ober-Ost moved to Kovno, a typical Polish town of mean

wooden houses and wide earthen streets. The view was restricted on all sides by low hills, but across the river was a
ruined castle which had belonged to the Teutonic Knights and a
hill from which Napoleon was said to have watched the *Grande
Armée* cross the Niemen in 1812. Every Sunday, the staff attended the garrison church parade, which the Lutheran chaplain,
Pastor Wessel, held in the requisitioned Orthodox Church. Ludendorff had not yet discovered that Christianity was a Jewish device designed to weaken the German people, and he thoroughly approved Pastor Wessel's weekly exhortations to the
troops. He remembered with special affection one hymn that
was often sung:

> *Ich hab'mich ergeben*
> *Mit Herz und mit Hand,*
> *Dir Land voll Lieb'und Leben,*
> *Mein deutsches Vaterland.*

In his opinion this hymn represented the zenith of religious experience; if he had had his way, it would have been sung every
Sunday in every church in Germany.[19]

With operations almost at a standstill, Field Marshal von Hindenburg had time to do some hunting in the Forest of Bialoviesa.
This sort of life suited the old man splendidly and his health had
never been better. He drank well, ate enormously, and, as always, slept a solid ten hours every night. The hunting, however,
was a little disappointing. One of the troubles with war, in the
Field Marshal's opinion, was that military operations cleared
away a good deal of the game and that poaching peasants, trying
to keep their families alive, accounted for even more of it. Since
the Forest of Bialoviesa provided inadequate sport, Hindenburg
went south to the Forest of Augustovo to take part in a wolf hunt
that had been arranged in his honor. It was pleasant to tramp
through the winter woods with deferential companions, so it did
not greatly matter that no wolves were sighted. There were few

traces of the terrible battle of the previous February — only a few scattered trenches filled with drifted snow.

Hoffmann had little work to do, but time never hung heavy on those small delicate hands. Day after day he would put on his high-peaked officer's cap and his magnificent fur-lined great-coat with its extra-wide lapels and drive off in a staff car to visit officers and men at the front or to look in at some field hospital.

Ludendorff had no more taste for this sort of thing than he had for hunting. He stayed in his office, growing more pallid and edgy as the days wore on. As early as the 3rd of November Hoffmann recorded in his diary: "Ludendorff is getting bored and keeps everyone on the run from morning to night. This restlessness — work for work's sake — is extremely uncomfortable for everyone around here." [20] This was when Hoffmann decided to get out and see the troops.

Ludendorff soon found congenial tasks to take up his time. Hindenburg put it this way: "To the former activities of my Chief of Staff were now added the duties of administering, reorganizing and exploiting the country with a view to procuring supplies for the troops, the homeland, and the local population. The increasing amount of work this involved would alone have been enough to take up the whole time and energies of one man. General Ludendorff regarded it as an appendix to his ordinary work, and devoted himself to it with that ruthless energy which is all his own." [21]

In fact, Ludendorff now began to administer an area the size of France. It was almost as interesting as directing battles. Six administrative provinces were created under *Ober-Ost:* Courland, Lithuania, Suwalki, Vilna, Grodno and Bialystok. Each was divided into large districts; a corps of gendarmes was formed and law courts were established with provincial courts of appeal and a high court of appeal in Kovno. Ludendorff issued a local coinage and levied taxes and customs duties; he nationalized industries and created monopolies on cigarettes, spirits, salt, matches, and confectionery; he established a chain of newspapers under strict censorship which provided the local populations with all the news he felt they should hear.

Railways had to be reorganized; branch lines had to be built; the Niemen bridges had to be repaired; the roads had to be made fit for all-weather transport; and the supply services had to be improved. Ludendorff established factories for the manufacture of barbed wire and workshops for the repair of military equipment. Russian machine-guns were altered to take German ammunition; billets were built for the troops; better hospital facilities were constructed; winter clothing was provided; and dozens of measures were taken to safeguard the health of men and horses; leave was arranged; and the mail delivery system put in order. To maintain morale Ludendorff established soldiers' clubs and field libraries and provided concerts, theaters, and field bookshops. Military training was intensified and altered to incorporate the lessons learned in action.

Ludendorff, determined that Germany would get everything possible out of the occupied territories, administered them with a ruthless hand. Because the war had created an enormous demand for lumber for field-works, railway ties, and cellulose, he set up forestry inspectorates and sawmills. He established a strict control over agriculture and supplied motor ploughs, agricultural machinery, and seed from Germany. German companies were formed to farm the conquered area, a census was taken of the peasants' cattle, and fishing was organized in the large lakes. Germany was supplied with Polish scrap iron, brass, copper, rags, skins and hides. Since horses were essential to the war effort, they were conscripted from the peasants, despite the hardship this involved. Ludendorff himself admitted: "The country was bound to suffer severely as the result of the continuous heavy demands made upon it, especially the constant levies of horses and cattle. The local administrative authorities often drew my attention to this fact, but there was nothing for it but to insist on these deliveries." [22]

Ludendorff was at least as brilliant an administrator as he was a soldier, and he thoroughly enjoyed using his powers. More ambitiously than Napoleon, he dreamed of the future German colonization of the East, especially of Courland. Even Hoffmann, for all his good sense, allowed himself to be carried away by dreams of grandeur. But Hoffmann was able to stand back and laugh at himself. Once when he had planned in his diary how to redivide the Balkans, he ended the ambitious paragraph: "But here am I disposing of kingdoms!" [23] It was a wonderful winter.

Yet a cold wind was blowing across Germany. Russia was still very much in the war; the French were holding out in the West; and the British Empire was just beginning to mobilize its resources. Although the German writ ran right across central Europe, the Fatherland was a beleaguered fortress. It was a spacious fortress, and the long goods trains made up in Hamburg's marshalling yards could roll without interference the 2200 miles to their destination in Baghdad. But Germany had solved nothing. With every tick of the clock her chances of ultimate victory perceptibly diminished. Falkenhayn realized this far better than Hindenburg and Ludendorff in eclipse in Kovno, but Falkenhayn was as fatally determined as ever to seek a decision in the West.

CHAPTER XI

THE SUMMONS TO SUPREME COMMAND

O SKAR VON HINDENBURG, the field marshal's son, leaned both elbows on the table and continued talking. His heavy face was a little flushed and his rather dull eyes glinted. He had rarely had so attentive an audience, and it was distinctly flattering to find the great Ludendorff and the legendary Colonel Hoffmann hanging on his words. When Oskar, who was serving as G.S.O.I. with the VIIth Corps in the West, had come to Kovno to visit his father in the middle of January, he had soon discovered he could hold the dinner table spellbound by telling stories about the "bungling" of the Supreme Command. The operations staff of *Ober-Ost* listened avidly, glad to hear confirmation of their belief that the war was being grossly mishandled and that Falkenhayn was even more inept than Moltke had been.[1]

This conviction did not prevent Ludendorff and Hoffmann from experiencing a brief resurgence of hope when Falkenhayn ordered Ludendorff to meet him at Lida at the end of the month. The strategy proposed by *Ober-Ost* seemed so obviously right that even Falkenhayn might have been converted to it. Perhaps he had at last admitted stalemate in the West and was now belatedly considering the brilliant combinations latent in the East.

Disappointment was general when Ludendorff returned on the 29th of January: Falkenhayn had wanted no more than a firsthand report on the morale and health of the Eastern armies. He had been formally courteous but had disclosed nothing of his intentions.[2]

Ober-Ost was now planning an attack of its own. The scheme, which had originally been suggested by General Otto von Below, was to cross the Düna River at Üxküwl, then thrust north to the Baltic, cutting off the main body of Russians in the Riga bridgehead. No great strategic results could be expected, but another 100,000 prisoners might well be captured. Apart from the loss inflicted on the Tsar, this would be a positive advantage, for industrialists and politicians had frequently intimated that the Fatherland could use more prisoner battalions. Agriculture especially needed extra labor, for Germany's food supplies were running short and the 1915 harvest had been the worst in 44 years. Although the attack at Riga would require seven or eight divisions from the West, the operation would not be protracted and, since it would shorten the German line, it would actually effect an economy in troops. Therefore when Ludendorff and Hoffmann completed the plan by the end of the first week in February, they submitted it to Supreme Headquarters hopefully.

Falkenhayn, however, was thinking on too grand a scale to be distracted by the lure of any minor success. He had pondered long in the loneliness of power, weighing possibilities and alternatives with goldsmith's scales, in his cold, enigmatic way. By temperament, however, he preferred a sharp exchange of pieces to subtle maneuvering, and he had already decided what 1916 was to bring. Partly because of his decision, it was to be the most blood-stained year in history.

As Falkenhayn saw it, Britain was Germany's principal enemy. But since Britain was primarily a naval power and since the British portion of the Western Front was unsuitable for offensive operations, he argued that Britain could best be injured by a blow at France. He wrote the Kaiser: "France has arrived almost at the end of her military effort. If her people can be made to understand clearly that in a military sense they have nothing more to hope for, the breaking-point will be reached and England's best weapon knocked out of her hand." [3]

This involved logic led Falkenhayn to an original strategic concept. He would attack some point "for the retention of which the French will be compelled to throw in every man they have," [4] then, by a series of limited advances, draw the French reserves into a killing-ground where they could be pulverized by artillery fire. If the battle went as he intended, France would bleed to death; if it proved too costly, Germany could at any time discontinue it. Having settled on his method, Falkenhayn looked about for a suitable slaughterhouse and eventually decided that the town of Verdun on the Heights of the Meuse met all his requirements admirably. It was perhaps the strongest fortress in the world; it had some military value as a menace to German communications; and for reasons of prestige the French would be forced to defend it regardless of cost. He gave his sanguinary plan the code-name *"Gericht"* ("a place of execution"), and obtained the Kaiser's consent to put it into effect.

Even outside *Ober-Ost,* some of the General Staff felt that Operation *"Gericht"* displayed less than military genius, especially since the Central Powers were overwhelmingly outnumbered by the Allies and desperately needed to conserve manpower. The German Crown Prince, who was to undertake the offensive, would have preferred to deal first with Russia, and Conrad, whose fiery temperament was his chief weakness as a strategist, dreamed night and day of striking the perfidious Italians a vicious blow in the Tyrol. In fact, Conrad asked for nine German divisions to replace Austrian formations on the Eastern Front, but Falkenhayn refused and extracted a promise that the Austrian line in the East would not be dangerously weakened for the sake of operations against Italy. No sooner had Conrad given this assurance than he began a steady withdrawal of troops from Galicia.

When Hindenburg and Ludendorff were told of Operation *"Gericht"* only a few days before it began, they were bitterly disappointed.[5] Verdun would be a worthwhile prize, but Ludendorff questioned the wisdom of attacking the enemy's strongest point. One would really think that Falkenhayn and Tappen had never heard of Schlieffen. In 1915, when *Ober-Ost* had been pleading for the wide envelopment across the Niemen and arguing that an attack on "the last exposed flank in Europe" might topple the whole edifice of Tsarist Russia, someone on Falkenhayn's staff had remarked contemptuously: "These people want to fight only when there is no one to oppose them." Ludendorff was still of the opinion that this was the more intelligent way to wage war.

Hoffmann was even more bitter. Like few among his generation of staff officers he had enough imagination to understand the human tragedy that lay behind casualty figures, and he was filled with rage whenever he remembered the *Kindermord* of 1914. He considered Falkenhayn "the evil genius of the Fatherland," [6] was convinced that he was losing the war, and feared that Verdun would become another senseless slaughter like First Ypres. Accordingly, he never ceased urging Ludendorff and Hindenburg to do all they could to frustrate Falkenhayn's plans. Ludendorff was easy to convince, but the old Field Marshal, who was shrewdly sensitive to the Kaiser's opinions, was sometimes surprisingly obstinate.

On the cold, dry morning of the 21st of February, the 15-mile long cloud of black smoke and dust that was the German barrage suddenly lifted, and the infantry clambered out of their trenches to advance on Verdun. Just as Falkenhayn had predicted, the French fought tenaciously, spending the lives of their young men for every yard of nitrate-tainted ground as recklessly as profligates squander money for vice. Falkenhayn was well pleased to see his troops inching their way forward into the charnel house, but some German staff officers worried about the extremely narrow frontage of attack and the unexpectedly heavy German losses.

The Verdun offensive certainly disrupted the Allied plans for 1916. In answer to French cries for relief, the Italians launched a fifth attack on the Isonzo, the British hastened their preparations for a major offensive on the Somme and the Russians once again gallantly sacrificed themselves for French interests. The Fifth

Battle of the Isonzo was as unsuccessful as the previous four had been, but the Russian offensive in March was a more serious matter. Ludendorff had heard rumors of an attack in the Lake Narotch region from Russian deserters who complained of the iron discipline imposed on divisions training behind the lines, but he had been skeptical, for the area was inadequately supplied with railways and provided little room for maneuver.

When he went to Berlin on the 11th of March to attend the wedding of Prince Joachim of Prussia, he did not believe an attack was imminent. The spring thaws were not far away and he thought it unlikely that the Russians would attempt any great operation during the time of "roadlessness" in Poland. Therefore he was surprised to receive an urgent summons to return at once to Kovno.

A Russian bombardment of unprecedented intensity opened on the 16th of March along the front between Lake Narotch and Lake Vischniev. Five relatively quiet months had refreshed Russia's strength. Her munitions crisis had passed and her armies now had enough ammunition, guns and rifles, as well as trained manpower to spare. On the 18th, masses of Russian infantry surged forward, attempting to cut out a sector of the German front by converging assaults on the flanks of the XXIst Corps.[7] For three days the situation was critical, for if the line was breached here, the road to Vilna and Kovno would lie open. By now the weather had broken and the expected thaw set in. As the snow melted, Eichhorn's Tenth Army fought waist-deep in icy water; breastworks dissolved; sandbags oozed away; and trenches became streams;[8] but the defense held, and the German rifles and machine-guns exacted a terrible toll. On the second day of the battle, German observers counted 9,270 Russian dead on the XXIst Corps' front, although German casualties amounted to only 560.[9] Although the Russians suffered appalling loss, they pressed on with fatalistic courage, but by the 26th of March Ludendorff was confident the crisis had passed.[10] By the end of the month the offensive had completely broken down, and even the Russians could scarcely afford the casualties they were suffering.

The attacks failed strategically as well as tactically, for not a man was moved from Verdun to the Eastern Front, and although the Tenth Army had given up some ground, it later won back all that had been lost. The German counter-attacks were remarkable for their preliminary artillery bombardments, which had been entrusted to a Lieutenant Colonel Bruchmüller, an unknown, middle-aged officer who had been brought back from the retired list to the staff of a Landwehr division. Bruchmüller proved to be one of the half dozen outstanding military technicians of the war, with a unique talent for divining exactly how much ammunition was needed to soften a position before an infantry assault. Ludendorff, always quick to recognize ability, was to promote Bruchmüller to greater and greater responsibilities.

In spite of his defensive victory of Lake Narotch, Ludendorff by May was even grimmer than usual. On the Western Front there were unmistakable signs that the British were about to attack on the Somme, and Falkenhayn was deeply committed at Verdun, where both sides were suffering fantastic losses. Some 60 French divisions had marched up the Sacred Way to be slaughtered in the few square miles of the nightmare battlefield, which was blasted and calcined as though by the fires of the Last Judgment. But, contrary to Falkenhayn's murderous intentions, the German casualties had been nearly as heavy as the French. Verdun was certainly a place of execution, but the killing had turned out to be indiscriminate, mindless, and seemingly perpetual. Still the insane fight raged around Douaumont, Thiaumont, Vaux, Le Mort Homme, and 304-Meter Hill — now mere names on the map, with their former features reduced to desolate anonymity — but still the French held Verdun. Although Falkenhayn had promised that the offensive could be broken off at any time, in practice this was not easy, for German prestige was now as deeply involved as the French.

In Kovno, the very word "Verdun" had an ugly sound.[11]

At the end of May, while German and French soldiers died daily by their thousands, suffered, and went mad in a small corner of the Department of the Meuse about Verdun, the Kaiser and Falkenhayn visited *Ober-Ost*. A formal banquet was given in their honor; the long tables set up in the headquarters mess gleamed with starched linen and sparkled with polished silver and crystal; the food was rich and plentiful; white-jacketed mess-waiters stood behind the chairs to fill the tall wine glasses; and to complete the illusion that everyone was still living in the world that had been lost, the dinner was followed by speeches. Hindenburg, as host, spoke first and dwelt eloquently on the importance of the Eastern theater — Hoffmann had written his speech for him the week before — but Falkenhayn countered with a masterly exposition of his "Western" strategy. He did it so well that even Hoffmann came temporarily under his spell and recorded in his diary: "If all that H.M. and Falkenhayn said is a correct statement of the present situation, then they are right, and we must acquiesce." [12] This mood did not last long. Hindenburg and Ludendorff took the Kaiser on a tour of the front, and by the time they returned, Hoffmann was himself again, and conspiring bitterly against G.H.Q.

On the final day of May, the last great European naval battle of history took place when the main British and German fleets clashed in the North Sea, 75 miles off the Danish coast. Although the British under Admiral Jellicoe considerably outnumbered and outgunned Vice Admiral Scheer's squadrons, the fighting at the Battle of Jutland favored the Germans. Jellicoe lost 3 dreadnaughts and 6274 men to Scheer's one dreadnaught and 2545 men. Nevertheless, at Jutland, as in the war as a whole, Germany's fate was a measure of brilliant tactical success, followed by slow but inevitable strategic failure. Since the Kaiser's High Seas Fleet returned to port and never ventured out to give battle again, the overall naval situation remained unchanged, with Britain dominating at least the surface of the oceans of the world.

Meanwhile, Conrad's offensive in the Tyrol made good progress. As the Austrians drove toward Verona, the King of Italy appealed to the Tsar who, as always, responded generously. General Brusilov, Ivanov's successor as the commander of the Southwest Front, had been preparing a set-piece attack for the end of June, and when the Stavka asked him if he could do anything to relieve the pressure on Italy, he replied with what was initially no more than a demonstration in force. After a single day's bombardment on the 3rd of June, his four armies moved tentatively forward along a 200-mile front. To their amazement the Austrian defences crumbled like a sand-castle before an incoming tide. In many places entire Austrian battalions surrendered and numerous Bohemian units fraternized with the enemy.

As soon as the Stavka recovered from its astonishment, it reinforced success. By the 9th, Russian reserves were pouring into the gap and by the end of the month Brusilov had captured 350,000 prisoners and had driven ahead 60 miles.

In all this scene of collapse and defeat only German divisions and Austrian formations stiffened with German troops had held firm. General Bothmer's *Südarmee* had stood like a rock while the waves of the attack washed by it on both sides and General Linsingen was still covering Kovel, but elsewhere the disaster was complete. Ludendorff sent every man he could to assist the Austrians, at the same time angrily demanding that the entire Eastern Front be placed under *Ober-Ost*.

Hopefully, the Russians attacked other parts of the line. After heavy fighting, the German front held, but time and again the Austrians broke, falling back by the end of June to a line running from the Dniester River through Kolomea to Kimpolung. Although Ludendorff sent Conrad five divisions and Falkenhayn dispatched four divisions from the West, the situation remained critical, and the German Foreign Office feared that Austria's difficulties might decide Roumania to enter the war on Russia's side.

At the end of June the Kaiser summoned Hindenburg and Ludendorff to Pless. Before the audience, Ludendorff talked to Chancellor Bethmann-Hollweg who looked even graver and more sorrowful than he had in 1915. He had long been disillusioned with Falkenhayn's conduct of the war and was appalled by the blood-letting at Verdun, but Ludendorff found him unwilling to take any positive action. Falkenhayn was present during the conference with the Kaiser, which was so innocuous as to be almost farcical. Nothing was discussed which could not perfectly well have been dealt with in writing, and Ludendorff received the impression that he had been summoned only because Falkenhayn wanted the Kaiser to believe that *Ober-Ost* was consulted in all operations.[13]

On the 16th, very large Russian forces poured out from the Riga bridgehead and attacked the Eighth Army west of the Dvina River. Conrad broke off his offensive in the Tyrol so that he could send Austrian formations back to Galicia, and although the British assault on the Somme had opened on the 1st of July, Falkenhayn dispatched two more divisions to the East. Nevertheless, by the end of the month, Ludendorff's only reserve for a front nearly 1,000 kilometers long consisted of a single cavalry brigade and some artillery and machine-gun units.[14] As the tension mounted at *Ober-Ost*, even Field Marshal Hindenburg was shaken out of his Olympian calm, while Ludendorff, according to Hoffmann, was "very much up in the air."[15]

The military situation by itself was not solely responsible for the frayed nerves. Ludendorff and Hoffmann now sensed that Falkenhayn's star was declining and that their own was in the ascendent. The difficulty was to get the old Field Marshal to do what they wanted. Although Hindenburg could never counter their arguments, he possessed a certain rustic shrewdness and a stubborn sense of loyalty that unfitted him for conspiracy. Ludendorff and Hoffmann would carefully compose letters to the Kaiser for the Field Marshal to sign, but, more often than not, Hindenburg would consider them ponderously, put them aside for a few days, and then carefully take out all those portions that contained comments on the general conduct of the war. Ludendorff went about with thunderous looks and even Hoffmann's air of mocking insouciance began to wear a little thin. They finally persuaded Hindenburg to demand unity of command on the Eastern Front, but they were continually on tenterhooks lest, when it came to the point, the old man might accept some unsatisfactory compromise.

Hindenburg was considerably distressed because these two clever men, who were his subordinates and friends, often seemed to be urging him toward unsoldierly courses. What was he to do when the Prussian virtue of obedience appeared in conflict with the good of the Fatherland? He had been told more than once that the Emperor "could not stand" Ludendorff [16] and he was deeply troubled by the imperial coldness to *Ober-Ost*.[17] The old man took to muttering to himself: "Yes, what my King commands, that I must do!" And Ludendorff would grow scarlet with suppressed rage, while in the background Hoffmann would roll his eyes to Heaven in exasperated supplication.[18]

July brought little improvement in the military situation. Although the British armies under Sir Douglas Haig suffered huge losses on the Somme for microscopic gains, they pressed their attacks as fiercely as ever. The Austrian Army was still so utterly unreliable that Hoffmann noted in his diary: "If after the war, anyone comes near me with a Nibelung's oath of fidelity and an offer to die at my side in battle, I shall certainly knock his block off." [19]

On the 27th of July, Hindenburg and Ludendorff were again called to Pless, but this time the atmosphere was noticeably different. Falkenhayn was definitely on the defensive, and — very significantly — the Kaiser seemed inclined to support Ludendorff's opinions rather than those of the Chief of the General Staff. Once, when Falkenhayn attempted to postpone a decision on a unified command in the East, Wilhelm burst out excitedly: "I tell you I'm not leaving here until this matter is settled! I owe this to my people." [20]

Full unity of command was not achieved, but Conrad had at last agreed that *Ober-Ost* should be responsible for the front as far south as Brody and that the armies of von Bothmer and von Pflanzer-Baltin should be united in a single army group under the Archduke Charles with Seeckt as his Chief of Staff. This army group would come under Austrian G.H.Q., but the appointment of Seeckt would ensure a large measure of German control. As Ludendorff pressed his advantage, the discussions at times became quite acrimonious. On the night of the 30th, Falkenhayn was so angered by criticisms of his conduct of the war that he did not appear at the Imperial dinner table, and Ludendorff hoped he might resign. Although nothing of the sort happened, Ludendorff was well satisfied with the conference. His sphere of command had been extended, and, even more important, a new wind was blowing in the capital.

With the extension of *Ober-Ost's* responsibility, Kovno was no longer a suitable location for operational headquarters. The administrative staff remained there but the operations staff set up a temporary headquarters in a special train. During the first week of August, Hindenburg, Ludendorff and Hoffmann toured the Austrian portion of the front. The Austrian commanders greeted them with perfect cordiality, criticized their own weaknesses with charming frankness, and had nothing constructive to suggest.[21] Although in some places between the Tartar Pass and the Roumanian frontier the Russians had reached the crest of the Carpathians, Ludendorff, surveying the situation coldly, concluded that he could stabilize the front with the resources at hand.

He now established his headquarters in the burnt-out town of Brest-Litovsk, which had been almost completely gutted in July. The railway station and the tall cathedral with its blue towers stood intact at the edge of the town and the ancient stone Citadel was unharmed, but nothing else remained except charred and blackened ruins. A sour odor hung depressingly over everything. Ludendorff found it difficult to operate his headquarters from a railway train on a siding; there was very little space; the large operational maps took up a great deal of room; the flat landscape shimmered with iridescent heat; and the August sun beat down mercilessly on the metal roofs of the coaches. Only Hoffmann managed to make himself relatively comfortable and continually amazed the other members of the staff by the way he made the most of what he called his "salon." [22] After a week or so in these cramped quarters, Ludendorff decided to move into the Citadel. The place was damp, musty and overgrown with nettles, but a small stream flowed through the grounds and graceful willows drooped their branches into its waters. Ludendorff energetically set about the task of housecleaning. The weeds were cut down, trees were felled to let in light and air, and the flagstoned corridors and large empty rooms were scrubbed with yellow soap and water until the lingering smell of cobwebs and disuse had completely disappeared. In a very short time the Citadel was habitable. "I took pleasure in putting things right," Ludendorff recalled.[23]

From about the middle of August, the Eastern Front was relatively secure, and Ludendorff had time to press his quarrel with Falkenhayn more vigorously than ever. On the 17th, after Hindenburg had declined to protest the removal of a division, Ludendorff sent an orderly to the Field Marshal with a request that he be allowed to resign. Hindenburg knew he would be lost without his Chief of Staff, but he had not yet reconciled his conscience to Ludendorff's view that a soldier might properly threaten resignation as a means of blackmailing superior authority. The old man refused to submit his own resignation to the Kaiser, and in fact Hoffmann had to persuade him that it would be disastrous to the Fatherland for Ludendorff to resign. The most Hindenburg would do was ask the Kaiser for an interview, and when this was refused, he let the matter drop.[24] Ludendorff and Hoffmann were by no means so amiable, for they sensed that supreme power was almost within their grasp.

On the 27th of August, Roumania declared war on Germany,

and something very close to panic descended momentarily on Berlin. This was a clear indication that small neutral nations whose vital interests were at stake believed Germany must ultimately lose the war. The Kaiser was particularly shaken, because Falkenhayn had assured him, only the day before, that Roumania would remain neutral. This, however, was no more than the final straw. The indictment against Falkenhayn was long — the *Kindermord* of First Ypres, the bloody failure at Verdun, the lost opportunities in the East. All Falkenhayn's own staff — with one notable exception — had secretly met and deputized Colonel Max Bauer to approach the Adjutant General, von Plessen, in an effort to persuade the Kaiser that Falkenhayn would have to be replaced. Only the optimistic Colonel Tappen had no part in this intrigue, perhaps because he knew who Falkenhayn's successor would certainly be.[25]

At all events, at one o'clock on the afternoon of the 28th of August, the telephone rang in the Operations Room in the Citadel at Brest-Litovsk and Ludendorff was summoned to take the call. The Kaiser's Chief of Military Cabinet, General von Lyncker, informed Ludendorff that the Kaiser required him and Hindenburg to report to Pless as soon as possible. When pressed for a reason, von Lyncker would reply only that: "The situation is serious," [26] but he did mention that Falkenhayn knew nothing about the visit and would be informed only after they had arrived. That afternoon at four o'clock, Hindenburg, Ludendorff and Major von Bockelberg steamed out of Brest-Litovsk in their special train, taking with them only enough personal effects for a three days' visit.

The next morning Lyncker met Hindenburg and Ludendorff at the railway station and informed them that Hindenburg had been appointed Chief of the General Staff and that Ludendorff would be entitled the Second Chief of the General Staff with a promotion to the rank of General of Infantry. Hindenburg accepted the highest military appointment with grave calm, but Ludendorff insisted on making certain conditions. He refused the title of Second Chief of the General Staff, for he felt there was something insulting about the word "Second," and he required an express assurance that he would have joint responsibility for all decisions taken. When von Lyncker agreed, Ludendorff accepted the post as First Quartermaster General.

After this conversation, Lyncker took Hindenburg and Ludendorff to see the Kaiser, who was found outside the royal castle, waiting for the Kaiserin to arrive from Berlin. With Wilhelm were Falkenhayn and Bethmann-Hollweg in a somber little group. The strain of the war had visibly aged Falkenhayn; in 1914 he had looked ten years younger than his age, but now he looked ten years older, and all the youthful vitality had gone from his face.[27] The Kaiser was sincerely sorry to see Falkenhayn go and had wept when he had taken the decision to replace him.[28] He neither liked nor trusted the men from *Ober-Ost*, for he considered Hindenburg to be wooden and unimaginative and Ludendorff, whom he called privately "the sergeant-major," to be humorless and thrusting. After the Kaiser announced the change in command, he sought for some royal banality to lighten the tension, but all he could find to say was that he hoped the crisis at the front would soon be overcome.[29] Bethmann-Hollweg expressed the same pious hope. Falkenhayn, very straight and handsome, drew himself up to attention and prepared to take his leave. He saluted the Kaiser, then bowed formally to Hindenburg and offered his hand. "God help you and our Fatherland," he said. With this he turned away, ignoring Ludendorff, his real successor.

CHAPTER XII

THE VIEW FROM THE SUMMIT

GREAT CHESTNUT TREES stood about the royal park at Pless and shaded the quiet streets of the town. The August of 1916 might almost have been mistaken for any of a hundred other Augusts under the cool greenness of the big trees, except that now their leafy serenity was an intolerable reminder of the world that had disappeared two years ago. So much had changed in so short a time. And to someone like Ludendorff, back from a theater of war, the change already had the bitter taste of finality. Trees and fields and hills remained as before, but thousands felt the same, sharp, intuitive pang, the sudden middle-of-the-night certitude of death or love betrayed, and knew beyond reason that the old Germany was gone.

Instinctively, Ludendorff resisted the revelation, although he soon discovered that from Pless the war looked very different than from Brest-Litovsk. At *Ober-Ost* he had been concerned almost exclusively with military problems, but at G.H.Q. he not only had to control all the military fronts but also to interest himself in international and domestic politics. Moreover, he inherited a far worse situation than Falkenhayn had done after the Marne. The Entente was everywhere fiercely on the offensive — the British attacking on the Somme, the Italians pressing the Austrians on the Isonzo, the Roumanians invading Transylvania with 750,000 men, and the Russians preparing to renew their assaults in Galicia. The Central Powers were dangerously outnumbered; the superior Allied industrial production was increasingly making itself felt; and, worst of all in Ludendorff's view,[1] morale at home was low, for the British naval blockade made food scarce and the 1916 harvest was not good.

His first problem was to find a sufficient force to deal with Roumania. A few exhausted Austrian divisions were in the interior of Transylvania, and a mixed force of about seven Bulgar-Turkish and German divisions under Field Marshal von Mackensen were on the southern bank of the Danube on the Bulgarian side of the Dobrudja frontier. Falkenhayn had intended that Mackensen should cross the Danube and march on Bucharest, but Ludendorff, feeling that this force was too weak, began to collect what troops he could from the Western and Eastern Fronts to form a new army in Transylvania. As a necessary corollary, he informed the Kaiser that the offensive at Verdun would have to be stopped immediately. Ironically, Falkenhayn was placed in command of the Roumanian campaign.

Ludendorff had been in his new post for less than 24 hours when Chancellor Bethmann-Hollweg came to him to discuss the question of unrestricted U-boat warfare.[2] In the United States an influential group of men favored intervention in the war on the Allied side. Their motives varied from idealism to a desire to protect their investments, but without some better case than they had so far been able to make they were unlikely to persuade the American people to disregard George Washington's advice against involvement in the controversies of Europe "without adequate inducement or justification." But if American ships were to be sunk by German submarines on the high seas, the interventionists would be presented with an irresistible battle-cry and would be reinforced by millions of patriotic Americans who had so far remained cool. The previous sink-at-sight campaign had been stopped in April after President Wilson had sent the German Government a virtual ultimatum, but the Admiralty, now headed by Admiral von Capelle, was pressing for resumption and arguing that Germany could win the war by this means alone. Admiral von Tirpitz had always claimed that his fleet of 148 U-boats would force Britain to sue for peace within six months. Bethmann, who distrusted Tirpitz's optimistic forecast and had a true appreciation of the effect of the United States' entry into the war, steadfastly opposed the Admiralty. When Ludendorff was inclined to underestimate American military potential, Bethmann told him that a resumption of the unrestricted U-boat campaign might lead to Denmark and Holland joining the Allies. Since Ludendorff simply could not find the troops to defend two additional frontiers, he agreed to support the Chancellor's position, at least for the time being.

Ludendorff was not long in making changes at G.H.Q. He organized a political department for liaison with the Foreign Office and centralized the control of the German Air Force under Supreme Headquarters. Colonel Tappen, who had so often stood at Falkenhayn's elbow with his obstinate slow-witted advice, was replaced as Chief of Operations by Lieutenant Colonel Wetzel, an intelligent, imaginative man, but of the staff at Brest-Litovsk, Ludendorff took only Major von Bockelberg with him to the West.[3] Prince Leopold of Bavaria became Commander-in-Chief East, and Ludendorff went to considerable trouble to see that Hoffmann was made his Chief of Staff, although he was only a colonel.

Military historians have frequently speculated as to why Ludendorff left Hoffmann on the Eastern Front, thus breaking up a consistently victorious team. Perhaps Ludendorff was subconsciously anxious to escape the influence of a personality at least as strong as his own and far more balanced in outlook, but the obvious reason — that Hoffmann knew the Eastern Front and was irreplaceable there — is much more probable. Certainly, the break was made without the least ill-will on either side. Hoffmann became, in everything but name, the Commander-in-Chief East, but in his new sphere Ludendorff was to miss his friend's wise counsel far more than he ever realized. Hoffmann's successor in the East as Chief of Operations was Major Brinckmann, the same immaculate officer who had distinguished himself at Liège.

The staff at Pless soon fell into a routine similar to that at *Ober-Ost*. Hindenburg did not begin his day until nine o'clock, but Ludendorff was invariably in his office by eight. Until noon, he dealt with reports from the various fronts, conducted short conferences with department heads, and issued instructions. Each day at noon Hindenburg went to the Neue Schloss for a brief, formal conference with the Kaiser, but Ludendorff, whose strong personality was already bearing down on the Emperor's weaker one, made no pretense of consulting his royal master about decisions. The afternoons passed in the same manner as the mornings. Dinner was at eight, and for a short while thereafter the staff sat around in groups until, sharp at 9:30, Ludendorff gave the signal to return to work. Ludendorff himself generally remained in his office until one or two o'clock, and everyone would be delighted whenever they saw his grim taciturn figure leaving a little earlier.[4] Few of his subordinates felt any personal devotion to Ludendorff, but all knew what a strain he was under and how much Germany's war effort depended on him.

In the more complex atmosphere of G.H.Q., where most problems had political implications, Hindenburg possessed even less real power than he had as Commander-in-Chief East. The old Field Marshal's ingrained distaste for politics made him only too willing to let his First Quartermaster General make all such decisions. That this would be so had always been obvious to those who knew the two men, and not all the Army had relished the prospect. On the 28th of August Colonel von Marschall of the Kaiser's Military Cabinet told General Gröner that he viewed Ludendorff's accession to power with terror because, "in his boundless vanity and pride," he would bleed Germany white, then make the Emperor bear the blame.[5] Although no one close to the heart of affairs regarded Hindenburg as anything but a figurehead, the German nation still reposed its complete trust in him. An extra aide-de-camp was appointed to deal with his vast, adulatory correspondence — a lady wrote from Chile complaining that she had lost her baptismal certificate and asking Hindenburg to obtain another; the burgomaster of a small provincial town asked his advice about the disposal of refuse; schoolchildren confided their troubles to him; and housewives pathetically begged him to end the war.

In the late summer of 1916 any responsible German soldier would have been glad to end the war if he had known how peace could be obtained on acceptable terms, but there was a good deal of disagreement about what terms would be acceptable. General Gröner, Colonel Hoffmann, or Bethmann-Hollweg would have been only too happy to return to the status quo, or something very near it. Belgium, they thought, should certainly be evacuated and Poland returned to Russia. When they looked hard at the military situation, they were even inclined to admit that some concessions might be made to France in Lorraine. But the majority of influential Germans would have regarded such terms as little better than treasonous. Ludendorff had recently written to a friend that after the war "Belgium's dependence [on Germany] must be an economic, military, and political one," [6] and Class and the Pan-Germans talked of vast annexations in Europe, the acquisition of colonies, and huge indemnities. One of the most remarkable aspects of the First World War was that the people of every country were utterly convinced of the justice of their own nation's cause, and even moderate men like Erzberger and Stresemann of the Center Party believed that Germany was entitled to some compensation for her wartime sacrifices. In any case, the debate about peace terms was meaningless, for the Allies had no intention of settling for anything but victory.

Early in September Hindenburg and Ludendorff set out on a personal inspection of the Western Front. Their tour was to begin with a conference on the 7th at Cambrai, the headquarters of Crown Prince Rupprecht of Bavaria. Margarethe came up from Baden-Baden to meet Ludendorff's special train at Frankfurt, and was prettily disconcerted when her husband told her she could accompany him only as far as Mainz. However, several officers joined their pleas to hers, and for once Ludendorff gave way. Margarethe stayed on the train as far as Metz, although Ludendorff had little time to spare for her. She was greatly impressed with the way Supreme Headquarters continued to function while it was being rushed across Germany at 60 miles an hour. Radio telephones kept Ludendorff in constant touch with all the fronts, and the Hughes Patent Machine ticked steadily away in the Operations coach producing printed tapes of situation reports.[7]

At Montmédy, the German Crown Prince met the Supreme Commanders and paraded a storm battalion in their honor. For the first time Ludendorff saw the new steel helmets, shaped like coal-scuttles, which had proved so useful on the Western Front. At Cambrai, in conversations with the Crown Princes of Bavaria and Württemberg, he learned that the German Army was very inferior to the Allies in aircraft, ammunition, and military equipment of all kinds, and that at the Somme the German defenders were beginning to suffer almost as much as the British attackers. German infantry divisions had to be relieved every few days, but because of a shortage of guns, the artillery remained constantly in action, with the result that some formations were becoming seriously disorganized. In general, the situation was much worse than Ludendorff had anticipated.[8] His decision to stop the fighting at Verdun was applauded, and it was agreed that Germany had no alternative but to stand on the defensive in the West for the foreseeable future. He promised to do what he could to remedy the supply situation, and on his return to Pless proposed to the Kaiser that a single command be established for the Quadruple Alliance in all technical and strategic matters. Wilhelm, as Supreme War Lord, would be nominal Commander-in-Chief, but in practice the power would be wielded by Ludendorff alone.[9]

At about this time Hoffmann visited Pless, and was at once borne off to Ludendorff's quarters for a long talk. There, over the tea-cups, Ludendorff spoke bitterly of the Army's failure to construct sufficient defensive positions on the Western Front, and even more strongly criticized both G.H.Q. and the War Office for not exerting enough control over the national effort. He said that there had been a general failure to co-ordinate G.H.Q. with the Civil Administration and that more pressure would have to be put on industry, especially on the munitions manufacturers. When Hoffmann asked if there was any possibility that Germany might obtain peace, Ludendorff answered that at the moment he did not think there was, but — perhaps because he knew Hoffmann's views on the subject — he assured him that G.H.Q. would miss no opportunity of coming to reasonable terms with the Allies.[10]

At the level of the Supreme Command, military and industrial problems were so closely related that Ludendorff would have been drawn into the matter even against his will,[11] and because of the poor co-ordination of government departments, he found it increasingly necessary to intervene in non-military matters. "All this is really no business of mine," he would protest, "but something must be done, and if I don't do it, nothing will be done at home." [12] Under his direction, General Gröner and Colonel Bauer drew up comprehensive controls over foodstuffs, raw materials, labor and munitions. This "war socialism," labeled the "Hindenburg Program," was administered by General Gröner from a newly established *Allgemeines Kriegsamt*. Like Hoffmann, Gröner was a far broader man than most General Staff officers. Highly intelligent, competent, humane, and of a transparent honesty, he got along equally well with soldiers and with labor leaders. As autumn drew in and the German people tightened their belts to face the "turnip winter," there was a good deal of grumbling and discontent, but Gröner's work was already beginning to show results in a greatly increased output of aircraft, ammunition, guns, and military equipment.

Ludendorff also interested himself in other aspects of the national life. He now attempted to do for all Germany what he had done in the conquered provinces of the East. He brought forward plans to raise the birth-rate, improve housing, reduce venereal disease, encourage rural resettlement, and counteract the dangerously successful Allied propaganda. One of his most important — and unpopular — measures was a compulsory labor law by which every German male between the ages of 15 and 60 would be pressed into the service of the state and an adequate number of female workers would be compulsorily employed in munitions plants. When Hoffmann again visited Pless early in November, Ludendorff admitted that some opposed his measures as too ruthless, and he complained in particular that Bethmann-Hollweg was indecisive. Although the Kaiser was at Pless, Hoffmann did not meet him. He was, Ludendorff said with a grim smile, "ill in his quarters." Ludendorff, who did not believe in the royal illness, thought the Kaiser had been frightened by the compulsory labor law and had taken to his bed to avoid approving further drastic proposals.[13]

Before the year was out, the labor law considerably eased Germany's manpower shortage, although the enrollment of female workers did not meet Ludendorff's expectations. However, large numbers of prisoners of war and Polish and Belgian "helpworkers" were coerced into the factories.

Bethmann-Hollweg, who was too much a humanitarian to relish Ludendorff's methods and too much a political realist to subscribe to his annexationist policies, found himself more and more at odds with G.H.Q. Nevertheless, he weakly agreed to Ludendorff's demand that the Foreign Minister, von Jagow, be replaced on the grounds that, although he was an intelligent man, he was "not one who can bang his fist on the table." Jagow's successor was Richard von Kühlmann, a cultured Bavarian, whom Ludendorff liked no better. Following the First Quartermaster General's example, staff officers at G.H.Q. now normally spoke with bluff, military humor of the Foreign Office as *"Das Idiotenhaus."*

In November, Hoffmann suggested that Ludendorff himself might become Chancellor, saying that he did not know of anyone else fit for the post.[14] Others were thinking along more radical lines, and as Germany's military situation darkened, some senior army officers and politicians began to speak of the possibility of a military dictatorship.[15] But when this was hinted to Ludendorff, he shook his big head impatiently, scowled, and replied that he was still too much the cadet to play the part of Cromwell.

In any case, he already possessed more real power than anyone else in Germany, although there were still some matters on which he could be overruled. One such instance was his attempt to promote battle-hardened soldiers and NCOs to fill the terrible gaps in the officer corps. The Military Cabinet refused, insisting that there should be no lowering of social standards, and created instead a new and much resented rank, that of *Offizierstellvertreter*. These classified officers were expected to endure the hardships and dangers of the front-line officer's life and then revert uncomplainingly to the non-commissioned ranks as soon as the war was over.

On a more important question, Ludendorff's views prevailed, with disastrous effect. In July, Germany and Austria-Hungary had signed an agreement to establish an independent Kingdom of Poland. Falkenhayn, who for all his faults had the sense to see the dangers inherent in this, had objected, and the Kaiser had supported him. The idea had been shelved but was revived again in the autumn when von Beseler, the Governor-General of Poland, unrealistically promised Ludendorff that Poland would provide him with at least five divisions by the spring of 1917 and a million men on the introduction of conscription. Ludendorff immediately became an ardent advocate of the Kingdom of Poland, which was duly proclaimed early in November.

The timing was unfortunate, for the Russian Prime Minister, Boris Stürmer, favored a separate peace with Germany,[16] and unofficial talks were already underway in Sweden. With the declaration of Polish independence, the Tsar had no choice but to break off negotiations, for Russia would never willingly accept the loss of her Polish territories. This outcome had been completely predictable, as had the complete failure of recruiting in Poland. The Poles were quite ready to accept independence as a right but had no intention whatsoever of shedding their blood for Germany. Having been brought up in Posen, Ludendorff should have realized this, but his desperate need for additional troops blinded his judgment. Hoffmann would never have made such a mistake, and it seems probable that if he had been brought into the Supreme Command at the end of August, Ludendorff would not have made it either.

In at least one theater, however, German arms had been brilliantly successful and German generals had proved again that in the conventional type of open warfare they had no equals. Late in August the Roumanians had invaded Transylvania, pushing through the high Carpathian passes with 23 divisions. Initially only seven divisions opposed them, but within a week Ludendorff had concentrated 16 divisions against them. At Hermannstadt on the 29th of September, at Kronstadt on the 8th of October, and at the Szurduk Pass on the 11th of November, Mackensen and Falkenhayn utterly defeated the Roumanian Army, driving its remnants north into Moldavia. On the 3rd of December, von Mackensen, mounted as usual on his white horse, and looking more like a dashing young captain of hussars than an elderly Field Marshal, rode in triumph through the streets of Bucharest.

That night as the winter dusk descended on Pless, Hindenburg and Ludendorff stepped out of headquarters to listen to all the church-bells of the town pealing forth the news of the victory. The brilliant little Roumanian campaign would raise morale, improve Germany's standing among the uncommitted neutral nations, and, most important of all, provide the wheat and oil without which the Central Powers could scarcely face another year of war. Yet as the two generals listened to the tumultuous clangor of the bells, they could not share wholeheartedly in the rejoicing. Although Roumania had been thoroughly beaten, she had not sued for peace, and a portion of her army remained in the field, needing only re-equipping and reorganizing before fighting again.

Nor did the defeat of Roumania greatly alter the overall military situation. At Verdun the French had counter-attacked and regained most of the ground lost earlier in the year. This defeat was especially galling, because Ludendorff knew that the German positions about Verdun were not worth defending, but — rightly or wrongly — he had believed that ground for which so high a price in blood had been paid could not be relinquished voluntarily. The fighting on the Somme had at last died down in mutual exhaustion, but on the Bulgarian front the French General Sarrail had taken Monastir, and King Ferdinand was urging that no more German troops be withdrawn from that theater, because his soldiers "liked to see spiked helmets" in their midst.[17]

The German cause was dealt another blow on the 21st of November when the 86-year-old Emperor of Austria, Franz Joseph, died. Franz Joseph's great-nephew, the Archduke Charles, ascended the throne, but all the divisive influences in the trembling, shaken Empire were strengthened by the passing of the old man who had so long been a living symbol of unity. Equally unfortunate from the German view was the fact that the Emperor Charles had definite opinions about Austria's role in the alliance. He moved the Austrian G.H.Q. from Teschen to Baden, near Vienna, to escape the influence of Pless and himself took over from the Archduke Frederick as commander-in-chief. Conrad was the next to go. He was strongly pro-German; his prestige had been shaken by Austrian defeats; and many Austrians considered his recent marriage downright frivolous in the midst of a world war. He was sent to command the Italian front, and was succeeded by General Arz von Straussenburg, a lesser man whom the Germans rightly regarded as little more than the Emperor's confidential servant.[18] In Vienna, the Empress Zita, well-known for her pro-Allied sympathies, whispered to her husband that nothing but peace could save the Empire from dissolution.

Hoffmann now suggested that if he were given a few extra divisions he could break through the Russian defenses near Zloczov and continue through Tarnopol along the main railway toward Odessa. This would place the Russian forces in the Carpathians in an untenable position and force them to retire. Ludendorff realized the strategic opportunity, but regretfully answered that he could neither spare troops from the Western Front nor transport them from Roumania because of the condition of the Roumanian and Hungarian railways.[19]

In the midst of these somber events, Ludendorff remained confident of ultimate victory, for he considered that, bad as Germany's situation was, that of the Allies was no better. At the end of the year he had some reason to be satisfied with what he had accomplished: the home front was far better organized than it had been in September and the battle lines seemed everywhere secure. Yet in spite of all he had done, he knew that Germany's position was relatively worse, largely as a result of the British naval blockade. This led him to change his mind about unrestricted U-boat warfare. That autumn he had drafted a memorandum for the Foreign Office to send to President Wilson, outlining the German position. Unless the United States made an almost immediate proposal for mediation, aimed at a peace which would leave Germany free to bargain on territorial questions, the unrestricted U-boat campaign would be resumed.

Ludendorff knew that unrestricted U-boat warfare would almost certainly bring the United States into the conflict, but he underestimated the fatal consequences this would have for Germany. He reasoned that an American declaration of war would make little difference to the industrial capacity of the Allies, since the United States was already supplying them with a maximum of war material. As a professional soldier, he was contemptuous of American military potential, for the United States had no army to speak of and could not field even green and untrained contingents for at least a year. Without in any way being able to examine the evidence, he accepted — possibly against his better judgment — the Admiralty's contentions that Britain could quickly be starved into surrender and that the United

States could be prevented from transporting any armed forces to Europe. Nothing more dramatically illustrates the shortcomings of Ludendorff's education and outlook than this totally erroneous appreciation. Lichterfelde, regimental service, and the rigorous training of the General Staff had made him a highly competent soldier who was nevertheless naïve to the point of imbecility in the wider realm of international politics. Bethmann-Hollweg still opposed unrestricted U-boat warfare but he was not the man to stand out long against Ludendorff. As the year ended, the Kaiser was coming under increased pressure to unleash the submarines.

Bethmann, like Hoffmann, had long ago realized that Germany could not win the war, but he still hoped for a reasonable peace. In England Lord Lansdowne had suggested that some compromise might be possible, and on the 12th of December, Bethmann formally proposed to President Wilson that he should mediate between the belligerents. Ludendorff had been unable to prevent these overtures, but he had no confidence in them and insisted that Bethmann make no positive proposals. This omission gave the Allied statesmen the excuse they sought for dismissing the tentative German peace-feelers out of hand. The war was to be fought to a finish for a prize called victory.

Bethmann-Hollweg was close to despair. "With Falkenhayn," he said, "we lose the war strategically, and with Ludendorff we lose it politically."

As 1916 passed into history, the trench-lines that festered like a polluted moat around the territory of the Central Powers were relatively quiet. Winter brought a lull in operations, but everywhere on the Continent the nations busily prepared for spring when they could start afresh on the half-finished task of tearing Europe to pieces.

CHAPTER XIII

THE MOST IMPORTANT MAN IN GERMANY

IN PLESS the morning of the 9th of January 1917 was cold and raw, with hoar frost whitening the bare branches of the chestnut trees and a low ground mist swirling about the cobbles of the streets. As Bethmann-Hollweg unfolded his long body from the back seat of his automobile and walked stiffly into the palace, he seemed hunched against the cold and his face was gray and haggard, as though he had not slept properly for weeks. There was a chill of apprehension in his heart which matched the exterior chill of the January morning. A telegram from Hindenburg had summoned him cavalierly to Pless for a conference, and he knew only too well what the Supreme Command intended to discuss.

With the spring, Germany would almost certainly be attacked simultaneously on all fronts, and Ludendorff was convinced that before then the American munitions shipments to the Allies would have to be stopped at all costs.[1] He was ready now to listen to the navy's claim that this could be done if its submarines were allowed to sink on sight all merchant ships found within the war zone. Using Hindenburg as a spokesman, he had already complained to the Kaiser that Bethmann-Hollweg was attempting to settle the question of unrestricted U-boat warfare without consulting the Supreme Command, but Bethmann had replied that more than military considerations were involved. With a wisdom that was denied the Field Marshal and his First Quartermaster General, the Chancellor had insisted that war with the United States was too grave an undertaking for him to approve;[2] he believed it would bring Germany what the Sicilian expedition had brought Athens.³ But as always, Ludendorff was determined to have his way.

On his arrival at Pless, Bethmann was disturbed to hear that the Kaiser had already made up his mind in favor of the Supreme Command, but he nevertheless spent a frustrating morning arguing with Hindenburg, Ludendorff, and the navy chiefs. He had sound arguments too, for he had been briefed by Karl Helfferich, the Vice-Chancellor, on the many fallacies in the navy's case.⁴ Hindenburg, briefed by Ludendorff, did not argue but replied flatly that the army would be substantially helped by unrestricted U-boat warfare and added that if the U-boat campaign did not begin by the 1st of February, he would not assume responsibility for the future course of operations.⁵

The audience with the Kaiser, which took place that evening, lasted only half an hour. Bethmann had always been a little afraid of the Emperor,⁶ and he found Hindenburg and Ludendorff intimidating personalities. They sat opposite him in all the professional prestige of their uniforms and rank and orders, Hindenburg massively impassive and Ludendorff grimly intent. Ludendorff presented the Supreme Command's case, and Bethmann, faced by men who were "no longer willing to allow themselves to be talked out of decisions they had already made," ⁷ rather weakly admitted that he was not prepared to challenge Ludendorff's statements of what constituted military necessity. Accordingly, the Kaiser formally decided to commence unrestricted U-boat warfare on the 1st of February.

Later that night, Valentini, the Chief of the Civil Cabinet, urged Bethmann to resign, but although he was depressed beyond measure by the events of the day, he decided, as statesmen so frequently do, that he had a moral duty to remain in office. His resignation would put Germany's fate irrevocably in Ludendorff's hands, all hope would be lost of more moderate counsels being heard, and an open split between civilian and military authorities could only damage the nation's morale.

Ludendorff had no such scruples. The next day, certainly at

the urging of the First Quartermaster General, Hindenburg went to the Kaiser and requested that Bethmann be replaced, but Wilhelm was not yet willing to go this far.

A few days later when Hoffmann had another long talk with Ludendorff at Pless, he was surprised to learn how bitterly the Supreme Command was opposed to the civilian power. Ludendorff told him, not without satisfaction, that when Bethmann had come to Pless for the U-boat conference, Hindenburg had not invited him to dine. This type of discourtesy was very unlike the Field Marshal and it may be surmised that he had only with difficulty been persuaded to take so hard a line. At all events, Ludendorff now asked Hoffmann to have a private talk with Hindenburg about Government policy, a sure indication that the old gentleman was having qualms of conscience. For half an hour Hoffmann briefed the Field Marshal on the wider aspects of the war. The treatment was effective, and that night Hoffmann noted in his diary: "At the end of it he was prepared to speak to H.M., provided I would put all I had said to him in writing." [8]

However, there was scarcely any struggle of wills between Hindenburg and his First Quartermaster General. It was not only that Ludendorff was a much stronger personality and much more intelligent; the real secret of his domination was the basic agreement between their views. After the war the Field Marshal admitted that he had "covered many expressions of opinion on political questions with my name and responsibility even when they were only loosely connected with our military situation," and one can almost hear the harsh accents of Ludendorff behind the old man's printed *apologia*.[9]

On the 31st of January Count Johann-Heinrich von Bernstorff, the German Ambassador in Washington, called on Robert Lansing, the United States Secretary of State, to tell him that the U-boats would be unleashed the following day. The two diplomats stared at each other grimly, for both knew that war was now inevitable.

In Germany the announcement of the resumption of the U-boat campaign was greeted with enthusiasm. The *Gasthaus* chauvinists were delighted, and von Mackensen expressed the opinion of most of the army when he said that "only people without a sense of reality and convinced enemies of the existing state order" would oppose the decision.[10] In the Berlin pension where Margarethe Ludendorff lived, a notice appeared at the entrance of the dining-room: "Any person who is particularly pleased at unrestricted submarine warfare will lend a hand this evening at clearing the snow away." Between nine and eleven o'clock that night, passers-by were startled to see a dozen ladies, all the wives of German generals, busily shoveling snow in front of their boarding-house.[11]

Albert Ballin, the Jewish shipping magnate who controlled the Hamburg-America Line, was a personal friend of the Kaiser's and certainly no convinced enemy of the existing state order. Yet he had so persistently opposed Tirpitz's U-boat war that Ludendorff always privately referred to him as "that damned Jew." When Ballin visited G.H.Q. to make a final, futile appeal against the folly of bringing the United States into the conflict, Ludendorff brushed his arguments roughly aside. As Ballin left headquarters, he turned to Ludendorff with tears in his eyes and said in front of half a dozen officers: "I may not live much longer, but you — you will end in a strait-jacket before the war is over!"[12]

In fact, many Germans, soldiers as well as civilians, were profoundly disturbed by Ludendorff's increasing authority. He typified all too completely one particular side of German national life, and this gave a nightmarish illusion of inevitability to his rise to supreme power. It was as though the Fates were deliberately encouraging the German hubris to rail so high in order the more terribly to exact retribution. Even Hoffmann, who was far more familiar with Ludendorff's outstanding military abilities than with his inept statecraft, was beginning to have his doubts. "We all know he is no politician," he wrote. "He is too impulsive. He always wants something to happen at once, while the politician must know how to wait." [13]

The Kaiser had always had his doubts, and these were strengthened early in February when Ludendorff told him that Hindenburg could no longer make the daily trip from Pless to the Neue Schloss to brief him on the military situation. Wilhelm suggested that Ludendorff come instead, but was curtly told that the Field Quartermaster General unfortunately had not the time.[14]

By now the Allies deployed 3,900,000 men* on the Western Front as opposed to Germany's 2,500,000. Ludendorff had searched desperately for some means of counter-balancing his numerical inferiority and by the end of 1916 had decided to adopt a new doctrine of defensive tactics. Colonel Fritz von Lossberg, the First Army's Chief of Staff on the Somme, had had the original idea. He had noted with alarm that rigid defense lines had been pulverized by artillery fire and that as the battle continued week after week, the defender's losses mounted until they were almost equal to those of the attacker. He had tried thinning out his forward line and sending his troops into No Man's Land to avoid the artillery barrage, but although this had resulted in some improvement, it was no sufficient answer. He then began to consider the alternative of deepening the defensive zone so that the attacker's artillery fire would be more dispersed and the defender's casualties fewer. Instead of attempting to hold the front-line trenches to the last, his new doctrine envisaged the defensive battle being fought in depth with a few machine-guns doing the work of many riflemen and with the forward infantry battalions being responsible for a zone some 2,500 yards deep. Strong counter-attack forces would be positioned three or four miles farther back, out of convenient range of the enemy's field guns; and echeloned behind these would be counter-attack divisions. The emphasis on counter-attack would also restore to the defense much of the initiative it had lost under the more inflexible system.

* French, 2,600,000; British, 1,200,000; Belgian, 100,000.

Ludendorff had not made up his mind to accept the new doctrine without considerable soul-searching, for there were obvious dangers in making drastic tactical changes in the middle of a war. Officers and men had long been trained in the old methods and — even more serious — the army of 1917 was no longer as good as that of 1914. It was not, in fact, as good as that of 1915 or even of 1916. Two considerations induced Ludendorff to accept the risk: Germany simply could not afford the manpower losses she had suffered in 1916 at Verdun and the Somme, and secondly, he believed that the German soldier, and more particularly the German officer, was still superior in training and military skill to his opponent. Once he reached a decision, he acted energetically, opening special schools for staff officers and commanders down to battalion level and disseminating the revised doctrine in a booklet ponderously entitled *Principles for the Conduct of Operations in the Defensive Battle in Positional Warfare.* Nevertheless, he awaited the first test of the new tactics anxiously.

Now that the Austrian G.H.Q. had moved to Baden, there was no reason why the German Supreme Command should remain at Pless. Accordingly, in the middle of February, it transferred to Kreuznach where Hindenburg and Ludendorff took up their residence in a villa that had once been the home of Emperor Wilhelm I. Hindenburg was sorry to go, for he had enjoyed hunting over the estates of Pless and Neudeck, but he was consoled by the welcome he received at Kreuznach and by the fact that daily during his stay there his quarters and mess were decorated with fresh flowers brought in by local maidens as though to a national shrine.[15] Ludendorff, for his part, was glad to be nearer the Western Front — it was really quite remarkable how in six months his views on the relative importance of East and West had changed — and he at once settled down to work in his office in the Oranienhof without in the least noticing whether there were any flowers for him or not.

Apart from political intrigue, the winter months were relatively quiet ones, but as Ludendorff became more and more the

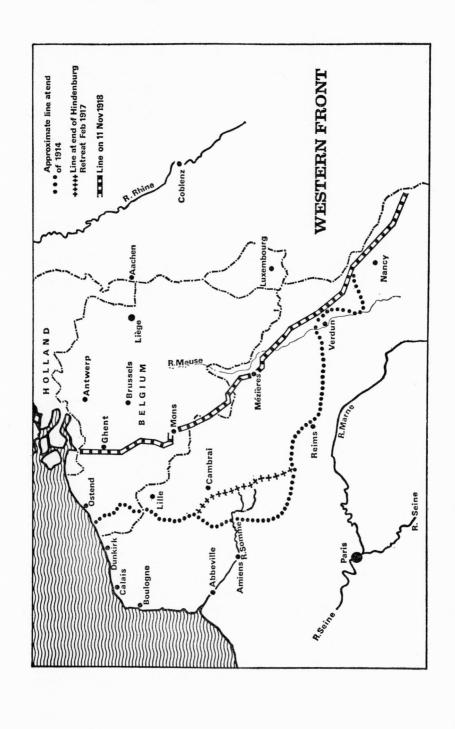

WESTERN FRONT

Legend:
- ● ● ● Approximate line at end of 1914
- ++++ Line at end of Hindenburg Retreat Feb 1917
- ▥▥▥ Line on 11 Nov 1918

HOLLAND

R. Rhine

Coblenz

Aachen

Luxembourg

Nancy

Liège

BELGIUM

Antwerp

Brussels

R. Meuse

Verdun

Ghent

Mons

Mézières

Ostend

Reims

R. Marne

Lille

Cambrai

Dunkirk

Calais

Boulogne

Abbeville

Amiens ● R. Somme

Paris

R. Seine

R. Seine

center of real power in Germany, corresponding efforts were made to influence him. In the middle of March, Deputy Matthias Erzberger of the Catholic Center Party appeared at Kovno to talk to Hoffmann who was paying a visit there. Erzberger was a short, dumpy little man, clumsy in his movements and with comical blunt features.[16] "Why he looks just like an ornamental beer-cork!" an Hungarian countess had once exclaimed after meeting him for the first time. A former Swabian school-teacher, he was a patriotic German who had not been above entertaining annexationist ambitions himself, but by now he probably represented the great, docile mass of the German people who knew in their hearts that the peace which came soonest would be the best peace of all. Hoffmann found him intelligent and interesting, but his journey to Kovno was in vain, for Hoffmann was far too shrewd to waste his time and diminish his position by attempting the impossible.

On his return to Berlin, Erzberger arranged to meet Margarethe Ludendorff, who found him fascinating. But when the Erzbergers invited Margarethe to dine with them before there had been a formal exchange of calls, she regretfully declined — "not being accustomed," she said, "to so loose a regard for the rules of society." [17]

Erzberger was not the only person who attempted to sway the Supreme Command by the roundabout route that ran through *Ober-Ost*. That same month Hoffmann noted in his diary: "I had a letter from Frau Ludendorff about my influence over her husband, and asking me to use it. Now the trouble is that by trying to influence anyone by letter one cannot meet his objections. One can influence a man in political questions only by talking to him . . ." [18]

Ludendorff had to withstand military as well as political pressures during the early months of 1917. Conrad was again requesting German divisions for an attack in the Southern Tyrol, and the Bulgarians wanted German help to drive the Allies out of Macedonia. Ludendorff rejected both pleas, for he had de-

cided that 1917 would have to be a year for the defensive. Moreover, operations in the West should be postponed as long as
possible so that the U-boat campaign might have time to take
effect.

Yet even the defensive form of war was shaped by Ludendorff's bold military imagination. Since German retirements at
the Somme had created a dangerous salient, he ordered a strong
defensive position known as the *Siegfried Stellung* to be prepared in the rear along a line Cobourg-Arras-St. Quentin-
Soissons. The area to be evacuated was some 20 miles deep,
and Ludendorff determined that nothing would be left behind to
assist the enemy. An unprecedented program of destruction was
prepared and given the code name *"Alberich"* after the mali-
cious dwarf of the Nibelungen Saga. Houses were leveled, trees
cut down, wells contaminated, mines and booby-traps planted,
and the bulk of the population moved out of the zone. Crown
Prince Rupprecht of Bavaria, the responsible Army Group Commander, opposed this ruthless destruction and thought of resigning rather than obeying, but when it came to the point he
merely refused to sign the *"Alberich"* order himself.

The German retirement, which began on the 16th of March,
was a complete success. Allied generals, accustomed to fighting
desperately for every foot of ground, were taken completely by
surprise and were slow to realize that they had suddenly lost contact with the enemy over nearly 100 miles of front. By the morning of the 19th of March, 29 German divisions had slipped cleanly
away to take up positions in the Siegfried Line or in reserve, and
the Allies did not re-establish contact along the entire front until
the 5th of April. By that time the Germans had shortened their
line, obtained better defensive positions, and freed 14 divisions
for employment elsewhere.[19]

Although the German Army, largely by virtue of its superior
staff work, could still perform military feats beyond the capabilities of its opponents, Ludendorff knew that the nation's strength
was gradually ebbing away. In Germany the spring of 1917 was

Ludendorff's birthplace, Kruschevnia in Posen

Margarethe Ludendorff,
the general's first wife

German reservists on their way to mobilization depots, August 1914

Hindenburg, Ludendorff and Hoffmann in East Prussia, August 1914
(from the painting by Hugo Vogel)

General Hermann von François, whose brilliant disobedience of orders
did much to win the battle of Tannenberg

General Erich Ludendorff, 1915

General Erich von Falkenhayn, Chief of the General Staff
from September 1914 to August 1916

Field Marshal
August von
Mackenson rides
in triumph into
Bucharest, De-
cember 1916

Colonel Max
Hoffmann and
Major Brinck-
mann in Brest-
Litovsk, winter
1917

Hindenburg, the Kaiser and Ludendorff in the Operations Room at Pless

Hindenburg, the Kaiser and Ludendorff in a French town, March 1918

Hindenburg and
Ludendorff in front
of General Head-
quarters, the Hotel
Britannique, Spa,
1918

The Kaiser at General
Headquarters in June
1918. From left to
right: Ludendorff,
Colonel von Rauch and
the Kaiser. The Ger-
man Crown Prince is
at the extreme right

Hindenburg, Mackensen and Ludendorff at the Tannenberg Memorial,
August 1924. *Below:* Hindenburg reviews troops at the Memorial.
Von Mackensen is behind him in the Death's Head Hussars shako

Ludendorff at a Nazi rally in 1926

Ludendorff and his second wife, Mathilde, at Tutzing on the general's seventieth birthday, 9 April 1935

Ludendorff at Munich, 1935

Ludendorff in his study at Tutzing, 1935

a hungry time. In the early mornings in Berlin long queues of women and children stood four abreast, waiting for hours for the food shops to open. The women were emaciated, with sunken cheeks and blue circles under their eyes, and many of the children had the thin, pathetic legs of storks. Often the shops had only turnips for sale, and housewives learned a dozen undreamed-of ways to serve them — as salad, as a vegetable, cooked with a bone or a thin slice of horsemeat, or as jam.[20] When the bread ration was reduced in March, an ominous series of wildcat strikes broke out and were settled only when General Gröner, in co-operation with the labor leaders, effectively reorganized the food distribution system.[21] *

But if times were bad in Germany, they were worse in Russia. Throughout January and February Ludendorff received intermittent reports of tension in Petrograd. Rasputin, the Tsarina's hated advisor, had been murdered on the 26th of December, but although the Russians greeted Rasputin's death ecstatically, they remained unmollified. Strikes broke out in Petrograd, and opposition to the Tsar and the war steadily increased. Although Ludendorff heard much of this, he did not believe that revolution was imminent.

Germany had been attempting to foment revolt in Russia since 1914, but there seemed very little to show for the millions of marks that had been spent. Part of the trouble was that the correct officials of the German Foreign Office could never take seriously the bearded Russian revolutionaries with whom they dealt. The exiles' obscure dialectic, their badly written little pamphlets, their endless squabbles over their samovars in second-rate rooming houses in Zürich or Geneva had been enough to mislead any diplomat. Colonel Nicolai, the head of military intelligence, who might have been more discerning, had other, apparently more important, matters to attend to, and so

---

* In December 1918, the Associated Medical Services of Germany estimated that 763,000 Germans had died as a direct result of the slow starvation imposed by the British Navy's blockade.[22]

for two and a half years the Tsar's most deadly enemies had been regarded as mere pawns on the international chess-board.

Nevertheless, the Germans, if often unlucky, were always thorough. They had maintained some contact with the Bolsheviks, Mensheviks, Anarchists and Social Revolutionaries, even although the officials of the Foreign Office regarded them as dim underworld characters who for more than half a century had subsisted on dreams of massacres and the tragical end of princes. In March 1915, Alexander Helphand, a dubious Russian exile who was better known by his cover name of "Parvus," had been employed by the Wilhelmstrasse; and since the spring of 1916, a little, bald man called Lenin, who lived quietly in Zürich with his wife, Krupskaya, had been on the German Government's payroll and in intermittent touch with Alexander Kekuela, a German agent.

The Wilhelmstrasse had almost concluded that these ventures were a complete waste of time. Indeed, it was no longer entirely certain that it wished to bring about revolution in Russia, for it appeared as though the Tsar might merely be replaced by a democratic government which would continue the war — and any alternative government would probably do that more efficiently. Prince Max of Baden was about to begin negotiating peace terms with Tsarist representatives when Petrograd was suddenly swept by a spontaneous wave of revolt. Bread riots flared up late in February; a strike occurred in the Putilov Metal Factory; angry workers roamed the streets; and on the 27th of the month, several units of the Petrograd garrison mutinied, killed their officers, and helped the mob sack the headquarters of the *Okrana*, the Tsarist secret police. By nightfall the Autocracy had lost the capital.

Ludendorff followed these events closely, but remained unconvinced. After all, the Russian Provisional Government, formed under Miliukov, had pledged itself to continue the war by the Allies' side. Then Erzberger, who was still searching desperately for peace on even one front, sent Helphand to Kreuznach to talk to Ludendorff. Helphand had led a variegated life on the fringes of most of the laws of Europe, but when he talked of Russian revolution he had all the earnest conviction of an itinerant preacher; he told the First Quartermaster General about Lenin, the exiled Bolshevik leader living in Switzerland with some 30 or 40 followers. This was the man Germany needed, Helphand insisted, with a note almost of awe in his voice. If Lenin were sent back to Russia, he would undoubtedly bring chaos with him. Moreover, he had publicly committed himself to a policy of immediate peace with Germany. Even if he failed to overthrow the Provisional Government and seize power — and Helphand was by no means certain that Lenin would fail — his mere presence in Petrograd would certainly vitiate the Russian war effort.

Ludendorff listened and came to a quick decision. The story that he did so only doubtfully and with a momentous sense of the probable consequences of his act is mere legend. In March 1917, it would have taken far more perspicacity than Ludendorff possessed to have recognized in the mild-mannered Lenin a world-shaking force.[23]

Lenin himself had not even heard of the revolution in Russia until the 15th of March and at first he had belittled its importance. Nine days later he was told of Ludendorff's decision to allow him and his revolutionary friends to pass through Germany on their way back to Russia. But Lenin was in no particular hurry to leave Switzerland. He was never one to brave avoidable physical risks, and Petrograd seemed a dangerously unsettled place. On the 27th Ludendorff sent an agent, Georges Sklarz, to Zürich to talk to him, but Lenin made so many conditions that it was not until the 4th of April that a formal agreement was drafted.

Much has been made of the sealed train that carried Lenin and his fellow conspirators through German territory like a "plague bacillus," but here again romance has placed its stamp upon events. The train that steamed out of Zürich on the 9th of

April carrying Lenin, Zinoviev, Sokolnikov, and 29 other Russians was indeed granted extraterritorial rights by the German General Staff and a guarantee that there would be no inspection of baggage or examination of passports at the border. This was done, not because Ludendorff feared that the Bolshevik virus might infect the workers of the Fatherland, but because Lenin and his fellow revolutionaries were afraid lest any social contacts in Germany should add color to the charge, which was only technically true, that they were paid German agents.

The sealed train wended its way slowly through Germany by way of Mannheim, Frankfurt, and Berlin. It was only one of hundreds of trains being routed by the General Staff and it had no very high priority. After spending several hours on a siding in the marshalling yards in Berlin, it was sent on via Stockholm to Helsinki. On the chilly evening of the 16th of April, a week after setting out from Zürich, Lenin stepped down from his carriage at the Finland Station in Petrograd and walked along the platform to meet his destiny. The pawn had queened.

Ludendorff, in all probability, had already dismissed the matter from his mind, for by now he had more urgent problems to consider.

CHAPTER XIV

THE SHADOWS LENGTHEN

THE ANTEROOM of the Headquarters Mess at Kreuznach was filled with officers smartly turned out in their best uniforms. They stood about with glasses of yellowish korn or kümmel in their hands, talking desultorily in little groups. Every time the door at the far end of the room opened, the buzz of conversation died and heads were turned to see who had come in. The 9th of April, 1917, was Ludendorff's 52nd birthday, and a small celebration had been arranged in his honor. But although it was well past the dinner hour, the First Quartermaster General had not yet appeared.

Everyone knew that the reports from the front were bad. At dawn that morning — it was a bitterly cold Easter Monday, filled with sleet and driving snow — the British First and Third Armies had launched a massive attack against General von Falkenhausen's Sixth Army about Arras. And for the first time in nearly three years of fighting, the British had made frightening gains. The Canadian Corps had stormed up the supposedly impregnable heights of Vimy Ridge and established itself firmly on the crest by mid-morning: the German first, second and third lines had all been broken; and German losses in casualties and prisoners were high. It looked as though the new defensive tactics might after all have failed.

Ironically enough, Ludendorff had been far more shaken by this possibility than by hearing on the 6th of April that the United States Congress, by a vote of 373 to 50, had declared war on Germany. He still woefully underestimated the effect of American intervention — which, in a way, was the complementary error to that made by the British and French High Commands, who still believed they could win the war by themselves and were anxious to do so before the Americans arrived to share the glory. Ludendorff had known the British were about to attack at Arras, for there had been no attempt at secrecy. Sir Douglas Haig's way of waging war was to mass his forces carefully, put his head down, and charge. Ludendorff had counted on this, but ever since the morning's reports had reached him he had been torn by anxiety. "I had looked forward to the expected offensive with confidence and was now deeply depressed," he admitted later. "A day like April the 9th threw all calculations to the winds." [1]

Field Marshal von Hindenburg, standing by the bar like a solid oak that had been planted there centuries before, was completely unruffled. But at last he glanced at the clock on the wall, set down his glass, and strode heavily from the room.

Ludendorff was in his quarters in a mood of black dejection when Hindenburg came in. The old man walked across to him and, with the characteristic gesture he always used for such occasions, took Ludendorff's right hand in both his own. "We have lived through more critical times than today together," he said in his deep voice.[2] And Ludendorff, reflecting that this indeed was so, was comforted.

As it turned out, the situation was not as bad as had at first appeared. Although the British had gained their first appreciable offensive success of the war, they soon demonstrated that they did not know how to exploit it. German reserves rushed up to seal off the gap, and by the 11th the danger had passed. Ludendorff's subsequent inquiries into the reasons for the breakthrough revealed that the trouble lay not with the new tactics but with the improper handling of the battle by army headquarters. The Chief of Staff of the Sixth Army was replaced by Colonel von Lossberg, and a little later General von Falkenhausen was appointed Governor-General of Belgium — "a post," Ludendorff said nastily, "in which he retained our complete confidence."

No sooner had the British attacks around Arras been held than the French struck in Champagne and on the Aisne. General Robert Nivelle, who had taken over command of the French Army from the discredited Joffre the previous December, was an eloquent, persuasive man who was convinced that he had found the secret of how to break the deadlock on the Western Front. As soon as he was made General-in-Chief, he announced that in the spring he would launch an offensive that would, "without chance of failure," destroy the enemy's forces and win the war. He was undismayed when his first plan was disrupted by the German withdrawal to the Siegfried Line and blithely undeterred by reports that Ludendorff had learned the details of his attack from captured French orders. His offensive, which opened on the 16th of April, was a murderous failure; in the first ten days of the battle the French lost 134,000 men;[3] mutinies shortly broke out in 54 French divisions; and by the end of the month the French Army was a broken sword in Nivelle's hand. Nevertheless, the Germans too had suffered severely, and Ludendorff believed that only the inactivity on the Eastern Front prevented a serious crisis.[4]

On the 17th of April, when Hoffmann was on his way to G.H.Q. to make a periodic report, he traveled between Berlin and Kreuznach in the same reserved compartment as Admiral von Müller, the Kaiser's Chief of Naval Cabinet. Von Müller, like Bethmann, was surprised to find a Prussian officer with such liberal opinions, for Hoffmann said quite bluntly that he had no faith in the U-boat campaign and that he wanted immediate electoral reforms in Prussia.

"The war must really be brought to an end sometime," he said with a beaming, boyish smile that seemed to take the seriousness out of his words. "Even if one is a soldier, one must agree to that."[5]

To Hoffmann, Ludendorff made no secret of his uneasiness about internal conditions in Germany and complained angrily of Bethmann's "want of decision." Both agreed that an offensive in

the West was desirable as soon as sufficient troops could be released from the East, but Hoffmann shook his head doubtfully
when Ludendorff described how he intended to conduct the operation.

"Conditions are very different here than in the East," Ludendorff explained. "In the West there is a continuous system of
fortifications which cannot be outflanked. I shall therefore
make a series of attacks which will probe for weak points capable of being exploited." Hoffmann suggested that German resources were insufficient for such tactics and that it might be
preferable to gamble everything on a single attack at a predetermined point.[6]

The two parted amiably, but Hoffmann sensed that there was
no longer the old rapport between them. In the past, Ludendorff
had generally allowed himself to be influenced by Hoffmann on
strategic matters, but now he was determined to go his own way.
For some time he had said openly: "It is better the German
Empire go under than that we make a renunciatory peace." [7]
One result of this all-or-nothing philosophy was that he increasingly adopted the most ruthless means to attain victory. The
"Alberich" Program had shocked many of his own countrymen;
the administrative districts were being exploited more harshly
than ever; large numbers of Polish and Belgian slave laborers
were sent to Germany; and Ludendorff now introduced two new
weapons which many thought violated the rules of war. The
first of these, the *Flammenwerfer,* proved of little military value,
but a fiendish new gas invented by Privy Councillor Haber, and
known as "Yellow Cross," or mustard gas, produced the most
terrible effects upon its victims. Haber had specifically warned
Ludendorff that it would be unwise to use Yellow Cross unless
he could guarantee that the war would be over within a year, for
he estimated that by then the Allies would be able to manufacture it in much larger quantities than Germany. In the summer of 1917 Ludendorff was certainly in no position to guarantee that the war would be over in a year, but he nevertheless
ordered that Yellow Cross be employed on the Western Front.

Although Ludendorff reacted with icy disbelief to any suggestion that Germany might not win the war, many intelligent Germans were beginning to despair of victory. One afternoon Margarethe Ludendorff and the committee of some patriotic society engaged in relief work were invited to tea at General von Moltke's house in Berlin. The former Chief of the General Staff, who had not seen Margarethe since the disastrous autumn of 1914, drew her to a corner of the room and talked very kindly to her about her husband and family. Suddenly, in the middle of the conversation, his voice faltered as he was overcome by his realization of Germany's plight and his share of the responsibility for it. Tears began to trickle slowly down his cheeks, and a moment later his shoulders were shaking with uncontrollable weeping.[8]

By now it was increasingly evident that the submarine campaign was not achieving the results the navy had predicted, and Ludendorff's oppressive awareness of danger grew day by day. However, he had convinced himself that by willing the end he could will the means. Surely, if only Germany had adequate political direction, the war could still be won. When Prince Henry of Prussia visited Supreme Headquarters on the 27th of June, the First Quartermaster General tried to influence him against Bethmann, but met with a cold rebuff.[9] Undeterred by this, he persuaded Hindenburg to write a letter to the Kaiser the same day:

> Our greatest anxiety at this moment, however, is the decline in the national spirit. It must be revived, or we shall lose the war. Even our allies need a powerful tonic, otherwise there is a danger of their deserting us. For this it is necessary to solve those economic problems which are the most difficult and are of the greatest importance for the future . . . the question arises whether the Chancellor is capable of solving these problems — and they must be correctly solved, or we are lost![10]

A few days later, Erzberger made a closely reasoned but sensational speech before a Reichstag committee. His ugly little face shone with sincerity as he frankly stated what many people already believed to be true — that the submarine campaign had failed and that Germany should now fight a purely defensive war, renouncing any thought of conquest.[11] When Ludendorff read Erzberger's speech he was furious and demanded an immediate audience with the Kaiser. Strangely enough, he blamed Bethmann more than Erzberger, for he felt that the Chancellor should have been able to prevent the Center Party leader from uttering his terrible truth in the Reichstag. But on the 7th of July, when Hindenburg and Ludendorff went to Berlin, the Kaiser courteously told them that he did not feel that what happened in the Reichstag was within the province of the Supreme Command, and two very disgruntled war-lords returned to Kreuznach that same evening.

Ludendorff soon convinced Hindenburg that the Allies would grant Germany only a "helot's peace" and that this fate was certain if Bethmann remained Chancellor. By the 12th the Field Marshal had been talked into writing out his resignation. Ludendorff did the same, and the two letters were dispatched to Berlin that afternoon. Ludendorff had taken the precaution of leaving Lieutenant Colonel Max Bauer in the capital to interview members of the Reichstag and inform them that this time he was in deadly earnest and that if Bethmann did not resign, he would.[12] Bauer, an unpleasant man who had a special talent for this sort of intrigue, had persuaded the Crown Prince to come to Berlin and had arranged for him to interview the party leaders on the morning of the 12th.

The war had not changed the German Crown Prince. He was as slim as ever, with the same greyhound profile and the same carefully cultivated resemblance to Frederick the Great. He received the party leaders standing, and addressed them as brusquely as though they were members of a corporal's guard. All of them but one, Friedrich von Payer of the Progressive Party, unhesitatingly agreed that if it came to a choice between Bethmann and Ludendorff, it would be Bethmann who would have to go. Very reluctantly the Kaiser bowed to this pressure, but he was outraged at Ludendorff's interference. "This kind of behavior on the part of a Prussian general has never been heard of before in the history of Prussia," he declared.[13]

The next day Wilhelm informed Hindenburg and Ludendorff that he had dismissed his Chancellor. After some discussion, Doctor Georg Michaelis, a nonentity who had been assistant state secretary in the Prussian Ministry of Food, was chosen as Bethmann's successor. With the evangelical simplicity so impressive to those who did not know him, Hindenburg rumbled: "He is a decent, God-fearing man, and I accept him in God's name." [14] Ludendorff said nothing, but when Erzberger was told of Michaelis' appointment, he snarled: "He'll die in the cradle! " [15]

In truth, it did not much matter who received the post, for from now on Ludendorff would be, in everything but name, dictator of Germany. His singular incapacity for such an office was revealed by his naïve comment that "I was surprised to find that the authorities concerned did not have a successor to the Imperial Chancellor always in readiness, and that in a matter of such decisive importance for its destiny, Germany had to live from hand to mouth." [16]

Germany was now committed to fighting to the bitter end, but Austria, for whom Germany had originally gone to war, sought an alternative solution. The Emperor Charles engaged in secret negotiations for a separate peace with Prince Sixt de Bourbon, an officer in the Belgian Army. These dealings came to nothing, but before they were finally broken off, the Austrian Foreign Minister, Count Czernin, asked Ludendorff if he would consider returning Alsace-Lorraine to France as a condition of peace. The answer was an uncompromising "Never!"

At the desperate urging of the western Allies, the Russian Provisional Government, now headed by Alexander Kerensky, had foolishly agreed to launch another attack in Galicia. Hoffmann was not unduly concerned when the "Kerensky offensive" opened at the beginning of July, and when Ludendorff telephoned him to ask if the breakthrough toward Tarnopol was still feasible, he "answered joyfully in the affirmative" but said that he would need at least four divisions from the West, and if possible six. On the Western Front, the British had captured Messines Ridge in a neat set-piece operation on the 7th of June, but had again been unable to exploit their success. Haig was undoubtedly planning another major offensive, which Ludendorff correctly believed would fall in Flanders, but General Sixt von Armin's Fourth Army was now defending this sector, and Armin's Chief of Staff, von Lossberg, assured Ludendorff that the German front would not break. Since Ludendorff knew that Lossberg was close to being a defensive genius, he unhesitatingly sent Hoffmann six divisions. The attack toward Tarnopol was launched on the 19th of July under General von Eben after an artillery preparation planned by Bruchmüller. On the first day the Germans drove forward 15 kilometers on a 20-kilometer front, and Tarnopol fell on the 25th. As Hoffmann had rightly calculated, the entire enemy position was rendered untenable, and by early August the Russians had evacuated Galicia and the Bukovina.

In the West, on the 31st of July, Haig at last began his great offensive in Flanders. He had dreamed of it for months and, with an assurance miraculously unshaken by previous failures, confidently claimed that it would clear the Channel coast and win the war. As it turned out, Gough's Fifth Army had only negligible success and on the first day the British suffered 31,850 casualties. Nevertheless, Ludendorff might at any moment need the six divisions he had sent to Hoffmann. Rather than withdraw them at once, however, he asked Hoffmann whether he could cross the Düna River and take Riga, an operation first suggested some two years ago. Hoffmann replied that the Riga attack was still feasible, but that he would not be ready until about the end of August. Ludendorff told him he could keep the divisions.

In Flanders the British, with incredible stubbornness and heroism, struggled heartbreakingly forward toward Passchen-

daele Ridge, and twice Ludendorff telephoned Hoffmann to tell
him that he would require the six divisions back in the West.
Twice he canceled the order and decided to leave them with
Ober-Ost. The Riga offensive was launched on the 1st of September under General von Hutier and was completely successful,
although the number of prisoners was less than had been expected because the Russians had already partly evacuated the
bridgehead.[17] After a successful attack at Jacobstadt on the 21st
of September, Hoffmann next mounted an amphibious operation
against the islands of Ösel, Moon, and Dagö in the Gulf of Riga.
Ludendorff was especially pleased to find some active employment for the surface fleet, for during the summer several small
mutinies had broken out in the German Navy. Many of the best
naval officers and men had been transferred to the submarine
service and some petty officers and ratings who had remained
idle in port had been influenced by the anti-war propaganda of
the Independent Socialists, Germany's communist party. The
amphibious operation in the Baltic met almost no resistance, and
the Russian commander, Admiral Vasili Altvater, later complained to Hoffmann that his troops had "melted away." [18]

While Hoffmann was winning easy victories in the East, and
Haig's soldiers were dying by tens of thousands in the Ypres
Salient, Pope Benedict XV attempted to bring about a peace of
"justice and reconciliation" based on a return to the *status quo
ante bellum*. His Holiness had always hated the war, and had
earned the bitter contempt of chauvinist Italians by publicly referring to it as "this senseless carnage." From the Vatican,
whose high windows looked out across the centuries, this, of all
the wars in history, seemed most certainly to be the war which
should never have been fought. In Germany the majority parties of the Center favored negotiating on the basis of the papal
note, but Ludendorff and the parties of the right felt that Benedict XV was much too well disposed toward the Entente. Not
being a military man, the Pope could scarcely be expected to appreciate the realities of the strategic situation. He seemed, for in-

stance, completely to ignore the fact that German armies were standing everywhere on foreign soil, and, not being a German, he failed to understand their right to remain in considerable portions of these territories after the war. At Ludendorff's direction, Chancellor Michaelis returned a deliberately vague reply to the papal proposal. As it happened, this made no difference, for the Entente rejected the peace note out of hand and with some indignation. In 1917 those in authority in Europe were generally agreed that, admirable as the Christian religion undoubtedly was, this was no time for intruding it into political life.

At the beginning of September, Margarethe Ludendorff was staying with friends in the resort town of Baden-Baden. In three years of war some of her beauty had faded and most of her gaiety was gone. All three of her sons were now in the Flying Corps, and Franz, the eldest, had already crashed once on the Eastern Front, sustaining a brain concussion and a badly smashed hip. After his convalescence, the German Crown Prince and Colonel Hoffmann had both offered him safe posts as an adjutant on the staff, but in spite of his injuries, Franz had managed to return to active duty in the Flying Corps, joining Bölcke's famous squadron. On the 7th of September, Margarethe received a telephone call from a staff officer at Kreuznach informing her that her husband was on his way to visit her. Once again, as so often during the war, she waited on a railway platform for him to arrive. The purple September twilight was closing in from the tops of the mountains when Ludendorff's special train halted at Baden-Baden. As he stepped out of the carriage, Margarethe ran forward to meet him, then stopped. His face was so drawn and sad that she stood aghast, her hand to her mouth.

"The boy, the child —" was all that Ludendorff could stammer out.

Margarethe looked at him with widened eyes, then finished his sentence "— is dead!"

His silence and the look in his eyes was confirmation enough.

Margarethe's scream pierced the summer dusk and Ludendorff caught her as she fell. She recovered consciousness to a sense of desolation that was to remain with her for life. Twice before, the long claw of the war had reached out for Franz and twice he had been saved. Margarethe had taken this as a sign that God intended to preserve him, and so the irrevocable realization of his death was the harder to bear. To spare her further pain, Ludendorff at first told her that Franz had been shot down behind the enemy lines. Only when she asked brokenly if nothing could be done to recover his body was she told that he had actually fallen into the sea. Some weeks later his body was washed up on the shores of the Dutch island of Wissekerke. The German military attaché accompanied his coffin back to Germany and Franz was buried in Berlin with full military honors.[19]

Ludendorff, too, felt Franz's death keenly, for he had been genuinely fond of his stepsons and proud of the part they were playing in the war. Only a week or two before his death, when Franz had met his stepfather at Lille, Ludendorff had found him full of energy and enthusiasm.[20] Margarethe, who was better informed, had a rather different picture of her son's last days. Just before he was shot down, he had written that he was flying up to twelve sorties a day, often having to meet the British aviators at odds of two or three to one. Nor had he been as enthusiastic for the war as Ludendorff had supposed, for he had written: "Mother, you cannot imagine what a heavenly feeling it is, when all the day's fighting is successfully over, to lie down in bed and to say to oneself before going to sleep: 'Thank God! You have another twelve hours to live.' The certainty of the thing is so pleasant." [21]

Ludendorff had no time to mourn. Each day he dealt with a hundred urgent items that came across his desk, and he was becoming more and more unwilling to delegate authority. German policy, as shaped by the First Quartermaster General, was no longer a system of alternatives, but had taken on all the close-knit consistency of a religious creed. Victory, annexations, future military security, colonies, and a long period of rich and peaceful development were inextricably linked together in Ludendorff's mind. He developed this theme at a Crown Council meeting on the 11th of September, when he proposed that the conquered territories in the East be divided into a Duchy of Courland and a Grand Duchy of Lithuania which would be united under the personal sovereignty of the Kaiser. These areas, which would be largely re-settled by German veterans after the war, would provide a buffer zone against any Russian attack, and he declared that it was necessary on military grounds to procure "defensive belts" to safeguard the coal fields of Upper Silesia and the iron mines of Lorraine. Moreover, Germany would have to insist on economic union with Belgium and a prolonged military occupation. Far from considering concessions in Alsace-Lorraine, he proposed that these provinces be incorporated into Prussia instead of administered separately as the Reichsland. He had plans for the seizure of all French property in the area, so that it could be handed over to German veterans, who would be encouraged to settle there. He was, however, willing to make a single concession, for he declared magnanimously that he was not interested in German naval bases on the Flanders coast, unless "the English keep a strip of French territory, e.g., Calais." [22]

October came in wet and gloomy, the sad herald of the fourth winter of war. Undernourished children went to school to be told tales of German heroism and victories, or stayed at home on cold days because they had no clothes to cover them. The women, hungrier than the children, prayed for an early peace. The industrial workers muttered among themselves, and on the lines of communication and in the rear areas of the armies, soldiers, in threadbare uniforms which were often ominously patched because they had been recovered from the dead, grew slack about saluting and stared sullenly at the young officers who tried to train them.

Ludendorff knew all this well, but it did not weaken his resolution. Hindenburg, celebrating his 70th birthday at Kreuznach early in the month, still felt a childish pleasure when his Kaiser came early in the morning to his house to congratulate him,[23] but the First Quartermaster General had never cared for such things and he was by now as contemptuous of the Kaiser as of most men. He was upheld by his belief in victory — and although this belief no longer had rational roots, he still had some reason on his side. The rot had not yet set in among the front-line troops, and on every battlefield German soldiers still fought as bravely and almost as skilfully as before.

There was to be one more victory in 1917. In October, the Austrian Supreme Command announced that their armies could not endure another winter of war. Although the Russians no longer threatened the Dual Monarchy, Austrian fighting power had sunk so low that if the Italians launched a twelfth offensive on the Isonzo, there was little prospect of withstanding it. Ludendorff knew that a passive defensive would be of no help, and his Chief of Operations, Lieutenant Colonel Wetzell, warmly advocated an attack against Italy. The First Quartermaster General sent General Krafft von Dellmensingen, who had commanded the Alpine Corps in Roumania, and Major Freiherr von Willinen to make a personal reconnaissance of the Italian front, and they returned to report that the thing was possible. Six or seven German divisions would be needed, and these would have to be re-equipped and receive special training, but if no time was wasted Italy might be dealt a deadly blow.

Ludendorff wasted no time. He formed a new Fourteenth Army of six divisions under General Otto von Below; pack artillery and special mountain equipment was scraped together; and on the early morning of the 24th of October, near Tolmino, the Germans and Austro-Hungarians attacked. The Fourteenth Army swept down from the mountains to strike the Italians like an avalanche. The entire Italian front crumbled, and the roads leading back into the heart of Italy were soon jammed with long columns of dispirited soldiers. The Germans pressed the pursuit with cold, professional ferocity. After some sharp fighting at Caporetto, the Fourteenth Army met little resistance. Von Below captured 275,000 prisoners, and the Italian Army lost twice as many more through casualties and desertions. Back and back the beaten masses fled, jostling to get out of the way of their terrible pursuers. At nights the autumn sky was bright with the flare of exploding ammunition dumps and petrol stores fired by the retreating Italians.[24] Not until the remnants had crossed the flooded Piave River on the 9th of November were they able to reform any kind of line. Ludendorff, who had already decided not to continue the operations beyond the Piave, brought his victorious divisions back to France.

For the time being at least, Austria was saved, although the Emperor Charles shrewdly suspected that it might be only for a worse fate. Ludendorff, too, was dissatisfied. He had won another great victory, but, as always in the past, it had brought him no nearer his final goal. Already his eyes returned to the West.

At the end of October Chancellor Michaelis resigned, unable to bear any longer the attacks made on him in the Reichstag. On the 2nd of November he was succeeded by the 76-year-old Count Georg von Hertling, a gentle professor of philosophy, who took office reluctantly and with the promise that he would follow policies more in keeping with the popular will. The promise was impossible of fulfillment, for the Chancellor, the Reichstag, and even the Kaiser no longer counted in Germany. The whole burden of the direction of the war, with its manifold responsibilities, now rested on the shoulders of one man. And that man, torn with anxiety and forebodings, went forward with the determined single-mindedness of a sleep-walker.

Meanwhile, the German lines in Flanders were still being assaulted by the British. In the Ypres Salient the most appalling conditions prevailed. The entire battlefield, where the drainage system had broken down from long shell-fire, was no better than a swamp, blasted and cratered like the face of some desolate moon. With a stubbornness and pertinacity that would have been admirable had it been lightened by any gleam of intelligence, Sir Douglas Haig launched attack after attack across this waterlogged waste. The British, Australians, and Canadians suffered the most terrible casualties, but the mere weight and persistence of their assault made Ludendorff deeply anxious. After each attack petered out in the mud and blood around Passchendaele Ridge, he consulted with the field commanders and staff. Unlike his British counterparts, he frequently went to the front himself to view conditions and he regularly interviewed front-line officers who had actually participated in the fighting. He analyzed the tactical experiences with General von Kuhl and Colonel von Lossberg and remained in constant touch with them over the telephone. His conclusions were that the German line would hold and that the new defensive system was working well, but he was worried lest in the end sheer weight of numbers should overwhelm him.[25] Throughout the latter stages of the battle the Germans probably killed three soldiers for every man they lost themselves, but the Allies could still find replacements for their dead. Across the Atlantic, vast American armies were training to take their place in the fighting line, and not even Ludendorff could any longer believe that the German Navy would be able to prevent their arrival.

Something much worse than the strain and loss of Passchendaele was in store for the German Supreme Command. Shortly after Haig had reluctantly broken off his futile offensive, General Sir Julian Byng's Third Army, supported by 324 tanks, launched a surprise attack at Cambrai. In the first six hours of the 20th of November, Byng's soldiers captured more ground than 51 British divisions had done at Third Ypres in four months of desperate fighting. The tanks drove triumphantly through the German lines to a distance of 10,000 yards, and 8,000 German prisoners were captured. British losses were remarkably small, only some 4,000 in all.

This blow was as unnerving as it was unexpected. Ludendorff frantically ordered several divisions to concentrate for a counter-attack, but he realized with dread in his heart that in most cases this would take at least three days. He need not have worried. Haig, who had so confidently massed his cavalry behind the Ypres swamps in the expectation that the horsemen would ride to the coast, had concentrated no reserves to exploit success at Cambrai. Indeed, he would have been hard put to do so, for the troops he might have used were — all too many of them — lying dead in the Passchendaele mud. By the evening of the 29th, Ludendorff had sufficient divisions concentrated for a counter-attack against the flank of the British penetration. The counter-attack duly went in the following morning and was completely successful, the British losing all and more of the ground they had so brilliantly won on the 20th.

Cambrai, however, had been a portent — and in more ways than one. The original breakthrough had been something with which a soldier could hope to deal, but on the evening of the 30th of November, in spite of the reports of success hourly being telephoned into his headquarters, Ludendorff was in a mood of black depression. For the first time in the war a good German infantry division that had fought bravely most of the day had suddenly stopped its pursuit of the beaten enemy in order to loot a captured supply depot.[26]

In the East, meanwhile, the war was as good as over. Early on the morning of the 25th of October, the Bolsheviks under Lenin and Trotsky staged a *coup d'état* in Petrograd, stormed the Winter Palace, overthrew Kerensky's Provisional Government, and seized power. Colonel Hoffmann's blue eyes twinkled benevolently behind their pince-nez when he heard the news, which was certainly gratifying. It was gratifying also to be told on the 30th that he had been promoted to major general, a full two and a half years before he could normally have expected such a distinction by seniority. Surely, in the whole of military history, no promotion was ever more amply justified, since for the past year and a half he had been virtual commander-in-chief of one-third of the German Army. Even Hoffmann was sufficiently a creature of his training and environment to be well pleased, for the time being at least, with this inadequate recognition, which was the sweeter because he would at last be called "Excellency." His promotion was a mark of Ludendorff's favor — the last as it turned out — for the Kaiser's Military Cabinet who controlled officers' promotions had been very reluctant to make such a departure from the seniority list, but Ludendorff had shouted, and pounded the table, and got his way.[27] Doubtless the members of the Military Cabinet consoled themselves with the reflection that they were generously rewarding merit.

On the 26th of November, Ludendorff received a wireless message from a man who had received much more rapid promotion than Hoffmann. Only a few months previously Corporal Krylenko had been one of the anonymous millions in the Tsar's army, but when the Bolsheviks seized power they made him commander-in-chief of the Soviet forces. Now, as one equal to another, he was inquiring of Ludendorff whether it would be possible for Russia to conclude an armistice.

Ludendorff had his doubts about all this. Early that summer he had personally drafted a set of armistice conditions for Russia,[28] but he had certainly not foreseen the present situation. He asked an orderly officer to get *Ober-Ost* on the telephone: General Ludendorff to speak to General Hoffmann.

When the call was put through, he told Hoffmann what had happened. "Is it possible to negotiate with these people?" he asked.

"Yes, it is possible to negotiate with them," Hoffmann replied immediately. "Your Excellency needs troops and this is the quickest way to get them."

Six days later, on the 2nd of December, the Russian armistice delegation crossed the German lines. They were met on the wooden railway platform of Brest-Litovsk by Major Brinckmann, heavier and grayer now than he had been at Liège, but as plausible and immaculate as ever. Brinckmann escorted the

Russians to the Citadel, where Hoffmann welcomed them with great amiability.

Ludendorff could now withdraw troops from the East, and there were still 80 good divisions there. In the spring, as soon as the weather broke, Germany could at last turn wholeheartedly and without distraction against a single set of her enemies. Ludendorff felt "as though a weight had been removed from my chest." [29]

But it was all illusion, for the crucial time had passed.

CHAPTER XV

THE LAST THROW FAILS

A T A CROWN COUNCIL meeting at Kreuznach on the 19th of December, the Kaiser, Hindenburg, Foreign Secretary Kühlmann, and the old Chancellor, von Hertling, listened to Ludendorff expound the final peace terms to be offered to Russia. He intended to carve a great slice out of Russia's flank from the Baltic to the Black Sea, because the timber, oil, minerals and grain from this area would ensure that Germany could survive any blockade in a future war. While he was talking, both Hindenburg and Hertling fell asleep, for the room was warm, they were old men, and they had heard it all before. Kühlmann, a Bavarian who had a European as well as a German conscience, tried to reason with Ludendorff, advocating a peace of conciliation with Russia. When he found the First Quartermaster General impervious to argument, he reached over and shook the old Field Marshal awake.

"Why do you want the Baltic territories?" he demanded.

Hindenburg raised his giant head and looked at the Foreign Minister through half-closed eyes. His mind took a moment or two to focus, then he spoke in the somnolent tones of the dormouse at Alice's tea-party: "For the maneuvering of my left wing in the next war."

Trying to reason with this attitude was an obvious waste of time, but Kühlmann did not abandon hope of making his views prevail. Since he knew Hoffmann agreed with him, he invited him to attend a second Crown Council meeting to be held on the Russian peace terms on the 2nd of January. Being a devious man, Kühlmann also arranged for the Kaiser to give Hoffmann a private audience at the Neue Schloss on New Year's Day.

His Majesty was so taken with Hoffmann's witty conversation that he asked him to stay for lunch, and during the meal inquired point-blank what he thought was the correct settlement of the Polish question. On this subject Hoffmann had long had his own very definite ideas, which were completely at variance with Ludendorff's. The latter's scheme for annexations and colonization appeared to Hoffmann the most fantastic folly. Apart from any other consideration, why should Germany coerce into the Reich millions of discontented Poles who would never become loyal subjects? In Hoffmann's opinion there were already too many non-Germans in the Empire, and he was apt to recall with regret that Bismarck had been overruled by the General Staff in his desire to let France keep Lorraine.

But Hoffmann had few illusions. He knew that if he expressed himself freely to the Kaiser, Ludendorff would certainly hear of it and be more determined than ever to have his own way. Accordingly, he begged to be excused from offering an opinion, saying — perhaps not without irony — that this was a purely political matter, entirely outside the province of the Chief of Staff, *Ober-Ost*. However, the Kaiser was intrigued by much that Hoffmann had already said and a little piqued at finding yet another soldier who declined to do as he asked. With a flash of the confident vanity that before 1914 had been habitual to him Wilhelm replied: "When your All Highest War Lord asks to hear your views on any subject, it is your duty to give them to him, quite irrespective of whether they agree with those of the Supreme Command or not."

However arrogantly phrased, this was indubitably true, and Hoffmann obeyed — as he always obeyed the voice of duty — but almost certainly with an ironical mental shrug. He explained exactly where he thought the Polish border should be drawn and why. Wilhelm was entranced and accepted every word with a disconcerting enthusiasm.

It was well on in the afternoon before Hoffmann could get

away from the Neue Schloss. As soon as he escaped from the Imperial presence, he went straight to the nearest telephone to get in touch with Ludendorff, but was unable to reach him. He had no chance to speak to the great man until the next morning at the Crown Council, and then, before he could talk to him, the Kaiser strode jauntily into the room with a map of Poland tucked under his arm.

What occurred next was entirely predictable; Hoffmann had anticipated almost every word of it. The Kaiser enthusiastically displayed his map with the Polish border marked in just where Hoffmann had suggested it should be, and then went on to expound, practically word for word, the arguments he had heard the previous day. What was worse, whether from native honesty or merely because of Hoffmann's presence, he blithely informed the company where the credit lay. Hoffmann watched Ludendorff with a sort of resigned fascination. The First Quartermaster General's face turned first pink, then purple, his neck swelled with rage, and the veins stood out on his forehead. He protested vehemently against the Kaiser's receiving advice through such unorthodox channels, declaring it was subversive of all military discipline. He damned Hoffmann's proposals root and branch and insisted that the whole matter be reconsidered. The Supreme Command, he said, desired to make further representations. He turned to Hindenburg to support him, and the old Field Marshal, who was not quite sure why his First Quartermaster General was so angry, nodded his head in mute approval. Completely taken aback, the Kaiser hastily agreed with Ludendorff's demands, but the rest of the conference was conducted in a strained atmosphere.

Ludendorff never forgave Hoffmann. He had Hindenburg write the Kaiser, demanding Hoffmann's dismissal, and saying that, if his proposals for the future of Poland were adopted, the Supreme Command would take it as a sign they no longer enjoyed the Imperial confidence.[1] Hindenburg had come a long way since 1914, when he would no more have thought of addressing his Emperor in such terms than his God. The Kaiser, who was becoming used to giving way whenever the Great Twin Brethren threatened to resign, did so now and agreed that Ludendorff's annexationist dreams would become German policy. However, no matter what his faults, Wilhelm was a gentleman, and he flatly refused to take any action against Hoffmann. With this Ludendorff had to be content, for he certainly had no intention of resigning. For a long time, however, he refused to speak to Hoffmann, even over the telephone, but dealt with him only through Colonel Bauer.

Even the Kaiser's personal friends now had to be sacrificed at the demand of Supreme Headquarters. On the 15th of January, Hindenburg, in a private audience, declared that he and Ludendorff could no longer tolerate Valentini as Chief of the Civil Cabinet, for the army had lost confidence in him. In translation, this meant that Ludendorff had heard of Valentini's support of Bethmann-Hollweg and of his criticism of the Supreme Command's encroachment on the civil power.[2] Wilhelm was "beside himself with rage" at the sheer impertinence of Hindenburg's demand. He turned deadly pale and for a moment could find no words, then he shouted at the Field Marshal: "I don't need your paternal advice!" and stalked out of the room, slamming the door behind him.

But it was no more than an ineffectual display of temper. Valentini resigned, to be replaced by von Berg, Ludendorff's nominee. Wilhelm knew very well who was really responsible and declared angrily in private that Ludendorff was "a malefactor" with whom he would never again shake hands.[3]

Meanwhile, the peace talks at Brest-Litovsk seemed to drag on interminably, and although Hoffmann was not unduly worried, since he was already sending back as many troops as could be spared, Ludendorff was "burning with impatience."[4] He insisted that *Ober-Ost* force the diplomats to press for a speedy settlement which would incorporate all his harsh demands on Russia. Count Czernin, the Austrian Foreign Minister, feared that, if the terms were too stiff, Russia might decide to continue the war, and he had instructions from the Emperor Charles to conclude peace at almost any price. At one point, he actually threatened that, if the Germans did not moderate their demands, Austria might make a separate peace. But, although Hoffmann was privately in sympathy with the Austrian view, he was a soldier under orders, and he was more than equal to this sort of thing. He smiled frostily and replied: "Splendid! That would enable me to redeploy the German troops I am now using to bolster the Austrian Front." Czernin winced and made no further mention of a separate peace.

At Kreuznach, Hindenburg, who remembered 1866, was indignant, but not surprised, that Austria should behave so, and he declared with some relish that "the next war will be between us and Austria." [5]

When Trotsky arrived to head the Russian delegation, the talks at Brest-Litovsk ground almost to a standstill. He was a striking figure with his pointed beard and clever Jewish face, but he would talk for hours about world revolution and say almost nothing on the subject of peace terms. His sharp eyes would flash behind their pince-nez while Kühlmann was speaking, then he would reply with a fine sweep of language and some sharp satiric thrusts. But it got him nowhere, for the truth was that the Russians held no cards at all. As Kühlmann cynically said: "The only choice they have is as to what sauce they'll be eaten with." Hoffmann finally brought the comedy to a close by bluntly outlining the German terms and declaring that Trotsky would have to take them or leave them. Obviously shaken, Trotsky requested an adjournment, which Hoffmann granted.

Ludendorff was displeased to hear of the adjournment, and again demanded that a treaty be signed without delay.[6] Trotsky returned to Brest-Litovsk on the 30th, but only to state that he could not accept the German terms. That did not mean, he hastened to add, that Russia was still at war with Germany. She was not. Although she refused to ratify an imperialistic peace treaty, she would not continue fighting. There would be "neither peace nor war." He declared that he was demobilizing the Russian Army and that hostilities were therefore at an end. This contained more than a touch of disingenuousness, for in truth the Russian Army was demobilizing itself as rapidly as the soldiers could make their way back to their homes. When Trotsky finished speaking, the startled silence around the conference table was broken at last by Hoffmann's affronted exclamation: *"Unerhört!"* It was perhaps the only occasion in the war when Hoffmann showed surprise.

However, he was not disconcerted for long, and soon found the perfect counter. On the 9th of February Germany signed a separate peace with the Ukraine. In spite of all their talk of self-determination and the rights of minorities, the Bolsheviks were enraged, and that night a wireless message from Tsarkoe Selo called on all German soldiers to mutiny and kill the Kaiser, the generals of the High Command and their regimental officers. Hindenburg promptly demanded that these bloodthirsty Socialists be taught a lesson, and Wilhelm, who strongly disapproved of people who advocated the murder of emperors, ordered Kühlmann to present Trotsky with a definite ultimatum and to insist as well that the Russians immediately evacuate the Baltic littoral. On receiving Kühlmann's strong protest, the Kaiser agreed to drop the second demand.

Trotsky's twilight state of "neither peace nor war" was not to last long. On the 13th of February, Ludendorff obtained the Kaiser's permission to denounce the armistice.[7] Hoffmann had long ago made his preparations and drawn up his orders; all that remained to do was issue them. On the afternoon of the 18th of February and on the morning of the 19th the German Army advanced all along the Eastern Front. The Russians put up no real resistance as German armored trains steamed from station to station, dropping off small detachments at intervals. The Bolshevik Government was appalled by this turn of events and naïvely indignant that an imperialist power should so persecute the revolution. Trotsky wanted to make a new pact with the Allies and renew the war, but Lenin was too much a realist for that. At his insistence, Russia abjectly surrendered on the 23rd of February, and the Bolshevik delegation returned to Brest-Litovsk five days later. Trotsky remained in Petrograd to avoid the humiliation of signing the new peace terms.

As usual, Hoffmann was in no hurry. Why should he be? While he smoked a good cigar and exchanged civilized pleasantries with Sokolnikov, the head of the Bolshevik delegation, the German Army was steadily pressing deeper and deeper into Russia. At last, at 5:30 on the afternoon of the 3rd of March, when the early winter twilight had already begun to close in around the grim old Citadel, Hoffmann presented the Russians with the treaty. As a final grand gesture, Sokolnikov did not even bother to read it before he signed. Hoffmann smiled mockingly beneath his diabolical eyebrows, clicked his heels together correctly, and took his leave. When the Russian delegation did read the treaty, they found that Finland and the Ukraine had gained independence; that Russia had given up Courland, Lithuania, Poland, Batum, and Kars; that Estonia and Latvia were to be occupied by Germany; that the Russian Army was to be demobilized; and that there would be an immediate end to Bolshevik propaganda.

Now only the relatively minor matter of peace with Roumania remained to be settled. Here again Germany and Austria had conflicting interests, for Austria feared post-war German influence in Roumania, while Ludendorff demanded that the country become a German satellite under a puppet government. Again Ludendorff urged that the peace negotiations be terminated speedily, and he ordered General Hell, Chief of Staff to old von Mackensen, to exert every possible pressure to that end. Unfortunately, Hell had only recently taken over from Colonel Hentsch, the same officer who had ordered the retreat from the Marne and who had climaxed a disastrous war record by dying unexpectedly at a crucial stage of the negotiations with Roumania. Hell was unable to exert much influence, and the treaty with Roumania was not signed until the 7th of May.[8]

Ludendorff found these political-military events in the East a worrisome distraction. If victory was to be had at all, it would have to be before summer came, and with summer the Americans. For weeks, troop trains had been rolling westward along the four great railway lines running across Germany. Corps after corps had come from Riga, from the flat plains of Poland, and from the Carpathians. Between November 1917 and the 21st of March 1918, German strength on the Western Front increased by 30 per cent, while the British Army was 25 per cent weaker than it had been in the summer of 1917. For a brief period in the spring — and for the first time in the war — the Allies would actually be slightly outnumbered in the West.

"I wish I could be there," Hoffmann noted rather wistfully in his diary on the 8th of March, "but I haven't a chance. Even the greatest personnages suffer from jealousy, so I don't think that Ludendorff is likely to let me have my finger in the pie." [9]

Neither the troops from the East nor those who had been standing on the defensive for two years in the West were ready to attack. Formidable problems of re-equipment had to be solved and huge quantities of ammunition amassed. Ludendorff initiated a crash training program and pushed it through with ruthless speed. Just as he had revised the defensive tactics of the German Army in 1916, so now he boldly instituted a new offensive doctrine which would have to be assimilated by all levels of the army before spring. He worked like a man possessed and drove all under him to do the same. He planned to attack shortly after the middle of March, for by then the training program would be completed and the fields of France would provide some grazing for horses, an important consideration because of the shortage of fodder in Germany.[10]

The first staff conference on the spring offensive, or *Kaiserschlacht*, had been held at Mons in 1917 — ironically enough, on the 11th of November. Ludendorff, General von Kuhl, Crown

Prince Rupprecht's Chief of Staff, General Schulenburg, the German Crown Prince's Chief of Staff, and Colonel Wetzell had met to decide the date and place of the first attack, which was codenamed "Michael." Significantly, not a single commanding general attended this vital conference, a clear indication of how the great Chiefs of Staff dominated the Army under Ludendorff. The war was being directed by a secret freemasonry of those who had known each other in the Red House on the Königsplatz before 1914.

In spite of the danger of alerting the enemy, the place of attack had to be decided early because of the tremendous build-up of material that would be necessary. Three possible areas were considered: the sector between Ypres and Lens in Flanders, that between Arras and St. Quentin in France, and the area on both sides of Verdun but excluding the fortress itself. Each sector had its advocates, but Ludendorff favored the center, between Arras and St. Quentin, because there the ground would be drier and the enemy, he believed, would be weaker. He decided to strike at the British rather than the French because he considered British commanders more inept and less flexible and because he rightly believed the British Army to have been seriously weakened at Passchendaele. Although from the strategic view an offensive in Flanders promised greater results, the British were strongest there, and Ludendorff refused to be tempted. "Tactics," he said, "had to be considered before purely strategical objects which it is futile to pursue unless tactical success is possible." [11] As usual, he had his way, but Crown Prince Rupprecht, when informed of the decision, commented in his diary: "Ludendorff underestimates the toughness of the British."

Ludendorff planned, not a single breakthrough, but a series of attacks to shake "the hostile edifice by closely connected partial blows so that sooner or later the whole structure would collapse." [12] Perhaps in the mud and filth of the Western Front there was bred some virus which infected generals with delusions of victory. For nearly four years the British and French

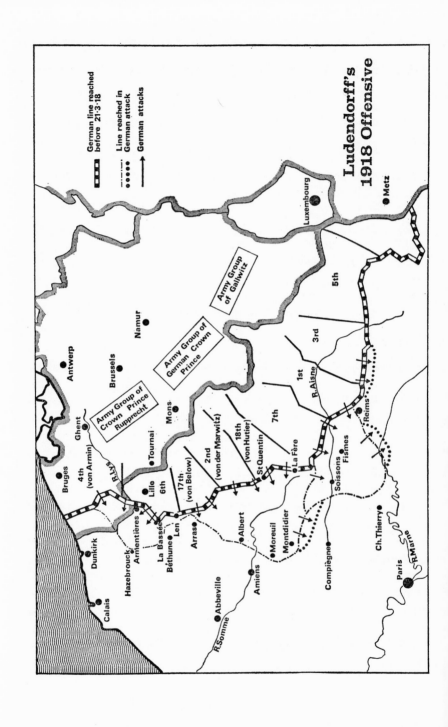

Ludendorff's 1918 Offensive

High Commands had had such delusions, and now Ludendorff assured the Kaiser: "It will be an immense struggle that will begin at one point, continue at another, and take a long time; it is difficult, but it will be successful." This sounded impressive, but Hoffmann's shrewder strategical brain had detected the fallacy, which was that each German attack, even if successful, would inevitably consume more and more reserves, while the Allies, confident of a steadily increasing stream of American reinforcements, had only to avoid utter disaster to be certain of final victory.

However, Ludendorff was certain that the thing could be done. As his way was, he had gathered around him a group of brilliant young officers and had set them to thinking about the best method of conducting an offensive under conditions of static warfare. He himself took a personal interest in the development of the new doctrine, and his was always the deciding voice. What eventually emerged was a series of pamphlets on *"The Offensive Battle in Positional Warfare."* The new German tactics would depend on basically the same weapons used on the Western Front for the past two years. Even had he wanted to, Ludendorff could not have obtained a significant number of tanks by March, and in any case, when he had seen his first captured tank in February 1918, he had not been much impressed. Tank production was not placed on the urgent list until after the 8th of August 1918.

How then did Ludendorff expect to accomplish, with a relatively weaker force, what the Allies had conspicuously failed to achieve in 1915, 1916, and 1917? Part of the answer was that the infantry assault would be based on a fundamentally new concept originated by Captain Geyer. There would be no mass attacks such as the British and French had launched at Loos, the Somme, Champagne and Passchendaele. Instead the fighting line would be kept thin, but would be fed constantly from behind. A new formation, the infantry group, consisting of a light machine-gun and a few riflemen, would be the tactical unit. Just as had been done on the defensive, Ludendorff was determined to replace manpower as much as possible by machine-power. The light machine-gun, "that concentrated essence of infantry," was to be given a much more important role and heavy machine-guns were to become almost supporting arms. Light trench mortars were supplied to the infantry in greater abundance, and some field guns were withdrawn from artillery formations and placed directly under the battalion as infantry guns. Groups of storm troopers, trained to probe for weak spots and taught to exploit success, would move forward in front of the main infantry assault, leaning hard against the barrage. Where they met resistance they would by-pass it, leaving it for later waves to overcome. No effort would be made to maintain a uniform rate of advance or to align formations. Thus the new German offensive would not be a battering-ram, pounding head-on against a wall, but rather like a flood of water, flowing around obstacles, isolating them, and following the path of least resistance deep into the enemy's territory.

Artillery tactics were revised under the direction of Captain Pulkowsky, and Ludendorff made drastic changes in the system of command and control. Headquarters of all formations moved closer to the front, and when a reserve division was committed to action it would come under the orders of the forward assault division instead of being controlled directly by corps headquarters.[13] These innovations, the thoughtful distillation of battle experience, demonstrated beyond question the excellence of some aspects of the German General Staff system. Schlieffen, who may be blamed for many things, had at least taught the General Staff that the field marshals were not necessarily the most intelligent men of all, and after that the generals. All through the war, the Germans — and Ludendorff especially — placed a far higher premium on brains than did the Allies. Hoffmann and Bruchmüller had been recognized as lieutenant colonels; Lossberg's defensive theories had been adopted when he was only a colonel; and the tactics of infiltration were devised by a mere captain. Germany's lack of colonies, felt as a grievance before the war, may very well have had something to do with this. Certainly, British and French generals who had spent their lives fighting against ill-equipped and unorganized enemies, were apt to place too high a value on rank and military discipline. The Allies had equally clever junior officers, especially in the tank corps, but whereas Ludendorff was always receptive to new military ideas, very senior Allied commanders seldom were. Even the belated Allied exploitation of the tank was more a result of superior industrial capacity than of astute military thinking, and the tank was accepted the more readily because it was a technical "gimmick" rather than an innovation in the sacred realm of military theory.

In preparation for his attack, Ludendorff inserted the Seventeenth Army, under General Otto von Below, into the line opposite Arras between the Sixth and Second Armies. General von Hutier's Eighteenth Army was placed between the Second and Seventh Armies opposite St. Quentin and La Fère. The Seventeenth and Second Armies were grouped under Crown Prince Rupprecht, but the Eighteenth Army came under the German Crown Prince. An army group headquarters could easily have controlled three armies, but Ludendorff intended "to exercise a far-reaching influence on the course of the battle" and rightly believed he could achieve this more easily and with less friction if two army groups were involved.[14]

By the beginning of February, the plan had been worked out in every detail, and Ludendorff fixed the date of the attack for the 21st of March. G.H.Q. moved forward from Kreuznach to Spa, where Ludendorff and Hindenburg took up their quarters in the Hotel Britannique. On the 18th of March an advanced headquarters was established at Avesnes.

Hindenburg and Ludendorff motored down to Avesnes that evening. Although the past few weeks had been fine, with clear, bright skies and fresh winds that dried the ground, the weather suddenly changed on the 18th, and Ludendorff and Hindenburg arrived at advanced headquarters in a violent thunderstorm. For the next two days, dark clouds piled high in a gloomy sky and violent winds and rain lashed the chosen battle area. In spite of the blustery weather, Hindenburg, who found himself in France again after an absence of 47 years, went out daily for his walk and looked about Avesnes with benign interest, speaking to people on the streets and patting children on the head.

The Kaiser, who had been assured that the longed-for victory was finally at hand, arrived on the 19th. Realizing that it would be better for everyone if he did not take up his residence in the headquarters, he lived in his royal train on a nearby siding. Whenever he found himself becoming bored, he steamed away to visit one of the armies.

For all his brittle confidence, Ludendorff was nervous. He was bad-tempered with subordinates and rolled his bread crumbs furiously with both hands at dinner, but he was utterly determined to go on to the end. A month previously, when Prince Max of Baden had bluntly asked him what would happen if the great spring offensive failed, he had glowered and given the terrible reply: *"Dann muss Deutschland eben zugrunde gehen!"* ("Then Germany will just have to suffer annihilation").[15]

On the 18th, two German soldiers deserted to the British near St. Quentin and betrayed the date of the attack. Ludendorff wondered if he should cancel Operation "Michael," for success in any case seemed uncertain. The initial bombardment depended on gas-shell, and all through the 20th the weather was stormy and rainy, entirely unsuited for gas warfare. However, after studying the meteorological reports at noon on the 20th, he decided to persevere.

Perhaps too his decision was based on less objective considerations. He had taken to studying a little prayer-book of the Moravian Brethren, a Bohemian sect who believed in the "total depravity of man" and the magical power of Scripture. The Brethren's prayer-book thoughtfully provided Biblical texts for every day of the year, and superstitious German evangelicals*

* Of whom Chancellor Bismarck had been one.

had long been in the habit of consulting these texts in order to regulate their conduct of the day's affairs. At lunch on the 20th of March Ludendorff turned abruptly to General von Tiescho-witz, who was seated beside him, and said: "Do you know to-morrow's watchword of the Brethren?" Tieschowitz obviously did not, and indeed had to rack his brains to recall who 'the Brethren' were, but Ludendorff went on: "It is — 'This is the day of the chosen people.' " The First Quartermaster General paused to allow General Tieschowitz to realize the significance of the final phrase, then said: "Can we fail therefore to look for-ward with confidence to the offensive which begins tomorrow?" [16] At the time, Tieschowitz could scarcely believe that Ludendorff was serious.

Sharp at four o'clock on the morning of the 21st of March, the massed German guns opened with a tremendous roar along 44 miles of front. The landscape was shrouded in mist and, as the sun climbed, the fog thickened. At Avesnes, Hindenburg and Ludendorff, in greatcoats and *Pickelhauben,* and with their ceremonial swords by their sides, walked out to stand together in front of their headquarters and peer into the gray murk. It made a fine picture for the army photographers, if it did nothing to win the war. All sounds were muted and the Supreme Com-manders could hear only a dull mutter of gunfire from the distant battlefield. The German infantry advanced at nine o'clock. To the north about Arras the Seventeenth Army attacked with 19 divisions along 9½ miles of front. Like all the German infantry that day, von Below's men were helped by the fog, but Byng's Third Army fought well and the second British line was not penetrated. In the center, von der Marwitz's Second Army of 18 divisions, attacking along a 9½-mile front, made better prog-ress, penetrating the second line. South of the Somme, where von Hutier's Eighteenth Army attacked on a 20-mile front with 24 divisions, General Gough's Fifth Army crumbled almost at once. Although this sector had been the weakest on the British front, Haig had placed only three of his eighteen reserve divisions behind it. As the storm troops pushed on and on, terrible confusion developed behind the British lines; vital railway bridges fell intact into German hands; 500 British guns were captured in the first two days; and as the advance continued, it seemed increasingly difficult for the British to make a stand.

On the second day of the battle, the Seventeenth Army was still making little progress, but the Second Army continued to move forward, and the Eighteenth Army was meeting practically no opposition. On the 24th, while the Germans were driving a deep wedge between the British and French south of the Somme, General Pétain gloomily informed Haig that if the advance was not soon checked, he would have to move French reserves southwest to cover Paris. This was nearly equivalent to saying that Pétain would leave the British on their own. By the 25th, von Below's Army was almost exhausted, but the Second Army had reached Albert. On the 27th the Eighteenth Army took Montdidier. A huge railway gun, especially constructed by Krupps and nicknamed "Big Bertha" by the Allies, now began to shell Paris at a range of 75 miles.[17] A chill of fear closed around the Allied world like a constricting hand, and those who knew the true situation looked gravely at each other, wondering in their hearts if this was indeed the end.

However, the new theories of the offensive were better understood at the tactical than at the strategic level. Ludendorff, contrary to his own principles, had concentrated his forces against the strongest portion of the British line, and when the more widely dispersed Eighteenth Army had unexpectedly broken through, he actually held it back while he tried again for success in the north, thus unwittingly coming to the Allies' rescue. Only after a fresh attack by the Seventeenth and Sixth Armies had failed to storm the heights about Arras, did he change his original plan.

If, in August 1916, Ludendorff had taken Hoffmann with him to Pless instead of von Bockelberg, he might well have fought this decisive battle better. But if Hoffmann had not been left in the East to win victories and free troops for the West, the battle might not have been fought at all. From the vantage point of half a century, this appears to be only another example of the perpetual German dilemma which Schlieffen, Moltke, Falkenhayn, and Ludendorff were each unable to solve. The truth was that the odds were always too great, and the tragedy was that so many Germans were too capable and too self-confident to recognize the truth.

Now, too late, Ludendorff reinforced the left wing of the Second Army and directed it and the Eighteenth Army towards Amiens. But by then the Allied resistance had hardened and Pétain had sent Haig 21 French divisions to bolster his front. On the 28th, General Ferdinand Foch was appointed Co-ordinator of the Allied armies in the threatened sector.

By the 4th of April, Ludendorff saw that the "Michael" offensive would make no more headway and ordered it to stop. On balance, he was satisfied with what had been achieved. The British and French had been terribly shaken by the speed and ferocity of the attack. For more than three years their own offensives, although fed remorselessly with the best blood of their nations, had never gained more than a few thousand yards of worthless ground. Yet, when every country was reaching the end of its endurance, the Germans in two weeks had smashed through on a front of over 40 miles and penetrated to a depth of 40 miles, capturing more than 80,000 prisoners and 975 guns. Although "Michael" had fallen just short of decisive strategic success, the Allied commanders knew how desperately close they had been to irretrievable disaster. If Amiens with its railway net had been captured, the British and French forces would have been thrust apart, the British to fall back towards the Channel and the French towards Paris. Had this happened, the war would have been lost. And although the worst had been averted, no responsible Allied general viewed the future with anything but the deepest foreboding.

However, there was another side to the story, and one which gave Ludendorff grave anxiety. Because of the rapidity of the

Eighteenth Army's advance, only captured stores had kept it properly fed.[18] In the British rear areas the Germans had come upon a land flowing with milk and honey. Before long German soldiers were hardly distinguishable from British, for all of them wore captured leather jerkins, waterproofs and fine English boots. An officer sent to the front on the 28th of March to ascertain why a certain division had halted when there seemed no tactical reason to do so, found that the troops were too busy looting to continue the attack. When he drove into the divisional area, he discovered hundreds of drunken soldiers with wine bottles in their hands, herding cows down the road and carrying hens under their arms.[19] This was bad enough, but what was worse was that when the troops had time to think about it, they were demoralized by these evidences of Allied abundance. For over a year they had been told that England was on the verge of starvation, but now they found the British far better fed and clothed than they were themselves. The resulting disillusionment and cynicism had far-reaching results.

One cloudy March afternoon just before he called a halt to his offensive, Ludendorff had climbed heavily into his staff car and been driven to the battle-zone. In an open field near the village of Nesles, a little group of sober-faced officers waited by the roadside. Not far away was an open grave marked with a crude wooden cross. Ludendorff bent forward and read the English inscription: "Here rest two German flying officers." As he straightened, an officer beside him made an apologetic little gesture to where the two exhumed bodies lay under a tarpaulin. Ludendorff nodded and moved slowly forward. When a corner of the tarpaulin was drawn back, he gazed sadly down at the dead face of his stepson Erich. For once, the First Quartermaster General looked positively pathetic as he stood there, his rounded shoulders slumped, and his eyes brooding. Then he climbed back into the staff car to return to the conduct of the war.

At Avesnes he telephoned his wife who had been waiting in torment of soul at Wiesbaden for just this call. On the evening of the 21st of March she had learned that her youngest son had not returned from a flight over the enemy lines. Now all her fears were confirmed by a few words spoken over a hundred miles of telephone cable. Margarethe collapsed completely and never fully recovered from this second blow. For years thereafter she was "always sick and sorry." Much later she looked back down the years and recalled how it had always been "one of my favorite dreams to see Ludendorff and my three boys sitting around our table as officers. How differently everything turned out." [20]

At conferences on the 1st and 2nd of April, Ludendorff, Kuhl, and Lossberg decided that the next attack should fall on the British in Flanders, on both sides of the River Lys. Unfortunately, it could not be mounted before the 9th, and then only 11 divisions would be able to participate, instead of the more than 60 divisions that had opened "Michael." Because the attack on the Lys would be on so small a scale, its code-name was changed from "St. George" to "Georgette." Hoffmann's doubts about Ludendorff's plan were already finding ominous confirmation.

Nevertheless, Ludendorff's 53rd birthday in 1918 was a much more pleasant occasion than it had been a year previously when the Canadian Corps had captured Vimy Ridge. At 4:05 A.M. an intense artillery bombardment, prepared by Bruchmüller, burst along the 11 miles of front between the La Bassée Canal and Armentières. When German infantry groups moved forward at 7:30, the weak 2nd Portuguese Division holding the line north of Neuve Chapelle broke, and before noon the Germans had penetrated three miles to endanger the entire British front.

Ludendorff, whose temperament was better suited to the attack than the defense, was pleased with the news that reached him that evening, but the Kaiser was exalted. Even after four disappointing years, he still fell all too easily into the "Shout Hurrah!" mood that Moltke had hated "like death." Wilhelm made a little speech, congratulating Ludendorff on his birthday and on the brilliance of his generalship, then presented a small iron statuette of himself to his First Quartermaster General.

By the 11th, Armentières had fallen and by the next day von

Armin's Fourth Army drove forward ten miles. Haig issued his famous order: "There is no other course open to us but to fight it out . . . With our backs to the wall, believing in the justice of our cause, each one of us must fight on to the end . . ." Haig had reason to be worried, for the British were far more vulnerable here than at St. Quentin. The leading German infantry were now only some ten miles from Hazebrouck, through which ran the only British lines of communications apart from the coastal railway. Moreover, Ludendorff had once again caught Haig on the wrong foot, for in spite of much evidence to the contrary, the British Commander-in-Chief had stubbornly insisted that the next German offensive would be another attempt to capture Vimy Ridge and the high ground about Arras. Perhaps Haig credited his German counterpart with his own bulldog tenacity and felt that Ludendorff was bound to attack again where he had previously failed.

Although by the 14th of April French divisions had arrived to reinforce the front, fierce fighting continued. The chill April weather was exceptionally clear, and each night British observers south of Bethune could see an ominous wedge of burning villages moving farther and farther westward toward the coast.[21] On the 25th, Mount Kemmel fell, but this was "Georgette's" last success. Once again the defense stiffened, and after a final, unsuccessful attack on the 29th Ludendorff called off the battle.

He was a bitterly disappointed man. For the second time victory had just eluded him. Worse still, some German divisions had shown no inclination to attack and there had been frequent reports of troops halting to loot depots and farmhouses in search of food. He reacted by railing against the Reichstag for having weakened military discipline and loudly regretted that, since the old Prussian military law had been modified, soldiers could no longer be tied up to a fixed object.[22]

Since the 21st of March, the British had suffered over 300,000 casualties and ten British divisions had been broken up for reinforcements, but German losses had been considerably higher.

Ludendorff pleaded desperately but without avail for a further combing-out of recruits on the home-front, for he knew that a quarter of a million American soldiers were now landing in France each month. After the failure of "Georgette," von Loss-berg concluded that further offensives would be futile. Hoff-mann had arrived at the same answer a month earlier — Germany had lost all hope of victory and should immediately go over to the defensive and negotiate for peace from a position of strength. Prince Rupprecht of Bavaria wrote privately to the Chancellor urging this course. He added that although even Ludendorff realized the time for this had come, he was hoping desperately "for the saving aid of some *deus ex machina*." [23]

Ludendorff would not allow himself to entertain such pessimistic opinions. There was a long pause before he attacked again, but at one o'clock in the morning on the 27th of May, 3,719 German guns opened up on a 39-mile front along the Chemin des Dames between Reims and Soissons. Fifteen German divisions struck four battle-worn British divisions which had moved to this "quiet" sector for rest and recuperation after the Battle of the Lys. By noon the Germans had crossed the Aisne River on unblown bridges and by sunset had driven forward 12 miles. At the end of the third day, Soissons and Fismes had been left far behind, and in the center the Seventh Army had reached the Marne.

The Kaiser, delighted with the success of the "Blücher" offensive, decorated Hindenburg and Ludendorff and gaily compared the defeat of the French on the Chemin des Dames to their defeat at Waterloo. Ludendorff, however, was far from satisfied, for although he had captured 65,000 prisoners and enormous quantities of stores and material, he had failed once again to achieve a clean breakthrough. Just as at St. Quentin and on the Lys, the defenders had been able to reinforce by railroad more rapidly than the attackers could press forward across country; the front had hardened as reinforcements arrived; and early in June he was forced to call off the attack. He was worried too by numerous reports of troops who had stopped fighting to loot and get drunk. Officers had frequently lost all control over their men, and it was reported that at Fismes "drunken soldiers were lying all over the road." A new attack, launched near Compiègne on the 9th of June, had to be halted after two days because of stiffening enemy resistance.[24]

Europe was to be spared nothing this terrible spring. For four years, war, death, and famine had ridden across the continent, and now the fourth horseman appeared, the rider of the pale horse of the Apocalypse, bearing an epidemic of Spanish influenza which, within a year, would slay more victims than the war had done. Morning after morning Ludendorff sat at Avesnes, listening to the telephone reports of the Chiefs of Staff of his armies. As the number of influenza cases mounted daily, army after army reported it was too weakened to withstand an Allied attack.[25] Yet Ludendorff, grasping at straws, hoped without reason that the Entente would suffer more from influenza than Germany. Predictably, the converse happened, for dietary deficiencies and actual starvation had weakened the Germans' resistance to disease.

The army still received far better rations than the rest of the population, and soldiers going home on leave were frequently appalled to find their wives and children visibly suffering from malnutrition. They returned to spread disaffection at the front, and new drafts, especially those from the East, also had a bad influence on discipline. Released prisoners of war from Russia often refused to go to the front, wrongly believing that, like the prisoners exchanged with the British and the French, they were under no obligation to fight again. Although the Conservatives, Junkers, Pan-Germans, and great industrialists still gave Ludendorff their complete confidence, a significant change had taken place in the sentiments of the people at large. They still viewed Hindenburg with superstitious veneration, but Ludendorff had lost a great deal of his popularity and was often spoken of as the man who was senselessly prolonging the war. And as the disruptive forces in Germany became stronger, the Independent Socialists under Karl Liebknecht and Rosa Luxemburg did their best to foment a Communist revolution.

Much Communist peace propaganda was conducted in trains. In the smoked-filled third-class carriages crammed with soldiers going back to the Fatherland on leave, agitators, dressed in field-gray and indistinguishable from their comrades, held long whispered conversations, urging the men not to return to the front. On the troop trains running in the other direction, the soldiers were urged to desert, mutiny, or offer passive resistance. Especially effective was the propaganda against officers. They were said to have better rations, (although in the field they ate from the same field-kitchens as the men), and were accused of hiding in deep dugouts while their men died in the trenches, (although in fact officer casualties were considerably higher than the over-all army average, and by now between 80 per cent and 90 per cent of the old Officer Corps was gone). With more truth, it was said that officers were more frequently given leave.

Ludendorff did his best to counteract these subversive influences. On the 23rd of June he published a hard order that promised death and the seizure of property to all deserters and made it clear that these penalties would never be lightened by any subsequent amnesty.[26] But many men who believed they had little chance of survival at the front felt it was better to chance being arrested by the military police than to participate in further attacks. An increasing number of deserters escaped into Holland to be interned.

The day after the publication of the order on deserters, Kühlmann declared in the Reichstag that Germany could no longer win the war by purely military means. When Ludendorff branded this outright defeatism and demanded his resignation, the Kaiser again gave way. Admiral von Hintze, the military Plenipotentiary at St. Petersburg, who replaced Kühlmann as Foreign Minister, visited Avesnes before he took office and asked Ludendorff directly:

"Are you certain of finally and decisively beating the enemy in the offensive now going on."

And Ludendorff replied: "I can reply to that with a decided *yes.*"

But by now he felt like a man who was slowly suffocating, and was convinced — possibly rightly — that the Allies would never grant Germany a reasonable peace. Although since the opening of the "Michael" offensive, he had suffered terribly from nerves and sleeplessness, he refused to delegate responsibility. According to Admiral von Müller, he fell into a fit of rage on the afternoon of the 30th of June at Spa, and raved incoherently against the Reichstag, the Foreign Office, the Independent Socialists, and the German people themselves. At about this time too, more than one army Chief of Staff was offended by his tendency to blame front-line soldiers and officers for their "failure." [27]

Ludendorff had now made three bulges in the Allies front, two of them of significant size. He would have liked to strike again in Flanders, but felt that the British were too strong there. Instead, he planned a diversionary attack on both sides of Reims for the middle of July, hoping that it would draw British reserves away from Flanders so that he could attack there about a fortnight later.

On the 15th of July the Seventh Army crossed the Marne east of Château Thierry, while the First and Third armies attacked east of Reims. The hazardous crossing of the Marne was accomplished without excessive casualties, thanks largely to Bruchmüller's artillery preparation. But this time the Allies, who had been warned by prisoners of the impending offensive, withdrew to hold firmly along their second line. These tactics were so successful and the French artillery inflicted such heavy losses on the German infantry[28] that at noon on the 16th Ludendorff was forced to order the First and Third Armies to switch to the defensive. However, he pressed the Seventh Army's attack south of the Marne toward the Reims hills, and for a day or two it looked as though Paris might be threatened for the first time since 1914. By the 16th of July Ludendorff was already beginning to ship artillery and aircraft by rail to Flanders, and he himself moved to Tournai the better to supervise his next offensive.

Foch and Pétain, however, had made different plans and had massed French reserves for a counterstroke against the shallow German salient south of the Marne. Ludendorff was at Prince Rupprecht's Army Group Headquarters at Tournai on the 18th when he heard that the French, attacking that morning with a large number of tanks, had penetrated deeply into the German lines near Villers-Cotterêts. Strong but unskilled American forces were also attacking near Château Thierry. Ludendorff at once boarded his special train and returned to Avesnes in "a state of the greatest nervous tension." [29]

Hindenburg was waiting on the station platform when the train pulled in at two o'clock in the afternoon. He reported that the six divisions in the Marne bridgehead, fighting with their backs to the river, were in grave danger. Ludendorff did what he could to reinforce the front, but the situation remained critical. For the first time Hindenburg lost some of his habitual optimism, and that evening wrote his wife that if the war was not won, it would not be his fault but due to Germany's lack of spiritual strength.[30]

For the next three days the French pressed their attacks with diminishing success, but on the evening of the 22nd, after sending von Lossberg to the front to make a personal inspection, Ludendorff decided to withdraw from the Marne Salient. It is a measure of how much fight was still left in the German Army that by the night of 1/2 August the front was successfully stabilized behind the Vesle. Nevertheless, in this one offensive, the Germans had lost 29,000 prisoners and suffered 168,000 casualties. When he had opened the *Kaiserschlacht* on the 21st of March, Ludendorff had had 207 divisions, of which 82 were in reserve. Now his reserve was reduced to 66 divisions, most of them seriously below strength, and ten divisions had to be broken up for reinforcements.

With this second retreat from the Marne the German Army

had launched its last offensive of the war; after the 18th of July the initiative passed forever to Foch. Very probably Ludendorff realized this, at least subconsciously, for his nervousness became much more pronounced. When von Lossberg came to Avesnes for a conference there was "a very painful scene" in which Ludendorff heaped wild and absurd reproaches on Colonel Wetzell and other members of the staff for having "failed" in their estimate of the fighting power of the Seventh Army.[31]

Before long the operations staff at Supreme Headquarters had more serious cause to worry about the stability of the First Quartermaster General. When Colonel Mertz von Quirnheim came in to see him one afternoon, Ludendorff gave him a significant look and said quite abruptly: "I am not superstitious." After a little pause he went on: "Or no. Rather I am. I had no confidence in the 15th of July." Colonel Quirnheim had some difficulty in following this until Ludendorff opened the drawer of his desk and took out his well-worn copy of the Moravian Brethren's prayer-book. Ludendorff read out the text for the 15th of July and shook his head over it gloomily. Then he thumbed through the book and read out the texts for the 21st of March, the 9th of April, the 27th of May, and the 9th of June. Quirnheim was "quite shaken" by this approach to strategy and was not much reassured by Ludendorff's parting words: "Let us hope that we shall not be abandoned by the good God." [32] It is not surprising that on the 29th of July, the Adjutant-General, von Plessen, noted in his war diary at Spa: "Morale at O.H.L. [Supreme Headquarters] very depressed. Especially Ludendorff, who has to be comforted by Hindenburg." [33]

By now the Allied generals had at last learned a trick or two. The attack launched on the early morning of the 8th of August at Amiens took the German Supreme Command completely by surprise. In dense fog Canadian, Australian, British and French troops, supported by 456 tanks, struck between Albert and Moreuil. Von der Marwitz's Second Army, holding the line with six weak divisions which averaged only about 3000 effectives each, had not bothered to do much digging or defensive work, both because labor was short and because they expected to resume the offensive soon.

Telephone reports from the front were slow in reaching Avesnes that day because of numerous breaks in the line,[34] but by mid-morning Ludendorff had a complete and gloomy picture of what had happened at Amiens. The penetration, especially in the Canadian sector, had been both deep and wide. Artillery positions had been overrun, divisional headquarters captured, and a corps staff at Proyart had been shot up by armored cars. Several German divisions had been completely broken in the morning's attack.

Ludendorff sent a staff officer to the battlefield and immediately began to move reserves to the threatened sector. Within 48 hours the situation was stabilized, at least temporarily, but Ludendorff was dismayed to hear that as fresh German divisions had gone into action, the retiring troops had shouted at them: "Blacklegs!," "Strike-breakers!," and "You are prolonging the war!"

The realization of Germany's terrible weakness was at last borne in upon the First Quartermaster General. "August the 8th," he later wrote, "was the black day of the German Army in the history of this war." [35] Germany's allies also regarded the defeat at Amiens as the final writing on the wall. The Emperor Charles ominously announced he was coming to Spa in mid-August for a "conference," and Hindenburg commented: "To fail in an attack was a very different matter from being vanquished on the defense." [36] The Kaiser heard the news of the Allied breakthrough with dignified calm, but said sadly: "We must draw only one conclusion: we are at the limit of our capabilities. The war must be ended." [37]

CHAPTER XVI

DEFEAT

AFTER THE 8th of August Ludendorff's nervous crises were more intense and much more frequent. The operations staff at Avesnes noticed the change, at first with incredulity, then with alarm. They spoke of it among themselves and, deciding it would be useless to appeal to Hindenburg, took action on their own. They arranged for a famous psychiatrist, Dr. Hocheimer, to visit headquarters on some pretext so that he could observe Ludendorff and advise them on what to do. At the end of his visit, Hocheimer told Ludendorff bluntly that he was "overworked" and that his "drive and creative power" had been damaged. Ludendorff did not remonstrate but said with a strange humility that he felt that way himself. Hocheimer prescribed a course of treatment and Ludendorff went on with his work, although he carried out all Hocheimer's medical instructions with typical thoroughness.[1]

But the inner resilience, which had so often brought him out of depression in the past, now failed him. For the few weeks that he remained in the Supreme Command he alternated between panic and irrational optimism. He realized something of this himself and, feeling that a fresh mind might take a better view of the military situation, "earnestly requested" Hindenburg to replace him if he no longer had confidence in him or thought it advisable for other reasons. He also discussed his replacement with the Chief of the Military Cabinet, who — possibly not unwillingly — broached the subject to the Emperor. When the Kaiser refused to retire him, Ludendorff wondered if His Majesty really understood the military situation.[2]

Bethmann-Hollweg had once told Admiral von Müller, the Chief of the Naval Cabinet: "You don't know Ludendorff, who is only great at a time of success. If things go badly, he loses his nerve. I've seen this happen in the Eastern campaign." [3] Now everyone was repeating and embellishing Bethmann's words, and informed gossip in Berlin spoke of the First Quartermaster General as "a completely broken man." [4]

On the 13th and 14th of August, Hindenburg, Ludendorff, Chancellor Hertling, and Foreign Minister von Hintze met in Hindenburg's suite in the Hotel Britannique at Spa. Ludendorff explained that since Germany could no longer force the Entente to sue for peace, the war would have to be ended, but he added that the Western Front would hold. Hindenburg, who began quietly to blossom as Ludendorff faded, took a considerably more optimistic view. The Field Marshal was not troubled with nerves himself and on several occasions in the past he had had to calm Ludendorff's fears. Naturally enough, he prided himself on this. Although his First Quartermaster General might think himself the brains of the combination, Hindenburg was sure who provided the character. Now he declared firmly that "with God's help" everything would still be well.

The next morning the Kaiser arrived at Spa and took the chair at the conference. After Ludendorff had repeated his report, von Hintze, with tears in his eyes, spoke of Germany's exhaustion and despair. Wilhelm, still very calm and dignified, ordered Hintze to open peace negotiations through the Queen of the Netherlands, but Chancellor Hertling protested that no official steps should be taken until the military situation improved, because any immediate appeal would be a confession of weakness. Hindenburg agreed and emphasized that the German Army still occupied much enemy territory. At this point, Ludendorff excitedly broke in to demand that stricter discipline be enforced on the home front and that there be a "more vigorous conscription of the young Jews, hitherto left pretty much alone." [5] With this, his spirits seemed to rise, and when Hintze, who was keeping minutes of the conference, wrote: "Hindenburg hopes, in spite of everything, that he will be able to stay on French soil and thus eventually impose our will on the enemy . . . ," Ludendorff abruptly seized the pen from his hand, struck out the word "hopes," and wrote in "explains that he will be able to . . ." [6]

The Allied governments and their military advisers would have disagreed with Ludendorff's amendment, for they were now beginning to realize that at long last the game was theirs. After the Battle of Amiens, Marshal Foch's strategy was to launch a series of fierce but limited attacks against the German lines. In each case, as resistance stiffened, the attack would be broken off and a fresh one opened elsewhere. This policy of "tapping," which was designed to take advantage of the Allies' growing manpower superiority and their abundance of material, was exactly the same strategy that Ludendorff had chosen for his spring offensive — but with the difference that Foch had the necessary resources to ensure its success. During August and September, as Foch struck, now here, now there, at the weakened German front, Ludendorff watched with deepening horror the approach of the disaster which it had been his life's work to prevent.[7] For the first time he realized that his daily responsibilities were too much for him and delegated some of them to Colonel Wilhelm Heye, who had succeeded Wetzell as Chief of Operations.

When the French Tenth Army attacked between the Oise and the Aisne on the 20th of August, Ludendorff managed to draw back his line before the French broke through, but he had the terrifying feeling that he could no longer depend on his divisions. For more than four years German soldiers had devotedly answered every demand of their commanders. Only now did they falter, and not because courage failed but because hope had gone. Colonel Nicolai, the Chief of Military Intelligence, noted in his diary that the First Quartermaster General seemed to dread his daily verbal reports and he added: "I recognize for the first time that [Ludendorff] seems to have reached the end of his strength." [8] Six days later, when the British First Army, spearheaded by the Canadian Corps, launched an offensive astride the Arras-Cambrai Road, Ludendorff was forced to withdraw his front from the Scarpe to the Vesle. With this retirement, advanced headquarters at Avesnes was no longer necessary, and Hindenburg and Ludendorff returned to Spa "much depressed." [9] A clear indication that Ludendorff considered the war as good as lost was that, when presented with a new and very efficient incendiary bomb which could have been used against Paris and London, he refused to allow its employment. [10] By the end of the first week in September the Germans had relinquished all the ground they had gained since the 21st of March, and Marshal Foch had decided to seek victory in 1918 instead of waiting until the spring of 1919, as he had previously intended.

Critical as was the German position in the West, the Central Powers were more secure there than on other fronts. Turkey was hard pressed as a British army advanced on Damascus, and when a Franco-Serb force under Franchet d'Esperey attacked in Macedonia on the 15th of September, several Bulgarian divisions abandoned their trenches and fled without fighting. Although Ludendorff hastily dispatched reinforcements, General von Scholtz, the German military "adviser" who was actually in command, could not reform the line. When the German reinforcements reached Sofia, they found the city calm but filled with masses of deserters pouring homeward with no other thought than to have done with the war. On the whole, the Bulgarian soldiers were good-humored and well-behaved but quite determined to fight no more. They turned in their arms and equipment at the depots, took leave of their officers and friends, and went their way, some promising to return to the army once they had had time to look after their farms. [11] In the face of this eminently sensible attitude, Tsar Ferdinand abdicated, and on the evening of the 29th of September Bulgaria signed an armistice.

Three days previously the French had attacked west of the

Argonne, and an American army had advanced between the Argonne and the Meuse. The harried First Quartermaster General was given no respite. On the 27th the British launched a new offensive between St. Quentin and Cambrai, and on the 28th the Belgian Army attacked toward Ghent. As the reports came in from the battlefields, they were brought to Ludendorff in his room at the Hotel Britannique by grave-faced orderly officers. In every sector where the enemy had struck, the German front had given way. Each situation report was more despairing than the last, and there were no adequate reserves. The divisions held for this purpose behind the lines were exhausted, pitifully under strength, and far too few, for the great offensives of the spring and early summer had cost Germany more than a million casualties. By the afternoon of the 28th of September, Ludendorff's nerves could stand no more. Suddenly shaken with rage, he lurched to his feet and began to storm and curse against the Reichstag, the Kaiser, the navy and the home front. Those who were with him hastily shut the door and watched appalled while he worked himself up into a frenzy.

At six o'clock that evening, still white and trembling, he went slowly down the stairs to Hindenburg's room one floor below. The Field Marshal and his First Quartermaster General looked at each other for a long moment without speaking, then Ludendorff haltingly began to outline his reasons for demanding an immediate armistice. As Hindenburg listened, his faded old eyes filled with tears, but at the end he nodded in agreement. Then he stood up and took Ludendorff's right hand in both his own. They parted without further words, "like men who have buried their dearest hopes." [12]

This then was the bitter end of Ludendorff's life's work. And it was the more bitter because his work had always absorbed so much of his life. At Plön and Lichterfelde, in the marine infantry, on the staff of formations, at the Red House on the Königsplatz, and most especially during the war, he had seldom relaxed or allowed himself to forget, even momentarily, his self-imposed duty. "He had never seen a flower bloom, never heard a bird sing, never watched the sun set," his doctor once said of him. "I used to treat him for his soul." [13]

He had had a passion for work — and it had brought him more work. Of course, it had brought him power too, terrible power, but he had never cared much for that for its own sake. Possessing none of the consuming personal ambition of an Alexander or a Napoleon, he had labored always in the shadow of another's legend, seeking nothing for himself. Looking back, he saw little with which to reproach himself. All that he had done he had done for what he thought was Germany.

His whole personality had been focused so intently on victory that the final realization of defeat left him without further inner resources. He had no religious faith and was too intelligent to hold in any high esteem what passed for religion in most of his contemporaries. He had entered the world naked in the naked East Elbian plains and had clothed himself with what philosophic rags he found to hand — love of country, pride in accomplishment, force of arms. Other men in his situation were saved from breakdown by stupidity or selfishness, but Ludendorff was not so fortunate.

That evening, he sent Major Erich Freiherr von dem Bussche-Ippenburg to Berlin to inform the leaders of the Reichstag of his decision,[14] and he summoned Foreign Minister von Hintze to meet with him at ten o'clock the next night at the Hotel Britannique. Hindenburg and Colonel Heye also attended this conference. In contrast to the confidence he had displayed only two weeks earlier, Ludendorff now told the Foreign Minister that catastrophe might result if an armistice was not obtained immediately. This was shocking enough, but, as they talked, Hintze slowly began to realize that Ludendorff appeared to regard an armistice as merely a temporary cessation of hostilities which would enable him to resume the war later after a period of rest. Hintze was amazed, both at what seemed to him a sudden worsening of the military situation and at Ludendorff's apparent belief that Germany could obtain an armistice without any intention of making peace. The Foreign Minister had not heard of Ludendorff's fit of uncontrollable rage the previous day, or he might have suspected that the First Quartermaster General had actually suffered brain damage. Hintze tried to explain that "such a sudden shift from fanfares of victory to the dirges of defeat would work upon the Army, the nation, the monarchy, and the Empire," and that ". . . along with the request for an armistice, indeed prior to it, there must exist a readiness for peace." At first Ludendorff would not hear of any permanent peace, but after some argument he finally admitted that peace might actually have to be made. At this point, incredible as it may seem, Hindenburg interrupted in his deep voice to growl that any peace treaty would have to allow for the German annexation of the mining districts of Longwy and Briey.[15]

Hintze, who must have felt that the Supreme Command had taken leave of its senses, did not bother to argue but went on to say that, if revolution was to be averted, Chancellor Hertling must resign and the government be reorganized on a parliamentary basis. Ludendorff at once objected, but Hintze firmly reiterated that it was essential. In reply to a query of Ludendorff's, Hintze admitted that the Kaiser's direction to approach the Queen of the Netherlands had not been obeyed,[16] but suggested that a peace proposal be made to President Wilson. Hindenburg and Ludendorff agreed, stipulating that identical notes be sent to the British and French Governments "for information." At this point the Kaiser joined the discussion. During these dark times Wilhelm showed to better advantage than he had ever done in the boisterous days of peace. He listened calmly to what his Foreign Minister and the Supreme Command had to say and agreed that President Wilson should be asked for an armistice. Hintze promised Ludendorff that the note to Wilson would be dispatched by Tuesday, the 1st of October, at the latest. At Ludendorff's request, Hindenburg accompanied the Kaiser back to Berlin on the evening of the 30th of September.

The next afternoon, Prince Max of Baden, who had been asked to assume the Chancellorship, arrived in the capital. It was a warm, sunny day, typical of the beautiful autumn of 1918, and the leaves were still green on the linden trees, but Prince Max found an atmosphere of despair in Berlin. When Major von dem Bussche briefed him that evening, speaking from notes drawn up by Ludendorff, he learned that German infantry battalions had an average strength of only 450 men and that even this figure had been obtained only by disbanding 22 divisions.

The next morning, when von dem Bussche spoke to the Reichstag party leaders, he said in part: "The German Army is still strong enough to stand against its opponents for months to come, to achieve local successes and to exact new sacrifices from the Entente. But each day brings our opponent nearer his goal, and will make him less inclined to conclude with us a peace which is tolerable. Therefore, no time must be lost. Every twenty-four hours can impair the situation and give our opponent the opportunity of clearly realizing our present weakness." [17]

The Reichstag leaders were appalled by this confession of military bankruptcy. Nothing they had been told in the last few months had prepared them for the disastrous situation they now faced. Many of them had concluded that Germany could not win the war, but they had not realized that when Ludendorff had gambled on his final offensives, he had accepted the stark alternatives of victory or utter defeat. The consistent tactical success of German arms between the 21st of March and mid-July had also misled them. The Reichstag leaders were demoralized by what they had been told, but what was worse, von dem Bussche's speech was immediately released clandestinely to the press by a socialist deputy, and the entire country felt a sense of shock and betrayal at the news. This emotion was thoroughly justified, for Ludendorff's pride and bitterness had led him to act with criminal irresponsibility. The real indictment against the Supreme Command and the extreme nationalists was that they had arrogantly and recklessly exploited the magnificent devotion of the German people and had, from ignorance and vanity, persisted in this course long after all reasonable hope of success had vanished.

Prince Max still demanded some cushion of time in which to negotiate, and at a Crown Council meeting on the 3rd of October he opposed Ludendorff's demand for an immediate armistice. The Kaiser quickly interrupted him with a comment that epitomized the whole tragedy of his reign — "The Supreme Command requests it, and you have not been invited here to make difficulties for the Supreme Command!" [18]

However, Prince Max persisted and begged for "ten, eight, or even four days, before I have to appeal to the enemy." Neither Hindenburg nor Ludendorff would hear of it. Ludendorff, his small mouth nervously pursed and his gray face ravaged, merely kept repeating over and over again: "I want to save my army!" With more dignity, Hindenburg, like a gigantic wooden oracle, rumbled that the gravity of the military situation meant that a peace offer would have to be made at once.

Hindenburg returned to Spa the next day, but Ludendorff remained in Berlin. When he saw Prince Max's note to President Wilson before it was dispatched on the 5th of October, he objected that it "betrayed weakness," but his demand for "a more manly wording" was ignored.[19] Wilson replied on the 8th, stating that the evacuation of occupied territories would be a first condition of an armistice. On the 12th Prince Max accepted Wilson's stipulation. On the 14th, Wilson wrote again, specifying that the U-boat campaign would have to be halted immediately and that the Allies would insist on dealing only with a democratic German Government.

At a meeting of the War Cabinet on the 17th Ludendorff strenuously opposed stopping the submarine campaign, but his words no longer carried their former weight. On the 20th, Prince Max accepted all Wilson's proposals. Now one of Ludendorff's fears found ominous confirmation, for three days later the American President responded to Prince Max by dispatching another note, even stiffer in tone than his previous one. In the days when the United States had still been a neutral, Wilson had spoken movingly of "peace without victory"; but when the United States became a belligerent, the winged goddess had promptly been restored to the American Pantheon. The righteous in their triumph would give no quarter but would insist upon virtually unconditional surrender. If the positions had been reversed, Ludendorff would certainly have done the same, and even more brutally, but now he declared that Germany should continue the war rather than accept humiliating peace terms. The next day he and Hindenburg went to Berlin to inform the Kaiser of their new resolve.

The previous night at Spa, Ludendorff had seen a proclamation signed by Hindenburg and addressed to the army. The proclamation had read:

For the Information of all Troops:

Wilson says in his answer that he is ready to propose to his allies that they should enter into armistice negotiations but that the armistice must render Germany so defenseless that she cannot take up arms again. He will only negotiate with Germany for peace if she concedes all the demands of the allies as to the internal constitutional arrangements of Germany; otherwise, there is no choice but unconditional surrender.

Wilson's answer is a demand for unconditional surrender. It is thus unacceptable to us soldiers. It proves that our enemy's desire for our destruction, which let loose the war in 1914, still exists undiminished. It proves, further, that our enemies use the phrase 'Peace of Justice' merely to deceive us and break our resistance. Wilson's answer can thus be nothing for us soldiers but a challenge to continue our resistance with all our strength. When our enemies know that no sacrifices will achieve the rupture of the German front, they will be ready for a peace which will make the future of our country safe for the great masses of our people.

In the Field, 24th October 10 p.m.

(Signed) VON HINDENBURG.[20]

This proclamation so exactly expressed Ludendorff's own opinions that there must always be a strong suspicion he wrote it himself. However, according to his own implausible account, before he countersigned the document, he asked the staff officer who had drafted it if it really represented the view of the Government and was assured that it did.[21]

Later that night Colonel Heye saw the proclamation and at once ordered that it be withdrawn. Unfortunately, far away in Kovno, an Independent Socialist telephone operator, on night duty at *Ober-Ost,* had taken it down word for word as it came over the line. The generals, he concluded, were up to their old tricks. If they had their way, the war would go on forever. In the early morning hours he put a call through the military switchboard to Berlin and told a representative of the Independent Socialist Party the whole story. By noon the proclamation was published in Berlin where it caused a great storm of protest in the Reichstag.

That evening Ludendorff was at the Ministry of the Interior talking to Vice-Chancellor von Payer. He got no satisfaction from the conversation, for by now no one but he and perhaps Hindenburg believed at all in the possibility of carrying on the war. At last he left and went downstairs to where General von Winterfeldt and Colonel von Haeften were waiting for him in the foyer. The First Quartermaster General looked like an old man as he walked heavily up to them. All he could say was: "There is no hope. Germany is lost." [22]

After a sleepless night, Ludendorff was back in the Red House on the Königsplatz early on the morning of the 26th of October. The specters and ghosts crowding in on his mind allowed him no rest. He sat down in the familiar office and wrote out his resignation for the last time. He had proffered it often enough before, although never with the intention that it should be accepted. Even now, perhaps, he hoped it would not be necessary to push matters that far. Hindenburg came in at nine o'clock, saw the letter lying on the desk, recognized it for what it was, and begged him not to send it. Ludendorff agreed. A little later, Colonel von Haeften arrived with the news that the previous evening Prince Max of Baden had persuaded the Kaiser to dismiss Ludendorff because of the proclamation he had countersigned. At eleven o'clock the Kaiser's adjutant telephoned to say that His Majesty wished to see Hindenburg and Ludendorff at Bellevue Castle.

The Kaiser received his two generals with cold formality but reserved his remarks for Ludendorff, upbraiding him bitterly for issuing a proclamation in direct conflict with the policy of the Government. Of those present that morning only Ludendorff has left us a verbatim account of the interview, and this, although certainly true in the main, is unreliable in detail. At all events, according to his own story, Ludendorff listened in silence until Wilhelm had finished, then said with dignity: "To my great regret I am compelled by Your Majesty's reproaches to recognize that I no longer possess the confidence of Your Majesty and that my labors at the front no longer find favor in Your Majesty's eyes. May I, with great submission, ask for my recall."

The Kaiser stood a moment in thoughtful silence, then said: "I thank you for your resignation. You are thereby rendering my position very much easier. I shall endeavor, with the aid of the Socialists, to build up a new Empire for myself." [23]

Ludendorff clicked his heels, saluted and took his leave. Rather haltingly, Hindenburg suggested that the Kaiser might like his resignation as well, but Prince Max had specifically requested that Hindenburg be retained because of his value as a symbol to the German people,[24] so the Kaiser brusquely vetoed the Field Marshal's request. Then Hindenburg also left.

Outside the palace, Hindenburg came up to his First Quartermaster General and suggested that they drive together to the Red House. Ludendorff turned and fixed him with a cold and hostile stare.

"I refuse to drive with you," he said.

Hindenburg asked why, and Ludendorff replied: "I refuse to

have any more dealings with you because you treat me so shabbily."

When Hindenburg protested that he could not leave without handing over his work to someone else, Ludendorff curtly suggested that General Kuhl could have the post, then he turned his back on the old man and climbed into his own staff car.[25]

Margarethe Ludendorff was standing at the window of her pension in West Berlin when her husband's car drew up. She was surprised to see him home so early. He came into the flat, looking as pale as death, and sank heavily into his usual chair. After sitting awhile in silence, he said tonelessly: "The Kaiser has sacked me. I have been dismissed." Margarethe tried to get him to talk about his troubles, but for a long time he only sat slumped in his chair, staring silently ahead of him. At last he jumped up abruptly and said: "In a fortnight we shall have no Empire and no Emperor left, you will see." [26]

That evening Ludendorff returned to G.H.Q. in his special train for the last time. The next day he packed his personal belongings, said his goodbyes to his staff and returned to Berlin. He was never stoned by the mob, as he had once predicted would happen, but that night when the news of his resignation was flashed as a special bulletin on the cinema screens in the capital, the audiences burst into applause.

On the 27th of October, the German Government replied to President Wilson's note, accepting all its conditions, but by now the German Empire was already in the process of dissolution. Prince Max, who had come down with influenza and been given a massive dosage of sleeping drops, lay in a coma between the 30th of October and the 3rd of November. When he returned to the Chancellery on the evening of the 3rd, he learned that mutinies had broken out in the German Navy, that Turkey had capitulated, and that the Austrian Government had signed an armistice that morning. The Kaiser had gone to Spa "to be with the army," but events now moved too rapidly for any of the old order to be saved. On the 5th of November, the red flag was hoisted over Lübeck and Hamburg and the Communists were on the verge of seizing power in Bavaria and the Ruhr. The next evening an armistice commission left Berlin for France. Since none of the right-wing politicians would assume any responsibility for the chaos they had helped bring about, the armistice commission was headed by Matthias Erzberger. Hindenburg had begged him to accept the task for the sake of the Fatherland and had clasped his right hand in both his own when Erzberger agreed, a gesture that by now had something almost ominous about it. One of the military members of the commission was Colonel Brinckmann, who more than four years previously had been with Ludendorff at Liège. On the 9th Prince Max resigned, turning over the control of affairs to a Provisional Government headed by the Majority Socialist, Friedrich Ebert; and on the same day, in a desperate attempt to forestall a revolution by a revolutionary gesture, the Socialist deputy Scheidemann, on his own initiative, proclaimed the Republic from a window of the Reichstag.

At Spa, General Gröner, Ludendorff's old rival of General Staff days, had dutifully taken over the appointment of First Quartermaster General. Because he was a South German and a convinced democrat, Gröner had frequently been given unpleasant tasks and he had always done them efficiently, loyally, and well. Now Hindenburg, who should have done it himself, left it to Gröner to inform the Kaiser that he would have to abdicate. When Wilhelm, with some of his old bluster, began to speak of the army's oath of loyalty to the Emperor, Gröner shook his head and said simply: *"Der Fahneneid ist jetzt nur eine Idee"* ("The oath of loyalty is now only a fiction"). In the early morning of the 10th of November the Kaiser, who had reluctantly signed his abdication the day before, crossed the frontier into Holland in his royal train. When "that damned Jew," Albert Ballin, heard of Wilhelm's abdication, he killed himself with an overdose of veronal.[27]

At five o'clock in the morning of the 11th of November Erz-

berger performed the last significant act of the war by signing
the Allies' armistice terms. Everything about the occasion — as
about any occasion so fearfully charged with emotions —seems
in retrospect to possess an incoherent symbolism of its own. A
cold, misty rain was falling and withered brown leaves drifted
sadly down from the tall beech and silver birch trees of the
Forest of Compiègne as the German delegation walked slowly
from their special train to Marshal Foch's private coach on another siding two hundred yards away. In many ways it had been
a railway war, and it was fitting that it should be brought to an
end in a railway compartment. It was fitting, too, that it should
end on the eleventh hour of the eleventh day of the eleventh
month of the year — although those who interpreted this to
mean that at the last moment Europe was being given one final
second-chance were to be disappointed.[28]

Back in his flat in West Berlin, Ludendorff sat day after day at
his writing desk without moving or speaking. Again and again
Margarethe attempted to get some response from him, but without success. The former First Quartermaster General sat there
as though he had been turned to stone.

CHAPTER XVII

NEW FRIENDS

ALL THAT November and December Germany was in chaos. Soldiers' and Workers' Councils sprang up overnight, and miniature Soviet Republics were proclaimed in Munich, Cologne, Frankfurt, Stuttgart, and Leipzig. When Karl Liebknecht and Rosa Luxemburg incited their followers to riot in the streets of Berlin, the Government had no means of protecting itself, for the old army dissolved as the returning troops reached the vicinity of their homes, and the new 100,000-man Reichswehr, which was all the armed force the Allies would allow Germany to possess, had not yet been formed. However, the news of spreading revolution and disaster did more than all Margarethe's solicitude to restore Ludendorff's interest in life. His scowl grew darker, but at least he left his writing desk and began to talk to people again.[1]

Ten million soldiers of all nations had been killed in the war and more than twice that number wounded. Civilian casualties, although certainly terribly heavy, could only be guessed at. Europe had supp'd full of horrors: her cities had been burned; her peoples starved, rendered homeless, and decimated by epidemics; her empires had been overthrown and her social structure overturned. It was not a time for moderation. Thoughtful men were not quite sure why all this had happened, but in all countries the less thoughtful were ready with their answers. The victors blamed the vanquished, and the vanquished, with more justification, blamed their own leaders. The Allies demanded the trial of German "war criminals" and proclaimed their intention of hanging the Kaiser and punishing Hindenburg, Ludendorff

and other prominent German soldiers. The common people of
the democracies supported such measures, for they knew nothing of the causes of the war and for more than four years had
been told repeatedly and with horrifying detail that their enemies
were fiends in human form. After the Armistice, irresponsible
newspapers and opportunistic politicians continued to pander to
the popular lust for revenge. The Dutch Government stoutly refused to extradite the Kaiser from his refuge in Holland, which
ultimately saved the Allies much embarrassment, and, as tempers cooled, only half-hearted attempts were made to indict German generals and politicians. But in Germany the Spartacists
and other left-wing extremists, whose tempers never cooled, still
clamored for Ludendorff's arrest.

His friends — already quite a different group of people from a
year ago — urged him to flee the country, and when he began to
imagine that suspicious-looking characters were loitering around
the street outside his flat, he agreed to take their advice. Margarethe disapproved of his decision, feeling that it was unworthy of him, but she was already beginning to disapprove
of many things her husband said and did, and she held her
peace.[2]

One dark November night, Ludendorff, disguised in a false
beard and a pair of blue spectacles, slunk out of Berlin and
made his way to Potsdam. He stayed there a few days with his
brother, a well-known astronomer, then on the 16th of November went on to Denmark.[3] In spite of his disguise, he was recognized on the steamer and when he landed at Copenhagen a
curious crowd was waiting to stare at him. Rightly or wrongly,
he felt that he was being followed everywhere he went in the
Danish capital, so he fled again, this time to take up residence
with a kindly stranger, a Germanophile Swede named Herr Dol-
son, who lived in a country house near Hesleholmgard outside
Stockholm.

Ludendorff's letters to his wife from Sweden betrayed deep
pessimism and anguished nerves:

My heart was torn at leaving you and having to leave you alone, and what made me saddest of all was the memory of my harsh words to you shortly before I left.

. . . To me it all seems like a bad dream. I do not know if I was right to go away. Things cannot go on like this forever. I say "forever," though the whole thing has only just begun.

. . . For four years I have fought for my country and now when so much is hanging in the balance I must stand aside. I am at war with myself and the whole world. Dearest, it isn't easy to pull myself together again.

. . . My nerves are too much on edge and sometimes my speech gets out of control. There is no help for it, my nerves have simply gone to pieces!

. . . Tell everybody how like my fate was to that of Hannibal. That will teach them to understand. Keep these letters, dearest, in time they will form my memoirs.[4]

Margarethe, meanwhile, was having trouble in Berlin. The Communists loudly urged that she be seized as a hostage to force the return of her husband, and after several hostile demonstrations outside her boarding-house, the other inmates of the pension demanded her expulsion for the common good. What made this the more bitter was that the persons seeking to be rid of her were mostly ex-officers' wives, who had been only too glad to claim her acquaintance when her husband had been First Quartermaster General. After the capture of Liège in 1914, they had brought her flowers and congratulations, but now they avoided her in the hall and complained that her presence endangered them all. Reluctantly the landlady gave way and turned Margarethe out into the street. On the 22nd of December, escorted by the former German naval attaché at Copenhagen, she set out to join her husband in Sweden. She arrived just before Christmas, driving in a sleigh the last few miles from the station over crisp, clean snow under a sky set with large crystal stars. Ludendorff greeted her eagerly, but she was shocked to see how even the few weeks of their separation had left their ravages on his face.[5]

The change in his appearance, in fact, was downright alarming. The thought lines seemed to have been smoothed away, and his former arrogance, although still retained as if by a conscious effort, was now pathetically touched with uncertainty. For the rest of his life Ludendorff's most typical expression was to be one of imperfectly concealed puzzlement.

Their Swedish hosts were very kind, but immediately after the gay family dinner on Christmas Day, Margarethe and her husband slipped quietly away to sit in their own room in silence, thinking their own thoughts. By now Ludendorff had begun work on his memoirs, and while he was organizing his thoughts, he would walk for hours in the spacious park of the estate, talking to himself continually. Margarethe stood it as long as she could, then announced that she was returning to Germany. She still had a married daughter and son there and was irked unbearably by the contrast between her comfortable life at Hesleholmgard and the privations her children must be suffering. Ludendorff was reluctant to let her go, but was much preoccupied with his autobiography and with his search for an acceptable explanation of Germany's defeat in the war. After an uncomfortable journey, Margarethe reached Berlin, so ill that she had to be admitted to a hospital. It was a considerable time before the tender care of the Franciscan nuns restored her to some semblance of health.[6]

Conditions had not improved in the Reich. Strikes, riots, and street-fighting were still almost daily occurrences in the capital and many other cities. By now, however, the supporters of the old regime had rallied, and, in defiance of the terms of the armistice, had formed their own volunteer defense organizations, the *Freikorps,* to combat the Communists and keep the workers in their place. *Freikorps* sprang up all over Germany, from the Polish Marches to the Austrian border, and by spring more than 400,000 men had been enrolled in some 200 para-military organizations. The members of the *Freikorps* were a mixed lot — idealists prepared to fight for the future of Germany; tough front-line veterans who knew no other trade but soldiering; aristocrats ruined by the war; and mere adventurers looking for excitement and three meals a day. Margarethe's son, Heinz Pernet, joined the Guards Cavalry *Freikorps,* the same organization that in January had been responsible for the murder of Karl Liebknecht and Rosa Luxemburg at the Eden Hotel. After the Communists had been suppressed in Berlin, Heinz went on to fight in Westphalia and Munich.

In Sweden the Social Democrats, inspired by working-class solidarity, demanded Ludendorff's expulsion. He was offered sanctuary in Finland, but by now the *Freikorps* were well on the way to "restoring order" in the Fatherland, and he felt it safe to return to Germany at the end of February 1919.[7] With the suppression of revolutionary elements in Germany, the nationalists, Junkers, great industrialists, and members of the Officer Corps quickly regained their former truculence and although there was still much public criticism of Ludendorff's conduct of the war, the reactionaries closed ranks to defend the Supreme Command. Officers who had recorded details of Ludendorff's nervous breakdown in their diaries now blankly denied that any such thing had occurred.[8] One result of this was that Ludendorff was never allowed to suffer the financial difficulties that beset so many ex-officers. Hoffmann was living with his wife and daughter in straitened circumstances in Berlin, eking out an inadequate pension with his small private means,[9] but as soon as Ludendorff returned to Berlin he and Margarethe were given a luxurious suite in the Adlon Hotel, the same building where the Allied Disarmament Commission had its headquarters. To avoid publicity he called himself "Karl Neumann," [10] and the hotel proprietor, Herr Adlon, thoughtfully provided him with a separate exit to the Wilhelmstrasse so that he would not be embarrassed by meeting Allied officers in uniform.

As a matter of fact, Ludendorff had no objection to exchanging reminiscences with senior officers who had recently been his enemies. And although the French military representatives were scrupulous never to address a single unnecessary word to a German officer, some British generals were curious to meet the man who had so long been their principal opponent.[11] One day when General Sir Neill Malcolm, the head of the British Military Mission, was visiting Ludendorff, he was surprised to be told that the German Army would never have lost the war if it had not been for the vacillation and weakness of the German Government and people. They had, Ludendorff said, proved themselves unworthy of their warrior ancestors. Ludendorff was none too coherent, and General Malcolm, in an attempt to pin down his argument, asked: "Are you trying to tell me, general, that you were stabbed in the back?" Ludendorff's prominent blue eyes lit up at the phrase. "That's it!" he shouted triumphantly. "They stabbed me in the back! They stabbed me in the back!" This casual catch-word was later to become notorious as Nazi propaganda.

By now Ludendorff was already well on the way to rationalizing the past. Like millions of other Germans, he found it impossible, after so many victories, to attribute defeat to natural military causes. He had not yet determined to his own satisfaction where the blame lay, but he reproached himself in only one particular. "I ought never to have let myself been dismissed," he used to say. "It would have been better if, while the war was still in progress, I had snatched the dictatorship for myself."[12]

Now that he was back in Germany where the *Freikorps* were loudly asserting their continued belief in the old order, he began to feel that Germany's former greatness might be restored: "The greatest blunder of the revolutionaries was to leave us all alive," he repeatedly declared. "If I once get back to power, there will be no quarter. I should hang up Ebert, Scheidemann, and their comrades with a clear conscience and watch them dangle!"[13]

The Adlon Hotel was too prominent a location for the sort of work he now had in mind, so when some friends offered to lend him a beautifully furnished flat in the Victoriastrasse with a view of the Tiergarten, he accepted. In the next few months,

Margarethe found her drawing-room invaded by a strange assort-
ment of men. Reichswehr generals like the dapper little von
Lüttwitz, commandant of the Berlin Garrison, and retired
civil servants like Dr. Wolfgang Kapp rubbed shoulders with
Captain Waldemar Pabst, a *Freikorps* tough, and with criminal
adventurers like Trebitsch Lincoln, a Hungarian Jew who had
been one of Colonel Nicolai's spies in England and America during the war. Colonel Max Bauer, whom Ludendorff had often
used for disreputable semi-political missions, was also a frequent
visitor. Margarethe could not help being aware that something
was being plotted, and, of course, that something could only be
the overthrow of the Republic, but since his return from Sweden,
Ludendorff no longer confided in his wife. She was hurt by this
but made no objection until she began to notice that women as
well as men were now having long private conferences with him.
Some women remained closeted with the general for hours behind his locked study door. When Margarethe protested, Ludendorff told her that it was all for her own protection. If she
knew nothing of any conspiracy, she could be summoned before
any court in the land and swear with a clear conscience that she
had taken no part in political intrigue. Margarethe was convinced and a little touched by this evidence of thoughtfulness,
which seemed to her "both chivalrous and devoted." [14]

In June 1919, in the Hall of Mirrors at Versailles, the German
delegation reluctantly signed the Peace Treaty. It was a hard
treaty and in some ways an unjust one, as treaties drawn up in
anger are apt to be. Certainly, it was unwise. Germany was
forced to admit her "war guilt" and formally accept sole responsibility for all the ancient prides and sins of Europe that had
in fact caused the war. To guarantee this enforced contrition,
she was to disarm almost completely and abolish forever the
German General Staff, and she was to pay huge but unspecified
indemnities. The German Government had had no choice but to
sign, and the right-wing nationalists knew it, but this did not prevent them from scurrilously attacking Erzberger as a "traitor"

and the members of the government as "the November criminals."

One of the disarmament clauses of the treaty called for the abolition of all military academies, and on the 10th of March 1920, Lichterfelde, the great cadet school which was the nursery of the German officer corps, was forced to close. That night the last class of Lichterfelde cadets, resplendent in their blue tunics and gold-mounted *Pickelhauben,* marched through the streets of Berlin to the stirring strains of *Fredericus Rex.* At the Potsdamerplatz a German general on a gray horse took the salute, and at the final parade on the great square at Lichterfelde, Ludendorff and Hoffmann were both present. As befitted such distinguished alumni on so tragic an occasion, they were coolly polite to one another, and in their speeches to the disbanding cadets both hinted that the great days of Lichterfelde's glory were only temporarily suspended.[15]

Although Hoffmann and Ludendorff both wished for the rehabilitation of Germany, they had very different ideas of how it was to be brought about. With Ludendorff's moral support, Captain Pabst formed a political organization called the *Nationale Vereinigung,* or Bureau of National Union, to co-ordinate the anti-Republican forces. He rented offices in the Schellingstrasse where he, Bauer, Trebitsch Lincoln, and a journalist by the name of Handke, who amazingly preferred to call himself "Dr. Schnitzler," began to draw up plans for a military seizure of power. Ludendorff was undoubtedly kept informed of this plot, but since he was somewhat erratic now and given to brooding on the dark forces that had encompassed Germany's defeat, the staff work of the *coup d'état* was left to others.

And a very queer crew they were. Apart from Ludendorff himself, General von Lüttwitz and the portly Dr. Kapp, scarcely one of them was any longer received in respectable society. Dr. Gottfried Traub, a Lutheran pastor who had formerly been court chaplain to the Kaiser, gave the conspirators his spiritual counsel, and Count Kuno Westarp, a former member of the Reichstag, tendered political advice. Margarethe was appalled at the company her husband was keeping, and for the first time the better class of people in Berlin began seriously to wonder whether Ludendorff might not actually be medically insane. But if in the spring of 1920, Ludendorff was a little unbalanced on the subject of German nationalism, he was not the only German who suffered from the same affliction, and he was still sufficiently plausible to persuade Hugo Stinnes, the financier, to donate a considerable sum of money to the Bureau for National Union.[16]

Matters came to a climax when the Defense Minister, Gustav Noske, under pressure from the Allied Control Commission, ordered the disbandment of Lieutenant Commander Hermann Ehrhardt's *Freikorps* which had fought the Communists in Brunswick, Dresden, and Munich and was now stationed at Döberitz Camp, 25 kilometers outside Berlin. Instead of disbanding Ehrhardt's brigade, General von Lüttwitz ordered it to march into the capital on the evening of the 12th of March. Lüttwitz intended to arrest the Majority Socialist leaders in their beds, declare martial law and form a new government headed by Dr. Wolfgang Kapp.

When Noske was belatedly warned of what was happening, he called an emergency meeting of senior Reichswehr officers, only to find that these gentlemen had no intention of supporting the Republic. While Noske outlined the seriousness of the situation, General von Seeckt, now the Reichswehr Chief of Staff, sat in shadow in a corner of the room, gazing coldly at him through his monocle. When Noske had finished speaking, Seeckt said in his soft voice: "Troops do not fire on troops. Do you perhaps intend, Herr Minister, that a battle take place before the Brandenburger Tor between soldiers who have fought side by side against the common enemy? When Reichswehr fires on Reichswehr, then all comradeship within the Officer Corps has vanished."

Seeckt rose to his feet, immaculate and supercilious in his field-gray uniform. He permitted himself a chilly smile when Noske declared that he would call a general strike.

"Then I'll mobilize the police!" Noske declared.

Again a grim little smile flitted across von Seeckt's face as he replied that unfortunately he would have to disappoint the Minister here too, since the police were already on the side of the rebels. He bowed stiffly and left the room followed by the other officers.

That night Ehrhardt's 5000 tough *Freikorps* fighters swung along the road from Döberitz, singing full-throatedly. They marched through a landscape that was silvered by a large full moon and their steel-tipped jack-boots rang smartly on the cobbles. They wore full battle order, and, in every particular but one, looked like a brigade of the old army — but one detail had been added, something that the Kaiser's army had never known. On the front of each man's steel helmet a black swastika was painted boldly on a white ground. This was the special insignia of Ehrhardt's *Freikorps*. Soon it would be adopted by Hitler's Nazi Party and become the most shameful symbol in history.

The marching column halted at the Pickelsdorfer Bridge where field kitchens served the men with steaming mugs of coffee. After the moon had set, they took the road again through the cool spring night, entering Berlin just as dawn was breaking. Ehrhardt halted them in the Tiergarten and broke them off to wait until seven o'clock. As they lay about on the grass under the large trees which were just breaking into pale green leaf, they smoked and talked together. Suddenly an excited whisper ran from group to group. Their voices stilled and they craned their necks to watch a familiar heavy figure walking across the park from the direction of the Victoriastrasse.

Ludendorff explained afterwards that he had merely "been out for a stroll" when he saw the brigade in the Tiergarten and innocently wandered over to investigate. This may even have been true, for the staff work of the attempted *coup d'état* was incredibly bad. Certainly, Dr. Kapp, who was to head the new government, had learned only accidentally and at the last minute that the Ehrhardt brigade was in the capital. While Ludendorff, Lüttwitz and Ehrhardt were talking, Kapp hurried up, correctly dressed in morning coat, striped trousers, top hat and spats.

Sharp at seven o'clock orders rang out and the troops formed up and turned into column of route. At their head marched Ludendorff, Lüttwitz and Kapp behind the old Imperial colors of black, white and red. A brass band played *Deutschland über Alles* as the *Freikorps* goose-stepped through the great arch of the Brandenburger Tor, up the Unter den Linden and on to the Wilhelmstrasse. When the rebels reached the Reich Chancellery, they found it deserted. The Republican Ministers had already fled to Dresden, leaving only the Vice-Chancellor, Dr. Eugen Schiffer, to stay behind as the representative of the legal government.

The *Freikorps* had captured the capital without a shot being fired, but it soon became obvious that they had no idea what to do next. The civil servants had all stayed away from work on this Saturday and there were surprisingly few officers to be found in the Ministry of Defense in the Bendlerstrasse. When Ludendorff turned up there in the course of the morning, he met Colonel Heye, who was now Seeckt's principal staff officer.

"Well, Heye," Ludendorff demanded, "what do you think of our affair?"

Heye had always been noted for his political sense, as he had shown when he had tried to suppress Ludendorff's rebellious proclamation to the army in October 1918, and he had no faith at all in Lüttwitz's *coup d'état*. Now he answered noncommittally that he did not know what was going on, adding: "But if you intend to make a *Putsch* against the Government, it seems strange to me that the Government you want to remove hasn't been arrested yet."

Ludendorff smiled jovially and called across the hallway to a room where Bauer and Lüttwitz were conferring: "Bauer, Heye here is of the opinion that we ought to arrest the Government."

Colonel Heye could not hear Bauer's muffled reply and Ludendorff was in a hurry to get away. He shook Heye's hand warmly as he dashed off, calling back over his shoulder: "We shall finish the job!"

Far from finishing the job, no one was doing anything to begin it. The rebels published a proclamation which truthfully announced: "We shall not govern according to any theory." [17] In fact, they were unable to govern at all. Kapp found that he could not form a Cabinet, since almost every prominent man he approached refused to have anything to do with the rebellion. Worse still, there was no money with which to pay the *Freikorps-kämpfer,* and when Kapp suggested that Ehrhardt march to the State Bank with some of his troopers and demand money in the name of the counter-revolution, the former lieutenant commander drew himself up in shocked indignation.

"Certainly not!" he exclaimed. "I'm no bank robber!"

The following night, in obedience to a proclamation signed by Ebert and Noske from their final place of refuge in Stuttgart, the trade unions declared a general strike. In an amazingly short time Berlin became like a city of the dead. The electric light was cut off, the trams and underground trains ceased to run, water ceased to flow from the taps, garbage rotted on the streets, and every place of business was deserted. The next morning in the Potsdamerplatz, when a crowd of civilians began to hoot and jostle some of Ehrhardt's men, the *Freikorpskämpfer* opened fire, killing and wounding several civilians. Later in the day, fighting broke out in the Moabit quarter and reports began to come in that serious disturbances were occurring in Frankfurt and throughout the Ruhr. That evening, Reichswehr commanders in Munich, Dresden and Munster announced their allegiance to the republican Government.

On Tuesday, Captain Pabst was sent to the Ministry of Justice to try to obtain terms from the Vice-Chancellor, but Dr. Schiffer refused to bargain with the rebels. That evening a Reichswehr battalion in Berlin mutinied, arrested its officers and declared for the Republic. This was all too reminiscent of the Soldiers' Councils of 1918, and the alarmed senior officers of the Reichswehr decided then and there that the *coup* had better be called off.

On Tuesday night, Ludendorff, Bauer, Ehrhardt, and Pabst

met in the Reichschancellery and quarreled bitterly among themselves. Bauer and Ehrhardt were inclined to blame von Lüttwitz for the failure of the *coup,* for the general had steadfastly refused their demands to allow the *Freikorps* to shoot
strike-pickets.[18] One of Ehrhardt's lieutenants later expressed
the rebels' point of view succinctly — "Everything would still
have been all right if only we had shot more people." [19] Great
tears rolled down Colonel Bauer's cheeks as he pleaded with Ludendorff to take over the leadership of the *coup.*[20] But although
Ludendorff had lost most of his former intelligence, he still retained sufficient caution to reject Bauer's suggestion. At last it
was decided that Bauer should go to General von Seeckt and offer
him the military dictatorship. When Bauer arrived at von
Seeckt's suburban villa, the general received him standing, glared
at him icily through his monocle, told him he was a fool, and
sent him packing. The inconclusive meeting in the Reichschancellery bickered on until daylight, when the rebels heard that the
Berlin Security Police were demanding Kapp's resignation, that a
Reichswehr unit in the Köpenickerstrasse had mutinied, and
that outbreaks of street fighting were occurring all over Berlin.

On Wednesday afternoon in the Wilhelmstrasse, Dr. Kapp
signed a proclamation which stated that, having completed all
his aims, he was resigning in favor of General von Lüttwitz.
Then he hurried down the great interior staircase, past the two
recumbent stone Sphinxes in the rotunda, and out into the
March sunshine. A soft hat was pulled low over his eyes and his
overcoat collar was turned up. Behind him a porter struggled
down the stairs, carrying his personal effects in a bedsheet tied
together at the corners. Kapp and his daughter were bundled
into a waiting taxi-cab and driven to Tempelhof Airport where
an airplane took them to Sweden.

Even after Kapp had gone, Ludendorff, Lüttwitz, Bauer,
and Ehrhardt were determined to carry on. Late that afternoon
they met in the Bendlerstrasse to plan their next move. Here
they were interrupted by Colonel Heye, who, as Seeckt's repre-

sentative, informed them that although the Reichswehr understood the motives that had prompted them to action, they must now abandon their plan in order to avoid civil war. At six o'clock that evening, Lüttwitz handed in his resignation to Dr. Schiffer in the Ministry of Justice. The *coup* was officially over, less than five days after it had begun.

One ugly little scene remained to be played out. The men of Ehrhardt's *Freikorps* fell in on the Wilhelmstrasse in bitter silence. No band played on this retreat and the storm-troopers had no heart for song as they moved off toward Charlottenburg. Their anger was directed against the German people, that generation which had shown itself "unworthy of its warrior ancestors," which had stabbed the front-line fighters in the back in 1918, and which now had refused to support their *coup d'état*. Sullen crowds along both sides of Unter den Linden gazed disapprovingly at them as they marched by. Suddenly a boy's spontaneous laughter broke the tense hush. Two of Ehrhardt's *Freikorpskämpfer* immediately broke ranks and knocked him down with the butts of their rifles, then kicked his small figure with their heavy jackboots until he lay still. Although the spectators were too frightened to do anything but hiss their disapproval, even this was more than one of Ehrhardt's officers could bear. He shouted an angry command: the storm-troopers halted and opened fire with rifles and machine-guns. In a few moments the civilians had vanished from Unter den Linden as if by magic, except for the dead and the dying who lay in little heaps on the street. The order to cease fire was given, and the *Freikorps* formed up again and moved off through the Brandenburger Tor. This time they sang on the march.[21]

While Ehrhardt's brigade was moving out of Berlin, the leaders of the conspiracy were going their separate ways. Ludendorff put on his blue spectacles again and fled incontinently to Bavaria where he sought refuge with Baron von Halkett in Stefanskirchen near Rosenheim.[22] Before he left, he shook his former Chief of Operations by the hand and declared: "Bauer, we are the richer for a bitter experience." [23] General von Lütt-witz and Colonel Bauer fled to Hungary, Captain Pabst went to Austria, and Pastor Traub and Dr. Schnitzler also escaped un-molested. Many of the less important rebels made their way to Munich where the writ of the Reich Government could scarcely be said to run.[24]

Margarethe Ludendorff was not left alone for long in her flat in the Victoriastrasse. Within a day or two she began to be plagued by the former employees of the Bureau of National Union whose salaries had not been paid and who looked to her for redress.[25] Since she had very little money herself, she was unable to help them.

Disgruntled secretaries were not her only visitors. A few days after her husband had slunk away to Bavaria, Margarethe was visited by a lady dressed in deep mourning. The visitor was visi-bly distressed to hear of Ludendorff's departure and, inform-ing Margarethe that she had important secret correspondence for the general, begged to be told his whereabouts. This Mar-garethe declined to do, but she did promise to forward any mail the lady might bring her. Her offer was accepted and for several weeks she scrupulously received the lady's bulky letters, placed each one within a second envelope and readdressed it to Bavaria under her husband's pseudonym. Only much later did she learn that this correspondence was in no way concerned with politics, but consisted of passionate love letters which the lady in black was sending to Ludendorff.[26]

Ernst Pöhner, the chief of police, invited the Ehrhardt Bri-gade to Munich, where its commander was made Chief of the Emergency Police and the *Freikorpskämpfer* were given jobs as agricultural laborers on the great estates about the city.[27] The next spring Ehrhardt formed a murder society, known as "Organization Consul," which proceeded to assassi-nate anyone the lieutenant commander considered an enemy of the German people. Within the next two years the *Feme* com-mitted at least 354 political murders,[28] operating with the approval and assistance of the Bavarian police under Pöhner.[29] The victims of Organization Consul were republican politicians, Germans who betrayed secret arms caches to the Allied Control Commission, or merely rival members of the innumerable patriotic societies, ex-servicemen's associations and defense leagues that infested Bavaria.

Matthias Erzberger, now Reichminister of Finance, was the first prominent politician to fall to Ehrhardt's gunmen. On the rainy afternoon of the 26th of August 1921, while he was walking in the Black Forest near Griesbach, he was suddenly challenged by two of Ehrhardt's thugs who asked him to identify himself and then fired twelve pistol bullets into his head. They left him lying there on the wet, coarse grass, and not even a Hungarian countess would any longer have considered that he looked like an ornamental beer-cork. The following June, Walther Rathenau, the German Foreign Minister, who favored fulfilling the armistice terms, was driving along the Königsallee in Berlin when three members of Organization Consul pulled alongside him in another car, emptied a pistol into his body and finished him off with a hand grenade.

These were the people around Ludendorff now and he was, in spirit at least, one of them. He moved to the little village of Ludwigshöhe, outside Munich, where he lived in a villa surrounded by high walls, guarded night and day by Ehrhardt's *Freikorpskämpfer*. Margarethe rejoined him there, and for the last time what was left of the family were reunited. Margot, her husband, a former naval officer, their young boy, and Margarethe's son, Heinz, all lived an uneasy life in the shadow of incessant conspiracy.

CHAPTER XVIII

WHIRLWIND HARVEST

ONE EVENING in the late spring of 1923, a big, square-jawed man walked past the *Freikorps* sentries posted outside Ludendorff's villa in Ludwigshöhe and was ushered in to see the general. Rudolph Hess had the fresh, youthful face and wide, intent eyes that often belong to religious fanatics — which was only fitting, for that, in a way, was what he was. On being invited to do so, Hess sat down very respectfully and at once began to talk about the National Socialist German Workers', or Nazi, Party which had recently been founded in Munich. At last he suggested that Ludendorff receive the Nazi leader, Adolf Hitler.

A few days later Hitler came out to the general's home, sat in his study under Vogel's portrait of the Great Twin Brethren at *Ober-Ost,* and spoke at length on the future of Germany. Ludendorff was impressed by Hitler's "driving determination" and by his opinions. He had often thought the same things himself, and he recognized that Hitler had one great advantage denied to many nationalists — his ability to appeal to the masses. Since Ludendorff had already come to believe that the German working class had to be won back to the patriotic cause,[1] he was far from being alienated by Hitler's uncouth manners and lack of breeding. In fact, these might be positive assets, appropriate to a man of the people. With the right guidance, Hitler would be invaluable.

Ludendorff himself, of course, had never quite belonged to the pre-war ruling class. He had been made to feel this at Plön and Lichterfelde — perhaps, indeed, as in the case of the young Napoleon, some subtle sense of social inferiority had accounted for his intense concentration on his work and for his aggressive personality. During the war the Kaiser had once offered to ennoble him to "von Ludendorff," but the First Quartermaster General had coldly declined, saying that he did not aspire to a name different from his father's. At all events, he found nothing socially objectionable about the Nazis of Munich.

Yet the men who had gathered around Hitler were a strange and sinister group. Most were professional veterans who intended to work no more — Captain Göring, air ace and drug addict, who had won the *Pour le Mérite* and been second-in-command of Richthofen's famous squadron; Captain Röhm, Reichswehr officer and homosexual; Rudolph Hess, who had served for a time in Hitler's regiment and now acted as his private secretary; Emil Maurice, ex-convict and bodyguard; Gregor Strasser, big, brutal, and socialistic; Lieutenant Rossbach, the head of a Munich *Freikorps;* Alfred Rosenberg, a Baltic German and wild racial theorist; and Heinrich Himmler, a sadistic former schoolteacher and bankrupt chicken farmer. All these people lived in Munich and from time to time went out to Ludwigshöhe to see the great gray eminence of German Nationalism.

During this period there was a visitor to Munich who did not make the pilgrimage to Ludwigshöhe. General Max Hoffmann was more grizzled now, a little grayer, but his conversation was as witty and his smile as boyish as ever, and he was still an astute observer of the German scene. When he heard rumors of what his former chief was up to, he decided to investigate the Nazi Party on his own. He spent six months in Munich, attempting to use "all his influence to delay a movement whose approach he regarded with horror." [2] Unfortunately, the former captains, lieutenants and NCOs who formed the backbone of Hitler's party had little use for an intellectual general, even for one as distinguished as Hoffmann.

By now, those who remembered could realize how completely the old world had changed. The wiser ones, like Hoffmann and

Margarethe, knew that they would never again see a linden tree, an old stone wall, or a misty morning as they had seen them before the war. Faces too had a different look. It could be noticed in people of all ages, including children and the old, but was most apparent in women — a sharper look, with something distrustful in it. Even ladies often had no serenity any more. And with this grace gone, they took to hideous new fashions, cut short their long hair, wore skirts awkwardly above their knees, shrilled their voices and mysteriously flattened their bosoms. This happened everywhere, but in defeated Germany the change was more rapid and more pronounced, for it came from a conscious rejection of all those values which might in any way, however remotely, be held responsible for the war.

Ludendorff had no time to reflect on these things. For a while he fell completely under Hitler's spell, and the embryo Führer was careful to treat the aging general with the utmost deference. "He is the greatest soldier of all time," Hitler used to say on occasions when he could be reasonably sure his words would be repeated back to Ludendorff. And Ludendorff in turn would boast of how his influence had broadened the former corporal: "I have watched the man grow," he frequently declared.[3]

Among the Nazi hangers-on was a certain Frau Mathilde Kemnitz, a widow who lived in the nearby village of Tutzing and whom Ludendorff had previously met in Berlin. Many might have found Mathilde unattractive, with her plain face and dumpy figure, but Ludendorff found her fascinating. He did not in the least mind her earnest way of speaking, her prominent, overbright eyes, her chubby hands that somehow had a predatory look about them, or even the disconcerting, sly, little half-smile of the nearly-mad that sometimes flitted across her face. But then, Mathilde really believed that Ludendorff was the greatest soldier of all time and said so, with unmistakable sincerity, in and out of season. Whereas Margarethe Ludendorff was inclined to be silently disapproving of her husband's new friends, Frau Kemnitz was always properly adoring. And she was a woman of intellect, not merely someone who knew how to dress well and preside over a drawing-room. In fact, Mathilde had evolved a theory of her own to account for Germany's defeat, and as Ludendorff listened to her expounding it, he was struck by its eminent reasonableness. He had long been looking for just such an explanation, and he eagerly read the little pamphlets that Mathilde shyly offered him. In his own words:

Gradually I recognized the pernicious forces which had caused the collapse of the people, and in them the real enemies of the freedom of the German race. More and more plainly I became aware of the fission-fungi within the structure of our society . . . in the form of secret supra-national forces, namely: the Jewish people and Rome, along with their tools, the Freemasons, the Jesuit order, occult and satanistic structures. . . . Moreover, I realized how the racial inheritance and national characteristics — the base for a people's life — were being systematically destroyed by these forces. Here too my insight deepened as time went on.

Of decisive influence on the course of my inner struggles was my becoming acquainted with the earliest works of Dr. Mathilde von Kemnitz . . .

I adopted it as my own view that the Christian doctrine and the way of life it had given to the people was the basic cause of the whole evil, and that it served solely as a means for obtaining for the Jew the mastery of the world, which had been granted to him by Jehovah. This through the utter disintegration of the peoples who had been christianized, by crushing each individual man's power to resist . . .

Thus . . . the Dictate of Versailles was signed . . . on the 28th of July, 1919, the fifth anniversary of the assassination of the Archducal pair at Sarajevo. At the time I did not suspect the parallelism of the dates nor have any idea that cabalistic beliefs had determined them. Even less did I realize that the murder of the Archducal pair had long been planned by the world brotherhood of the Freemasons, in order finally to unleash in the Jehovah year 1914 the World War which had been decided upon by the Grand-Orient Lodge of France at Paris and furthered by Rome.[4]

Since the terrible afternoon of the 28th of September 1918, when he had railed against fate and the world in the Hotel Britannique at Spa, and possibly suffered a stroke in the process, Ludendorff had thought incessantly about what had gone wrong. Now he had his answer. Under Mathilde's guidance, he began to share her vision of a vast international conspiracy, moving nations and statesmen like pawns for their own dark, unTeutonic purposes. He came to believe that the Catholic Church, international Jewry, and the Freemasons were plotting in improbable combination to overcome the chosen *Volk*. Germany could never have been defeated in open battle. There was treason here and sorcery. In a way, these fantasies were a bleak, East Prussian version of the old German fairy world of dwarfs and glass mountains, magic spells, and Frederick Barbarossa asleep for a thousand years under the Kyffhäuserberg. But there was no poetry in Mathilde or Ludendorff, and from the long talks at Munich and Tutzing, in which Hitler, Rosenberg, and Himmler from time to time participated, came the horrors of Belsen, Ravensbrüch, Dachau, and Buchenwald. Ludendorff accepted all Mathilde's vicious nonsense, partly because his critical sense was quite dead, and partly because the roots of these wild hatreds had always been present in his soul. He became interested in astrology, took up with the mountebank alchemist Tausend (and, like most people, lost money through the relationship),[5] and withdrew more and more into a twilight realm where reality and illusion were indistinguishable shadows of the mind. In truth, the man who had been dictator of Germany during the two most perilous years of her history was now scarcely sane.

Nevertheless, he still had a tremendous reputation with the uninformed masses of the German people, and his alliance with Hitler, which he formally announced on the 2nd of September 1923, at a Sedan Day rally of the *Kampfbund* at Nuremberg, was extremely useful to the Nazi Party. To the discerning, however, his association with Hitler completely discredited the former general.

Unfortunately, the times favored extremists. In January 1923, President Poincaré of France, alleging as excuse that Germany had failed to deliver 140,000 telegraph poles on time, had ordered French troops to occupy the Ruhr. No sooner had Poincaré swooped down on the iron and coal deposits of the Ruhr than Poland had demanded that its frontier with the Reich be "rectified" and Lithuanian troops had marched into the city of Memel. Patriotic Germans — and these were the overwhelming majority of the nation — were outraged, desperate, and undecided. To renew the war against France seemed out of the question; it seemed equally impossible to relinquish the Ruhr. Even the coldly calculating von Seeckt toyed with the idea of military resistance and warned the British Ambassador, Lord D'Abernon, that "the road from Dortmund to Berlin is not very long, but it passes through streams of blood." [6] However, the new 100,000-man Reichswehr was not ready to fight, and Seeckt reluctantly decided that, if the worst befell, he would have to employ the *Freikorps*. He asked both Ludendorff and Hitler if he could count on their support if the French invaded Central Germany. Hitler's reply is not recorded, but Ludendorff answered that he would lend his "world historic" name, provided he were given supreme command in the event of war. [7]

Possibly this fantastic reply helped von Seeckt make up his mind: Germany was still a sick nation and overt resistance was out of the question. Seeckt persuaded the Republican ministers that, although for the time being Germany must accept the occupation of the Ruhr, the government should finance a reserve army, or "Black Reichswehr," composed of various *Freikorps* organizations. [8] By September, Seeckt had some 80,000 men enrolled in his illegal force. [9]

But by September the French occupation of the Ruhr was not the most serious of Germany's difficulties. All through 1923 the value of the mark had fallen with terrible swiftness. On the 11th of January, when the French had occupied the Ruhr, the mark had been worth 50,000 to the pound sterling. By the end of the month the rate of exchange was 250,000 to the pound, and by August 20,000,000. Although some industrialists and land-owners profited from the nation's distress by purchasing on a falling market, the savings of the middle class were wiped out and the working class saw nothing ahead but unemployment, starvation, and despair.

Against this black background Hitler decided to make his bid for power. He persuaded Ludendorff to approach General Otto von Lossow, the commander of the Reichswehr in Bavaria, in an attempt to enlist the army's support in overthrowing the Berlin government. As an inducement, Ludendorff offered von Lossow the post of Reich Minister of Defense, but Lossow was unimpressed: "I thought [Ludendorff and Hitler] were like children playing at 'you be the Emperor and you be the Pope'," he recalled. ". . . I was no unemployed *comitadje;* at that time I occupied a high position in the state." [10] Indeed, because of Ludendorff's vicious attacks on the Catholic Church, most Bavarians agreed with Lossow that the former First Quartermaster General was "a wild man [with] . . . evil in his head." [11] The Nazis were not unduly depressed by Lossow's attitude, for they felt that, when it came to the point, the great gray cat of the Reichswehr would jump down on their side. Munich simmered with conspiracies. At Nazi headquarters in the Brown House, in chalets in the nearby mountains, and behind the high walls of Ludendorff's villa at Ludwigshöhe, Hitler's followers talked interminably of *Der Tag.* Nevertheless, when the Führer finally decided to strike, he consulted no one but himself.

On the 26th of September Ritter Gustav von Kahr, a swarthy little Bavarian monarchist who wanted an independent South German kingdom under the Wittelsbachs, was appointed State Commissioner with dictatorial powers. In the next few weeks the separatist government in Munich quarreled seriously with the central government in Berlin on several issues, but Kahr was firmly supported by General von Lossow and Colonel von Seisser, the Chief of Bavarian Police. When this triumvirate an-

nounced that they would address a meeting at the Bürgerbräuhaus on the evening of the 8th of November, Hitler decided he
could wait no longer, for he feared that Kahr and Lossow might
be intending to proclaim Bavaria's independence and the restoration of the Wittelsbach monarchy.

The Bürgerbräuhaus was a huge beer-hall on the south bank
of the Isar River on the outskirts of Munich. At 8:30 P.M. on
the 8th of November the great main room of the place was filled
with patriotic citizens, and Kahr had just begun his speech from
the platform, when the doors were suddenly flung open and a
mob of steel-helmeted Nazi storm-troopers under Captain Göring dashed into the room. Hitler, dressed in an ill-fitting morning suit, followed close behind his brown-shirted thugs. He
jumped on a table, drew a pistol from his pocket, and fired it
twice at the ceiling. Having thus attracted attention, he shouted:
"Silence!" Admiral von Hintze, who was in the audience, remembered the scene as ludicrous, almost pathetic. As the former
Foreign Minister looked at Hitler waving his arms on the table-
top, his only thought had been: "The poor little waiter!" [12]
When the first astonished murmurs were stilled, the Nazi leader
continued: "The National Revolution has broken out. This hall
is occupied by 600 fully armed men. If there is not immediate
silence, a machine-gun will be placed in the gallery." To give
point to his words a machine-gun was actually trundled into
the hall and a storm-trooper swiveled it menacingly around to
threaten the crowd.

Making his way to the platform, Hitler hustled Kahr, Lossow
and Seisser into an adjoining room. There he explained what it
was all about. This was the beginning of a *coup d'état* that
would sweep away the government of the "November criminals."
The Munich police chief, Pöhner, was to be Bavarian Prime
Minister with full dictatorial powers. Von Kahr was to be administrator. The Reich Government itself would be headed by
Hitler, and the National Army would be commanded by General Ludendorff. Seisser would be Reich Minister of Police, a post

which, at least at first, would be nothing but a sinecure, since in Germany all police were under state control. Hitler was very excited and almost incoherent: "If things go wrong," he declared, "I have four bullets in my pistol — three for my colleagues if they foresake me, the last for myself." With this, he pointed his revolver at his own head.

Kahr shrugged his shoulders: "You can arrest me or shoot me," he said. "Whether or not I die doesn't matter."

At this point Ulrich Graf, Hitler's simian body-guard, thoughtfully arrived on the scene with a large stein of Munich beer which he passed to his master. Hitler, too overwrought to remember his teetotal convictions, accepted the tankard and absentmindedly swigged at it as he continued to talk. When General von Lossow interrupted to ask about Ludendorff, Hitler replied: "Ludendorff is holding himself ready. He will be here in a moment."

In fact, at about this time Ludendorff was being bundled into a car by Dr. Max von Scheubner-Richter, who had been sent to Ludwigshöhe to fetch him. The general was wearing an old tweed shooting jacket and had time only to snatch up a hat before he left for Munich. When he arrived at the Bürgerbräuhaus, he was amazed and far from pleased to find that so much had been done without him. Hitler was still haranguing Kahr, Lossow and Seisser in a back room, and Göring stood like a tubby monument on a chair in the main body of the hall, trying to quieten the crowd. The national revolution was not directed against the Reichswehr or the police, Göring assured the Munichers, but only against "the Jewish Government in Berlin." When this statement was met with murmurs of dissent, Göring raised his voice and shouted for silence at the top of his lungs. He had a sergeant major's voice and the room fell still. Göring looked about him with satisfaction: "That's right" he said. "After all, you have your beer."

Ludendorff pushed his way through to the anteroom where Hitler was still talking about the government he intended to establish. "The task of the Provisional National Government," he was declaiming, "is to organize the march on that sinful Babylon, Berlin. Tomorrow will either find a National Government in Berlin or us dead." Ludendorff's arrival brought a calmer atmosphere, and the Nazis put their revolvers back in their pockets. Perhaps Kahr, Lossow and Seisser were genuinely won over by Hitler's eloquence and Ludendorff's presence, or perhaps, as they claimed later, they merely decided to humor a group of armed madmen. In any case, the three Bavarian leaders agreed to cooperate with the *coup d'état*. Kahr declared that he could accept the post of Bavarian administrator only as a representative of the Wittelsbachs, but when Hitler at once agreed, the two men shook hands. General von Lossow (although he later denied it) is said to have told Ludendorff: "I take Your Excellency's words as a command. I shall organize the army in fighting order as Your Excellency requires."

The little group then emerged onto the main stage of the hall, where Hitler announced to the fascinated audience that the nationalist revolution had begun. Ludendorff had the last word. He drew himself up and said: "Deeply moved by the greatness of this moment, and profoundly surprised, I place myself, by virtue of my own right, at the disposal of the German National Government."

Shortly afterwards, the crowd in the Bürgerbräuhaus was allowed to go home. Kahr, Lossow and Seisser were also permitted to leave, and when someone objected to this, Ludendorff frowned him down, saying grandly: "I forbid you to doubt the word of a German officer." Ludendorff then went to the War Ministry on the Schönfeldstrasse and Hitler hurried away to settle a dispute that had broken out when the *Freikorpskämpfer* of the *Bund Oberland* had attempted to take over a Reichswehr barracks.

General von Lossow went back to his headquarters, where he was met by his second-in-command, Lieutenant General von Danner, who was in charge of the Munich garrison. Danner had heard what had happened at the Bürgerbräuhaus and did not approve of it. He looked Lossow squarely in the eye and said with a silky threat in his tone: "All that, of course, was bluff, Excellency?"

General Lossow, reflecting that in all Munich only Danner actually had troops under his command, began to think that it had, after all, perhaps been bluff. This suspicion was confirmed later that night when von Seeckt telegraphed from Berlin to say that, if the army in Bavaria did not immediately suppress the *Putsch,* he would do so himself. Sometime after midnight Crown Prince Rupprecht of Bavaria, who was living in his castle near Berchtesgaden, dispatched his adjutant to Munich: Rupprecht sent his compliments to von Lossow and would the general please be advised that neither the Crown Prince nor Cardinal Faulhaber would have anything to do with any *coup d'état* led by Ludendorff.

When Hitler and Ludendorff met again at the Bürgerbräuhaus at dawn, the Nazi leader was seriously worried. He had sent several liaison officers to von Lossow at the 19th Infantry Regiment's barracks, but none had returned. Which was not surprising, since they had been arrested as soon as they appeared. The Führer now announced that he would establish a "national tribunal" to court-martial criminals "likely to endanger the existence of the people and the state." Those found guilty would be shot within three hours of sentencing. In his lust for bloodshed he ordered the execution of a number of left-wing politicians who had been arrested by Nazi squads during the night. Fortunately, this order was not obeyed. Von Kahr had already moved the Bavarian Government to Regensburg, and from this sanctuary declared that he was revolted by "this repulsive orgy of violence," that the Nazi Party was outlawed, and the *Kampfbund* dissolved. When word of Kahr's announcement reached the Bürgerbräuhaus later in the morning, Ludendorff said in disgust: "I will never again trust the word of a German officer."

Meanwhile, Munich was rapidly filling up with armed men.

Various *Freikorps* formations converged on the city, but by eight o'clock Reichswehr reinforcements had also moved in and set up machine-guns on the Ludwigstrasse. When Hitler learned that the Reichswehr would oppose him, he could see plainly enough that the *Putsch* had already failed. He then suggested that Crown Prince Rupprecht be asked to mediate between the Bavarian Government and the *Freikorps,* and rather nervously proposed that the rebels should retire to Rosenheim. Ludendorff looked at him coldly. "We march!" he declared curtly. When Hitler excitedly objected that, if they marched, they would be fired on, Ludendorff looked down at the little man and barked: "We march!" [13]

They marched. At a little after eleven o'clock several thousand *Kampfbündler* set out across the Isar bridge toward the center of Munich. They walked eight abreast, with their rifles slung over their shoulders. Ahead of them strutted an S.A. man bearing a large swastika flag. In the front rank were Ludendorff, Scheubner-Richter, Ulrich Graf, Hitler, and three other Nazi leaders. A detachment of Bavarian police was guarding the bridge over the Isar, but when Göring threatened to shoot the political hostages, the procession were allowed to pass. Most of Munich had turned out to see the parade, and the Nazis were cheered loudly as they reached the Marienplatz. On they marched, down the Residenzstrasse toward the Odeonsplatz, singing as they went. Since the Residenzstrasse was very narrow, the files had to crowd together, and at the end of the street, where it debouched into the Odeonsplatz, a cordon of police was drawn up, blocking the way. Ulrich Graf ran forward, shouting: "Don't fire, Ludendorff and Hitler are coming!"

Fortunately for the Republic, the police detachment here was under the command of Freiherr von Godin, a courageous and conscientious officer. As the brown-shirted mob pushed on toward him, he gave the order to fire. When his policemen hesitated, he repeated the command, then impatiently snatched a rifle from one of his men and fired it himself. Immediately a fusilade of shots rang out. Scheubner-Richter, marching between Ludendorff and Hitler, fell dead; Hitler dived ignominously to the pavement; and in a moment sixteen Nazis and three policemen had been killed. The entire procession, nearly 7,000 strong and including some 2,000 Nazi storm-troopers, ran panic-stricken in all directions. Within a minute the Residenzstrasse was cleared — except for two men. Ludendorff, his hands thrust into the pockets of his old shooting coat, continued to march straight ahead, and his adjutant, Major Streck, kept pace beside him. This was the last great gesture of the hero of Liège. He approached the line of leveled rifles, brushed them contemptuously aside, and walked through unopposed toward the Feldherrnhalle.

Not one of the Nazis followed him. Hitler was being bundled into a little yellow Fiat on the Odeonsplatz and driven away to hiding. Göring, slightly wounded, scrambled to safety, and so did Rosenberg and all the rest. When it was obvious that the single volley had broken the revolt, the police respectfully approached Ludendorff and asked him to accompany them to the central police station for questioning. They kept him there all afternoon and most of the night, but eventually released him on parole.

Margarethe spent an agonizing twenty-four hours, for she had not heard from her husband, her son Heinz, or their servant, Kurt Neubarr, since they had hurried away separately on the evening of the 8th of November. Not until the 10th did she learn that neither Ludendorff nor Heinz had been injured, and then her relief was soon spoiled by word that poor, stupid Kurt Neubarr, who had served the family faithfully for years, had been killed. In the afternoon Heinz returned to Ludwigshöhe, looking rather sheepish, although all he had done was drive his stepfather's car. A little later the police arrived and took him away to prison where he was to wait nearly five months before his trial. On the 11th, the police picked up Hitler in the house of a supporter, Ernst Hanfstängl, in the village of Uffing. The Nazi Führer was found cowering at the back of Frau Hänfstangl's wardrobe closet, imperfectly hidden by his hostess's dresses.

Except with the Nazis, the Beer Hall fiasco destroyed whatever reputation Ludendorff still possessed. As he marched proudly through the police cordon on the Odeonsplatz, he was, in fact, marching out of history. All the rest of his life was excruciating anti-climax. Perhaps after all, it would have been better if von Godin's men had dared to shoot their wartime leader down.

Ludendorff, Hitler, and eight other Nazis were brought to trial in the Munich *Volksgericht,* or People's Court, between the 26th of February and the 27th of March 1924. The General did not show up well at the trial. Unlike Hitler, who boasted of what he had done and became something of a hero in the process, Ludendorff attempted to exculpate himself. Although Hitler and the eight Nazis were all found guilty and sentenced to terms of fortress detention, Ludendorff alone was acquitted. The court explained this strange verdict by saying that he had been so emotionally overwrought at the time of the *Putsch* that he had not known what he was doing. Ludendorff, who had elected to wear his general's uniform throughout the trial, stormed out of the court in a furious rage, saying: "I consider my acquittal a disgrace to the uniform and decorations I wear." Few Germans disagreed with this, but few thought that the explanatory rider added to the jury's verdict was unjust.

Shortly after his acquittal, Ludendorff was elected to the Reichstag as a Nazi deputy, but he made no impression there, and even his fellow Nazis did not take him very seriously any more. That August, on the tenth anniversary of the Battle of Tannenberg, most of the commanders who had made great names for themselves on the Eastern Front gathered at Hohenstein for the laying of the foundation stone of a Tannenberg Memorial. Ludendorff, of course, was present, as were Mackensen, von François, and Hindenburg. By now Hindenburg was back on friendly terms with his First Quartermaster General, for the old field marshal shrewdly realized that for all posterity Ludendorff would be the inescapable *Doppelgänger* of his legend. Hoffmann, however, could not come, for he was ill. The war had strained his giant frame, as perhaps had his cognac and incessant cigarette smoking. He lived quietly now, for he had never been able to save money, having always held that "a man should know how to part with a twenty-mark piece gracefully upon occasion." (As a subaltern, he had once prompted his colonel to remark: "My corps of officers seems to consist mainly of the rich sons of poor fathers.") [14] And he was at once too proud and too humble to accept other people's money as Ludendorff did. He spent his time between Berchtesgaden and Berlin, telling all who would listen to him that Russian Communism was the great future menace to Western civilization.

In March 1925, when President Ebert's death made an election necessary, Hitler persuaded Ludendorff to stand as a candidate for President of the Reich. Hindenburg begged him not to, warning him that it would lead only to ignominious defeat, and Margarethe also tried to dissuade him, but Ludendorff went his own way.[15] When the election results were in, Ludendorff was found to have polled only 280,000 votes of the nearly 24,000,000 cast, or slightly over one percent. This revelation of how he had fallen in the estimation of his countrymen was only slightly offset by the torchlight procession which the Munich Nazis organized for him on his 60th birthday, for even Ludendorff realized that this was a political rather than a personal tribute.

Since no candidate had gained the necessary plurality in March, the election had been inconclusive and a second ballot was necessary. This time the Nationalists persuaded Hindenburg to stand for President, and he succeeded triumphantly where Ludendorff had failed. On the 27th of April the 77-year-old field marshal began the last phase of his public life as President of the Republic. That summer, for the first time in three or four years, Hindenburg wrote that he was unable to pay his annual visit to the Ludendorffs at Ludwigshöhe, giving as an excuse the fact that he was President and therefore no longer his own master. Ludendorff "foamed with rage" at this rejection,[16] and never again spoke of Hindenburg except in terms of bitter vituperation.

But by now Ludendorff had quarreled with everyone. After the Beer Hall *Putsch,* a certain coldness had developed between him and Hitler, for he did not quite accept the story that when the police had opened fire, Hitler had been dragged to the ground in the death-grip of Scheubner-Richter. However, the final break was caused by Hitler's unwillingness, for political reasons, to join in Ludendorff's attacks on the Catholic Church. Before the Nazis came to power, Ludendorff published an angry pamphlet entitled: "Hitler's Betrayal of the German People to the Roman Pope." [17] He quarreled with Crown Prince Rupprecht, who reluctantly brought a libel action against him and won it easily. All the prominent German officers associations passed resolutions protesting the slanders against Rupprecht, and 37 generals signed an indignant manifesto, excluding Ludendorff from their society. He quarreled with the German Crown Prince and with the other members of the royal family.[18] He quarreled with prominent Freemasons like Count Dohna, who long ago had refused to bet with Hoffmann on the number of prisoners captured at Tannenberg. He quarreled with Admiral von Tirpitz and after he publicly referred to the political party Tirpitz supported as "a gang of perjured renegades," the Admiral never spoke to him again.[19] This sort of phrase now slipped easily off Ludendorff's tongue, so it is not surprising that he lost the respect of all his former comrades.

Margarethe followed these developments with "silent horror," [20] and now Ludendorff turned against his last and most faithful friend. In 1926, at the age of 61, he obtained a divorce, and on the 14th of September of that year, dressed in full uniform with sword and medals, he married Frau Mathilde von Kemnitz in Tutzing. "Hereafter," he said, "[we] fought jointly against the supra-national forces and their tools . . . mutually enriched our minds, and widened the struggle for freedom." [21] A few years later Margarethe, who probably needed the money, published a charming, unorganized book of memoirs, *Als Ich Ludendorffs Frau War,* which was remarkable for the unmistakable note of affection with which she spoke of Ludendorff in the days before his decline.

Ludendorff now took up his residence in Tutzing, in his new wife's house, and these two pathetic people got down in earnest to the business of publishing scurrilous pamphlets. Some they wrote jointly and some were individual efforts. Typical of Ludendorff's work was one entitled *The Secret of the Might of the Jesuits and Its Aim.* He described another, entitled *The Destruction of Freemasonry Through Disclosure of Its Secrets,* as "The revelation, based on secret sources, of how the rite of Freemasonry breaks the race consciousness, the national pride and the masculine will of men and makes them artificial Jews — the tool of the Jews that has no will of its own." These ridiculous and contemptible effusions of hate enjoyed considerable popular success, but none did as well as a pamphlet Mathilde wrote, entitled *Salvation from Jesus Christ,* which sold over 400,000 copies. Ludendorff was not jealous of his wife's greater literary success, and declared roundly that "on the dissemination of *Salvation from Jesus Christ* depends the liberation of every single German, of the German nation, and of all nations."

In August 1927, when Ludendorff attended the dedication of the Tannenberg Memorial, he created a scene by refusing to stand by Hindenburg's side during the ceremony. Hindenburg, much incensed, left before Ludendorff spoke, and after the dedication, the former First Quartermaster General found himself shunned by all his former comrades and left rather pathetically to make his way to his car alone. Once again Hoffmann had not been present. He had died the previous month at Berchtesgaden at the age of 58, and only his own circle of friends realized how fine a German gentleman had passed away.

Although Hindenburg had given his solemn word that he would never make "that Bohemian corporal" Chancellor of Germany, he was persuaded to do exactly that on the 30th of January 1933. The old gentleman had stubbornly resisted Hitler's appointment, but when he realized that only a government headed by Hitler would be able to suppress an investigation into the corrupt use of public money by the East Prussian landed aristocracy, he changed his mind and declared that he accepted Hitler "in God's name." Thus, although they had never received more than 37 per cent of the popular vote, the Nazis came to power, with terrible and tragic results for the entire world. Perhaps Hindenburg's final betrayal may be partly excused by the fact that he was in his 86th year and almost senile.

A story, possibly apocryphal, went around Berlin at this time. On the night Hitler was appointed Chancellor, the Nazis staged a great torchlight procession through the streets of the capital. Twenty-five thousand brown-shirted S.A. men and seemingly endless files of Stahlhelm in field-gray marched along the Wilhelmstrasse while Hitler beamed down on them from the balcony of the Reich Chancellery. A few yards away at the Presidential Palace Hindenburg stood on another balcony, listening to the military bands and beating time with his crooked old walking-stick. As the brown and field-gray ranks swung by below him, his faded blue eyes lit up. Suddenly he lifted his head and spoke over his shoulder: "Ludendorff," he said, "how well our men are marching! And what a lot of Russian prisoners they've taken!" [22]

The next year Hitler confirmed his power by the murderous blood-purge of the 30th of June, in which Röhm, Gregor Strasser, and other S.A. leaders were shot. Von Kahr was also killed, in belated vengeance for the part he had played in the Beer Hall *Putsch.* Someone drafted a telegram which Hindenburg signed, expressing the President's "profound thanks" for Hitler's "resolute and courageous" action. Almost the only man in Germany who dared publicly condemn Hitler's new system of government by murder was old Field Marshal von Mackensen, who at 84 was almost as bright-eyed and quite as slim as ever. He spent the weekend of the blood-purge on the telephone, furiously trying to reach Hindenburg to get him to stop the killings. Those around the old gentleman prevented Mackensen from speaking to him, however, and when Mackensen demanded the punishment of the murderers, no one paid any attention. Less than a month later Hindenburg died peacefully on his family estate at Neudeck, which a grateful Hitler had enlarged the previous year by the tax-free grant of an additional 5000 acres. What Ludendorff thought of the blood-purge is not recorded, but presumably he approved of it. He still attacked the Nazis in pamphlets and in his little newspaper — and was the only man in Germany who was allowed to do this with impunity — but his attacks were in the main complaints that Hitler was displaying too much tenderness toward Catholics and Jews.[23]

In 1935 Ludendorff again came briefly into the limelight with the publication of a book entitled *Der totale Krieg*. In this book he developed the theory that "War is the highest expression of the national will to live, and therefore politics must serve warmaking,"[24] which, of course, was a complete and insane reversal of Clausewitz's famous dictum that war was only a continuation of policy by other means. Although Ludendorff's extreme and ruthless doctrines were rejected by the German General Staff, they had considerable influence on Hitler. One passage in the book was of particular interest, since it showed Ludendorff's own assessment of his life's work: "A nation deserves to have a great general only when it places itself at his service, that is, in the service of the totalitarian war which is waged for its assistance. In this case, the great general and the nation are one and indivisible, otherwise the general is wasted on the nation." On Ludendorff's 70th birthday that year Hitler offered to make him a field marshal, but he declined, for he had already created for himself the more high-sounding title of "Field Lord of the World War."[25]

On the 20th of December 1937, Ludendorff's stormy odyssey came to an end in the Josephinium Hospital on the Schönfeldstrasse in Munich. He died at the age of 72 of a bladder ailment, having been attended tenderly at the last by the nuns of that church which he had viciously attacked for the final fifteen years of his life.[26] Two days later, on a cold, windy morning, Hitler followed the coffin through the streets of Munich to the Feldherrnhalle where Field Marshal von Blomberg, the Nazi Minister of War, delivered the funeral oration. Ludendorff's body lay in state in the Feldherrnhalle, the casket draped with a huge swastika flag and guarded by four Nazi soldiers. In his will Ludendorff had expressly stated that he did not wish to be buried either in the Invaliden Cemetery in Berlin or in the crypt of the Tannenberg Memorial but at Tutzing, and Hitler, although reluctant to leave Ludendorff's remains in the sole charge of Mathilde when they might have served a party purpose in a Nazi shrine, did not overrule the dead man's wish.[27]

✠

The First World War, coming as it did when Europe stood within grasping distance of a golden age, was the most tragic episode in modern history. And Ludendorff's domination of German policy from August 1916 to October 1918 was central to the tragedy and profoundly deepened it. The defensive and offensive doctrines developed under his direction displayed a tactical brilliance not shown elsewhere in the war and seldom equalled in any war. While Hoffmann stood behind him, he was also capable of strategical brilliance of the highest order. His administrative ability was even more pronounced, and he must be ranked as one of the very greatest military organizers of all time. In purely military matters he demonstrated a commendable readiness to accept the intelligent opinions of others, even of very junior officers.

Yet his direction of Germany's affairs led to utter disaster. He was completely unequipped, by background, training, or talent, to cope with political problems, but with a rash self-confidence which was typical of him, he forced his will upon the Kaiser, the civil government, and the German nation. Completely unable to work with moderate men on equal terms, he imposed his own short-sighted policies and pursued them with criminal obstinacy. His harshness towards Russia, his credulous belief in the mirage of Polish corps, his foolish contempt of American strength, and his rejection of all possibility of a compromise peace brought Europe to ruin. The three great empires came crashing down, and although they had certainly been imperfect, there was soon to be good reason to regret their fall. In a sense, Ludendorff was well suited to the terrible new world he had been instrumental in creating, for by temperament he preferred ruthless and extreme courses, and it was only fitting that he should find his spiritual home in the Nazi Party.

Although the First World War was a heart-breaking blunder which, with a little more good will and a little less pride on both sides, might have been avoided, the aftermath of the war, the rise of Hitler, and the second world conflict bear the imprint of inevitability. For this Ludendorff must assume a large share of the responsibility. Hitler might well have come to power without Ludendorff's support (although that support was an incalculable advantage to him in the early days), but Hitler could never have come to power had not Germany been so grievously strained by the war that Ludendorff had carried on too long.

All men's lives are a struggle between good and evil forces contending within them. There was much good in Ludendorff's early and middle life — personal courage, intelligence, determination, and a high and selfless sense of duty — but none of these was a truly heroic virtue, and nothing less than heroic virtue could have met the challenge of supreme command. In Ludendorff the darkness encroached steadily upon the inadequate light. In the course of time, pride drove out selflessness, the intelligence blurred and faded away, and even personal courage was replaced by a false beard and a pair of blue spectacles.

It was catastrophic for Germany and the whole world that Ludendorff should have attained the power he did. There were certainly other men who could better have discharged his great responsibilities — Gröner or Hoffmann or von Seeckt — but in the empire of Wilhelm II none of these could well have been considered. Their very moderation would have argued against their appointment to the Supreme Command. Had it been otherwise, there might have been no war at all.

REFERENCES

INDEX

✠

Note: Works frequently cited in the References are identified by the following abbreviations.

BÜLOW   Prince von Bülow, Memoirs (transl. Geoffrey Dunlop) (4 vols., Boston 1931).

GOLOVINE: General Nicholas N. Golovine, *The Russian Campaign of 1914* (transl. Capt. A. G. S. Muntz) (London 1933).

HINDENBURG: Field Marshal von Hindenburg, *Out of My Life* (transl. F. A. Holt) (New York 1921).

HOFFMANN: Major General Max Hoffmann, *War Diaries and other Papers* (transl. Eric Sutton) (2 vols., London 1929).

IRONSIDE: Major General Sir Edmund Ironside, *Tannenberg: The First Thirty Days in East Prussia* (London 1925).

KNOX: Major General Sir Alfred Knox, *With the Russian Army* (2 vols., London 1921).

LUDENDORFF: Erich Ludendorff, *My War Memories, 1914–1918* (2 vols., London 1919).

LUTZ: Ralph H. Lutz, *Fall of the German Empire, Documents, 1914–1918* (2 vols., Stanford 1932).

MARGARETHE LUDENDORFF: Margarethe Ludendorff, *My Married Life with Ludendorff* (transl. Raglan Somerset) (London 1929).

MÜLLER: Admiral Georg von Müller, *The Kaiser and His Court* (London 1961).

RITTER: Gerhard Ritter, *The Schlieffen Plan* (transl. Andrew and Eva Wilson) (London 1958).

UDZ   German Official Documents, *Untersuchungausschuss über die Weltkriegsverantwortlichkeit* (12 vols., Berlin 1925–1929).

REFERENCES

CHAPTER I

1. Theodor Wolff, *The Eve of 1914* (transl. E. W. Dickes) (New York 1936), 296.
2. Margarethe Ludendorff, 31, 36.
3. Schlieffen's "Memorandum of 1892," quoted in: Ritter, 25.
4. Ritter, 162.
5. Ritter, 51–52, 95–96; Friedrich von Bernhardi, *Vom heutigen Krieg* (Berlin 1912), II, 42–43.
6. Bülow, III, 132.
7. Bülow, II, 201.
8. Eugen Zimmermann, article in *Süddeutsche Monatshefte,* March 1921.
9. Hoffmann, II, 33–34.
10. Erich Ludendorff, *Kriegsführung und Politik* (Munich 1922), 71; *Mein militärischer Werdegang* (Munich 1933), 125–28.
11. H. von Moltke, "General Observations on the Schlieffen Plan," quoted in: Ritter, 165–67.
12. Erich Ludendorff, *Süddeutsche Monatshefte,* 1920–21, Bd. 18, I, 375.
13. Schlieffen's "Memorandum of December 1905," quoted in: Ritter, 143.
14. Golovine, 25.
15. Henny von Tempelhoff, *Mein Glück im Hause Ludendorff* (Berlin 1918), 177, 186, 229, and *passim.*
16. Ludendorff, I, 50.
17. Ludendorff, I, 22.
18. Margarethe Ludendorff, 17.
19. Walter Görlitz, *The German General Staff: Its History and Structure 1657–1945* (transl. Brian Battershaw) (London 1953), 139.
20. Schlieffen's "Memorandum of 1905," Ritter, 146.
21. Margarethe Ludendorff, 18.
22. Margarethe Ludendorff, 19.
23. Margarethe Ludendorff, 16.
24. Friedrich von Boetticher, *Schlieffen* (Berlin 1957), 102.
25. Schlieffen's "Memorandum of 28 December, 1912," Ritter, 175.
26. Margarethe Ludendorff, 39–49.

CHAPTER II

1. Margarethe Ludendorff, 51–52.
2. Ludendorff, I, 29.
3. Theodor Wolff, *The Eve of 1914,* 443.

316

4. Winston S. Churchill, *The World Crisis 1911–1918* (4 vols., London 1949), I, 188.
5. Bülow, III, 184.
6. *German White Book (Collected Documents Relating to the Outbreak of the European War)* (H.M.C., London 1915), No. 342, p. 302.
7. Lutz, I, 4.
8. Theodor Wolff, 509.
9. Ludendorff, I, 25.
10. Baron de Bassompierre, *"La nuit de 2 au 3 août 1914 aux Ministère des Affaires Etrangères en Belgique,"* in: *Revue des Deux Mondes,* 15 February 1915.
11. Quoted in Bernadotte E. Schmidtt, *The Coming of the War* (2 vols., New York 1930), II, 390.
12. Ludendorff, I, 38.

CHAPTER III

1. Ludendorff, I, 35.
2. Lieut. Gen. E. J. Galet, *Albert, King of the Belgians in the Great War,* (transl. Maj. Gen. Sir Ernest Swinton) (London 1931), 54–55.
3. General von Kluck, *Der Marsch auf Paris und die Marneschlacht 1914* (Berlin 1920), 19.
4. Sewell Tyng, *The Campaign on the Marne 1914* (London 1935), 53.
5. Ludendorff, I, 31.
6. *Der Weltkrieg 1914–1918* (German Official History) (14 vols., Berlin 1925–1944), I, *Die Grenzschlachten im Westen,* 110–11.
7. Reproduced in: Henri Davignon, *German Posters in Belgium: Their Value as Evidence* (London 1918), 2.
8. *Times History of the War,* I, 336.
9. Ludendorff, I, 34.
10. *Der Weltkrieg,* I, 115.
11. Ludendorff, I, 35.
12. Captaine Commandant R. de Wilde, *De Liège à l'Yser, Mon Journal de Campagne* (Paris 1918), 18.
13. Bülow, III, 160.
14. Feldmarshall Franz Conrad von Hötzendorff, *Aus Meiner Dienstzeit 1906–1918* (5 vols., Vienna, 1921–25), II, 193.
15. Ludendorff, I, 32.
16. Generaloberst Helmuth von Moltke, *Erinnerungen-Briefe-Dokumente 1877–1916* (Stuttgart 1922), 24.
17. Raymond Poincaré, *Mémoires* (transl. Sir George Arthur) (4 vols., New York 1929), III, 7.
18. Ludendorff, I, 35–36.
19. Lutz, I, 13.
20. *Source Records of the War* (7 vols., n.p., n.d.), II, 50.
21. Ludendorff, I, 39.
22. "General Leman's Diary, Magdeburg, Germany," quoted in: *Source Records of the Great War,* II, 46.
23. Ludendorff, I, 39.
24. Margarethe Ludendorff, 74.
25. Ludendorff, I, 41.
26. Ludendorff, I, 44.

CHAPTER IV

1. Ludendorff, I, 44.
2. Colonel Max Bauer, *Der grosse Krieg im Feld und Heimat* (Tübingen 1921), 45.
3. Bauer, 48.
4. Admiral Georg von Müller, *The Kaiser and His Court* (London 1961), 24.
5. General Hermann von Kuhl, *Der Weltkrieg 1914–1918* (Berlin 1930), I, 47.
6. *Der grosse Krieg 1914–1918* (ed. M. Schwarte), 289–90.
7. Ludendorff, I, 45.
8. Ludendorff, I, 46.
9. Margarethe Ludendorff, 80.
10. Hindenburg, 69.
11. Hindenburg, 81.
12. Hindenburg, 82.
13. Margarethe Ludendorff, 84.
14. Hoffmann, II, 33.
15. Ludendorff, I, 147.
16. Hoffmann, I, 37; II, 22.
17. Ironside, 145–48.
18. Golovine, 167–71.
19. Hoffmann, II, 263.
20. Ludendorff, I, 50.
21. Hoffmann, II, 36.
22. Knox, I, 88.
23. Hoffmann, II, 41.
24. Hoffmann, II, 263.

CHAPTER V

1. Hoffmann, II, 273.
2. General von François, *Marneschlacht und Tannenberg* (Berlin 1920), 206.
3. Hoffmann, II, 273.
4. Golovine, 171.
5. Second Russian Army Order of 25–26 August 1914, quoted in: Ironside, 155.
6. Princess Evelyn Blücher, *An English Wife in Berlin* (London 1920), 37.
7. Hoffmann, II, 282.
8. Hoffmann, II, 282.
9. Hindenburg, 95.
10. Hoffmann, II, 282.
11. Hoffmann, II, 41–42.
12. Ironside, 176–77.
13. Knox, 68–69.
14. Quoted in: Ironside, 164.
15. Hoffmann, I, 41.
16. Ironside, 158.
17. Golovine, 234.
18. Ludendorff, I, 52.
19. Hoffmann, II, 37–38; François, *Marneschlacht und Tannenberg*, 213–14.
20. Ludendorff, I, 55.

318   REFERENCES

21. Hoffmann, II, 310.
22. Hoffmann, II, 305.
23. General von François, article in *Reichsflagge,* 17 September, 1925.
24. Hoffmann, II, 311.
25. Ludendorff, I, 57.
26. Hindenburg, 96.
27. Ludendorff, I, 57.
28. Knox, 73–75.
29. General Martos, "Outline of the Operations of the XVth Army Corps in Eastern Prussia in 1914," quoted in: Golovine, 262–63.
30. Golovine, 298–300.
31. General Postovsky, "The Offensive of General Samsonov's Army into Eastern Prussia," quoted in: Golovine, 300–01.
32. Martos, quoted in: Golovine, 317–18.
33. Hoffmann, II, 322; Hindenburg, 97.
34. Martos, quoted in: Golovine, 327.
35. Hoffmann, II, 322–23.
36. Ironside, 195.
37. Hindenburg, 99.
38. Hindenburg, 99.
39. Ludendorff, I, 58.

CHAPTER VI

1. Ludendorff, I, 61.
2. Ludendorff, I, 62.
3. *Der Weltkrieg,* II, 268.
4. Ludendorff, I, 59.
5. *Der Weltkrieg,* III, 232.
6. Hoffmann, I, 41.
7. Hoffmann, I, 41.
8. Ludendorff, I, 58.
9. Hoffmann, I, 42.
10. Ironside, 212.
11. *Der Weltkrieg,* II, 269, 288.
12. Ironside, 206.
13. Hoffmann, II, 44.
14. Ludendorff, I, 64.
15. General Basil Gourko, *Russia 1914–1917: Memories and Impressions of War and Revolution* (New York 1919), 83.
16. Ludendorff, I, 63.
17. François, *Marneschlacht und Tannenberg* (Berlin 1920), 259–60.
18. Ludendorff, I, 67.
19. Quoted in: Ironside, 244.
20. Ironside, 244.
21. Ironside, 250–51.
22. Ironside, 257–58.

CHAPTER VII

1. Hindenburg, 108.
2. Ludendorff, I, 72.

3. Ludendorff, I, 73.
4. Margarethe Ludendorff, 111.
5. Ludendorff, I, 75–76.
6. *Österreich-Ungarns letzer Krieg* (Austrian Official History) (7 vols., Vienna, 1934–38), I, 344–45.
7. Major General Sir Alfred Knox, "Hindenburg's Second Offensive in Poland: The Operation of Lodz, November 1914," in: *The Army Quarterly*, vol. II, April-July 1921, 335.
8. Hoffmann, I, 45.
9. Hoffmann, II, 56.
10. Ludendorff, I, 88.
11. Hoffmann, I, 46.
12. Ludendorff, I, 90.
13. Hoffmann, I, 46.
14. Hindenburg, 121.
15. Hoffmann, I, 47.
16. Hoffmann, II, 60.

CHAPTER VIII

1. General von Sturgkh, quoted in: B. H. Liddell Hart, *Reputations* (London 1928), 63.
2. Hans von Zwehl, *Erich von Falkenhayn, General der Infanterie* (Berlin 1926), quoted in: *The Army Quarterly*, April 1926, 148.
3. Ludendorff, I, 95.
4. Hindenburg, 124.
5. Ludendorff, I, 118.
6. Hoffmann, II, 81–82.
7. Knox, I, 203.
8. Ludendorff, I, 106.
9. Knox, 339.
10. Knox, 339.
11. Knox, 341.
12. Hoffmann, II, 77.
13. Winston S. Churchill, *The Unknown War* (New York 1931), 260.
14. Ludendorff, I, 107.
15. Knox, I, 211.
16. Hoffmann, II, 82.
17. Müller, 46.
18. Hoffmann, II, 80.

CHAPTER IX

1. Hoffmann, II, 83.
2. Ludendorff, I, 114.
3. Ludendorff, I, 114.
4. Prince Hohenlohe, quoted in Emil Ludwig, *Hindenburg and the Saga of the German Revolution* (transl. Eden and Cedar Paul) (London 1935), 93.
5. *Der Weltkrieg*, VII, 11–12.
6. Ludendorff, I, 116.
7. Margarethe Ludendorff, 169–70.

8. General von Falkenhayn, *General Headquarters 1914–1916 and its Critical Decisions* (London 1919), 58.
9. Hoffmann, II, 35.
10. Hoffmann, II, 85.
11. Ludendorff, I, 118.
12. Hindenburg, 36.
13. Hindenburg, 136.
14. Ludendorff, I, 120; Hoffmann, II, 90.
15. Hindenburg, 137.
16. Hindenburg, 137–38.

CHAPTER X

1. Grand Admiral von Tirpitz, *My Memoirs* (2 vols., London n.d.), II, 553.
2. Hindenburg, 144.
3. Ludendorff, I, 128–29.
4. Hoffmann, II, 96–97.
5. Margarethe Ludendorff, 99–112.
6. Hoffmann, II, 96–97; Ludendorff, I, 135.
7. General H. Kannengiesser, *The Campaign in Gallipoli* (London 1928), 26.
8. *Der Weltkrieg*, VIII, 132–35.
9. Hoffmann, II, 107.
10. Hoffmann, I, 62.
11. Hoffmann, I, 63.
12. Margarethe Ludendorff, 140.
13. Ludendorff, I, 155.
14. Hindenburg, 142.
15. Hoffmann, I, 76.
16. Hoffmann, I, 60.
17. Falkenhayn, *General Headquarters 1914–1916 and its Critical Decisions,* 145–48.
18. Hoffmann, I, 80.
19. Ludendorff, I, 180.
20. Hoffmann, I, 194.
21. Hindenburg, 147.
22. Ludendorff, I, 198–99.
23. Hoffmann, I, 82.

CHAPTER XI

1. Hoffmann, I, 100.
2. Hoffmann, I, 105.
3. *Der Weltkrieg*, X, 1–16.
4. *Der Weltkrieg,* X, 1–16.
5. Hindenburg, 155.
6. Hoffmann, I, 22.
7. Hindenburg, 151.
8. Hindenburg, 152.
9. Hoffmann, I, 114.

10. Ludendorff, I, 213.
11. Hindenburg, 155.
12. Hoffmann, I, 121.
13. Hoffmann, I, 135–36.
14. Ludendorff, I, 236.
15. Hoffmann, I, 131.
16. Tirpitz, *My Memoirs*, II, 519.
17. Tirpitz, *My Memoirs*, II, 552–553.
18. Hoffmann, I, 137.
19. Hoffmann, I, 141.
20. Müller, 188.
21. Hindenburg, 158.
22. Ludendorff, I, 233–34.
23. Ludendorff, I, 234.
24. Hoffmann, I, 143.
25. Bauer, *Der grosse Krieg in Feld und Heimat*, 103–04.
26. Hindenburg, 158–59.
27. Gröner's unpublished Memoirs, quoted in: Gordon A. Craig, *The Politics of the Prussian Army 1640–1945* (Oxford 1955), 306.
28. Letter by Wilhelm II to Falkenhayn, quoted in: Zwehl, *Erich von Falkenhayn*, II, 13; Müller, 198.
29. Ludendorff, I, 239.

CHAPTER XII

1. Hindenburg, 167.
2. Ludendorff, I, 243.
3. Hoffmann, I, 154.
4. Hindenburg, 190.
5. Gröner, unpublished Memoirs, quoted in Craig: 306n.
6. G. von dem Knesebeck, *Die Wahrheit über den Propagandafeldzug und Deutschlands Zusammenbruch* (Munich 1927), 158.
7. Margarethe Ludendorff, 134–37.
8. Ludendorff, I, 246.
9. Ludendorff, I, 258.
10. Hoffmann, II, 159.
11. Hindenburg, 237.
12. Crown Prince Wilhelm of Germany, *Memoirs* (New York 1922), 159.
13. Hoffmann, II, 159–60.
14. Hoffmann, II, 161.
15. Walter Görlitz, *The German General Staff*, 139.
16. Crown Prince Wilhelm of Germany, *Memoirs*, 136–37.
17. Hindenburg, 299–300.
18. Hoffmann, II, 161.
19. Hoffmann, I, 160–61.

CHAPTER XIII

1. Erich Ludendorff (ed.), *Urkunden der Obersten Heeresleitung über ihre Tätigkeit 1916–1918* (Berlin 1920), 315ff.

2. Rudolph von Valentini, *Kaiser und Kabinettschef* (Oldenburg 1931); *German Official Documents, Untersuchungausschuss über die Weltkriegsverantwortlichkeit* (Berlin 1920), 214.
3. Friedrich Meinecke, *Strassburg, Freiburg, Berlin, 1901–1919, Erinnerungen* (Stuttgart 1949), 247.
4. Karl Helfferich, *Der Weltkrieg* (3 vols., Berlin 1919), II, 397–98.
5. Valentini, *op. cit.*, 144–45.
6. Daisy, Princess of Pless, *From My Private Diary* (London 1931), 286.
7. Theobald von Bethmann-Hollweg, *Betrachtungen zum Weltkrieg*, (2 vols., Berlin 1919–21), II, 137–38.
8. Hoffmann, I, 168.
9. Hindenburg, 220–21, 233.
10. Fieldmarshall August von Mackensen, *Briefe und Aufzeichnungen des Generalfeldmarschalls aus Krieg und Frieden* (ed. W. Förster) (Leipzig 1938), 339.
11. Margarethe Ludendorff, 125–26.
12. Johannes Steel, *Escape to the Present* (New York 1937), 19.
13. Hoffmann, I, 169–71.
14. Müller, 240.
15. Hindenburg, 258.
16. Bülow, III, 233.
17. Margarethe Ludendorff, 154.
18. Hoffmann, I, 173–75.
19. *Der Weltkrieg*, XII, 143–45.
20. Lilo Linke, *Restless Flags, A German Girl's Story* (London 1935), 16.
21. Dispatch of Prince Hohenlohe to Count Czernin, 23 April 1917, quoted in Lutz, I, 222–24.
22. Lutz, II, 199.
23. Philip Scheidemann, *The Making of New Germany* (New York 1929), 365–67.

CHAPTER XIV

1. Ludendorff, II, 421.
2. Hindenburg, 265.
3. *Les Armées françaises dans la Grande Guerre* (French Official History) (Paris 1922–38), Tome V, vol. II, Annexes 1914 and 1917.
4. Ludendorff, II, 427.
5. Müller, 258.
6. Hoffmann, II, 173–74.
7. Müller, 296.
8. Margarethe Ludendorff, 139.
9. Müller, 277.
10. Ludendorff, II, 451.
11. Helfferich, *Der Weltkrieg*, III, 111.
12. Müller, 284n.; Erich Eyck, *A History of the Weimar Republic* (transl. Harlan P. Hansen and Robert G. L. Waite) (2 vols., Cambridge, Mass. 1962), I, 17.
13. Müller, 286.
14. Richard von Kühlmann, *Erinnerungen* (Heidelberg 1948), 502.

15. Conrad Haussmann, *Schlaglichter, Reichstagbriefe und Aufzeichnungen* (Frankfurt am Main 1924), 102.
16. Ludendorff, II, 457.
17. Hoffmann, II, 178–85.
18. Hoffmann, II, 178–85.
19. Margarethe Ludendorff, 111–16.
20. Ludendorff, II, 483.
21. Margarethe Ludendorff, 114.
22. Ludendorff, II, 471, 516, 519–20.
23. Hindenburg, 259–60.
24. Hugh Dalton, *With British Guns in Italy* (London, 1919), 105.
25. Ludendorff, II, 489.
26. Ludendorff, II, 489.
27. Hoffmann, I, 202.
28. Ludendorff, II, 510.
29. Ludendorff, II, 413.

CHAPTER XV

1. Erich Ludendorff, *The General Staff and Its Problems*, II, 524–28.
2. Valentini, *Kaiser und Kabinettschef*, 245.
3. Müller, 324–25.
4. Ludendorff, II, 553.
5. Richard von Kühlmann, *Erinnerungen,* 516.
6. Ludendorff, II, 553.
7. Ludendorff, II, 560–61.
8. Ludendorff, 569–70.
9. Hoffmann, I, 208.
10. Ludendorff, II, 544.
11. Ludendorff, 590.
12. Hindenburg, 356–57.
13. *Manual of Positional Warfare for All Arms (The Attack in Positional Warfare)* 1 January 1918, Collection of German Military documents, Hoover War Library.
14. Ludendorff, II, 592.
15. Erich Eyck, *A History of the Weimar Republic,* 127.
16. Siegfried A. Kaehler, *Zur Beurteilung Ludendorffs im Sommer 1918.* (*Nachrichten der Akademie der Wissenschaften,* Göttingen 1953), I, 17.
17. *Der Weltkrieg,* XIV, 160, map 6.
18. Hindenburg, 354.
19. Rudolph Binding, *A Fatalist at War* (transl. Ian F. D. Morrow) (London 1928), 208, 210.
20. Margarethe Ludendorff, 128–33.
21. Captain D. G. Brown, *The Tank in Action* (London 1920), 319.
22. Ludendorff, II, 634.
23. UDZ, II, 191.
24. Ludendorff, II, 634.
25. Ludendorff, II, 630.
26. Reproduced in Lutz, I, 655.
27. Müller, 367; Colonel Albrecht von Thaer, quoted in: Kaehler, *Zur Beurteilung Ludendorffs im Sommer 1918,* I, 15.

28. Hindenburg, 375.
29. Ludendorff, 668.
30. Görlitz, 196–97.
31. F. von Lossberg, *Meine Tätigkeit im Weltkrieg 1914–1918* (Berlin 1939), 344–46.
32. Diary of Colonel Mertz von Quirnheim, 22 July 1918, quoted in: Wolfgang Förster, *Der Feldherr Ludendorff im Unglück* (Wiesbaden 1952), 25.
33. Förster, 29.
34. Hindenburg, 390.
35. Ludendorff, 679.
36. Hindenburg, 394.
37. UDZ, II, 223.

CHAPTER XVI

1. Siegfried A. Kaehler, *Zur Beurteilung Ludendorffs im Sommer 1918,* I, 21.
2. Ludendorff, II, 684.
3. Müller, 240.
4. Müller, 388*n*.
5. UDZ, II, 390; signed protocol of Conference at General Headquarters on August 14, 1918.
6. Erich Eyck, *A History of the Weimar Republic,* I, 31.
7. Ludendorff, II, 707.
8. Quoted in Förster, *Der Feldherr Ludendorff im Unglück* (Wiesbaden 1952), 62.
9. Ludendorff, II, 699.
10. Ludendorff, II, 700.
11. Hindenburg, 410.
12. Ludendorff, II, 721.
13. Quoted in John W. Wheeler-Bennett, "Ludendorff, the Soldier and the Politician," in: *The Virginia Quarterly* (Spring 1938), 187–202.
14. Müller, 397*n*.
15. UDZ, II, 400–05.
16. Ludendorff, II, 723.
17. Ludendorff, II, 723.
18. Max von Baden, *Erinnerungen und Dokumente* (Stuttgart 1927), 346.
19. Ludendorff, II, 730.
20. Ludendorff, II, 761–62.
21. Ludendorff, II, 761–62.
22. Ludendorff, II, 761–62.
23. Ludendorff, II, 761–62.
24. Max von Baden, *Erinnerungen und Dokumente,* 500.
25. Müller, 412–413; Margarethe Ludendorff, 172.
26. Margarethe Ludendorff, 173.
27. Johannes Steel, 19.
28. General Maxime Weygand, *Le 11 novembre* (Paris 1932), 23*ff*.

CHAPTER XVII

1. Margarethe Ludendorff, 176.
2. Margarethe Ludendorff, 177.

3. Erich Ludendorff, *Vom Feldherrn zum Weltrevolutionär und Wegbereiter Deutscher Volkschöpfung: Meine Lebenserinnerungen von 1919–1925* (Munich 1940), 34.
4. Margarethe Ludendorff, 179–81.
5. Margarethe Ludendorff, 199.
6. Margarethe Ludendorff, 205.
7. Ludendorff, II, 628.
8. Wolfgang Förster, *Der Feldherr Ludendorff im Unglück*, 77–80.
9. Karl Novak, Introduction to *Hoffmann Diaries*, 32.
10. David Lampe and Laszo Szenasi, *The Selfmade Villain: A Biography of I. Trebitsch Lincoln* (London 1961), 109.
11. John W. Wheeler-Bennett, "Ludendorff, the Soldier and Politician," in: *Virginia Quarterly Review* (Spring 1938), 200.
12. Margarethe Ludendorff, 280.
13. Margarethe Ludendorff, 177.
14. Margarethe Ludendorff, 230.
15. Brigadier J. H. Morgan, *Assize of Arms* (London 1945), 56–58.
16. David Lampe and Laszo Szenasi, *The Selfmade Villain*, 109.
17. *Deutsche Reichsgeschichte in Dokumenten 1849–1934: Urkunden und Aktenstücke zur innern und äussern Politik des deutschen Reiches* (ed. J. Hohlfeld) (Berlin 1934), II, 793–94.
18. J. Benoist-Méchin, *Histoire de L'Armée Allemande 1919–1936* (2 vols., Paris 1938), II, 102–03.
19. Rudolph Mann, *Mit Ehrhardt durch Deutschland: Erinnerungen eines Mitkämpfers von der 2. Marinebrigade* (Berlin 1921), 91.
20. *L'Europe Nouvelle*, 9 April 1921, "Les Dessous de la Politique Reactionaire," 457–75.
21. J. H. Morgan, *Assize of Arms*, 74.
22. Margarethe Ludendorff, 234.
23. Lampe and Szenasi, 137.
24. E. J. Gumbel, *Verschwörer: Beiträge zur Geschichte und Soziologie der deutschen Nationalistischen Geheimbünde seit 1918* (Vienna 1924), 33.
25. Margarethe Ludendorff, 232.
26. Margarethe Ludendorff, 234–35.
27. E. J. Gumbel, "Le Capitaine Ehrhardt et l'Organization C," in: *l'Europe Nouvelle*, VI (25 August 1923), 1073.
28. Gumbel, *Vier Jahre politischer Mord* (Berlin 1922), 144–45.
29. Ernst Röhm, *Die Geschichte eines Hochverräters* (Munich 1934), 131.

CHAPTER XVIII

1. Erich Ludendorff, *Vom Feldherrn zum Weltrevolutionär*, 161; Kurt G. W. Ludecke, *I Knew Hitler: The Story of a Nazi Who Escaped the Blood Purge* (New York 1938), 60–65.
2. Margarethe Ludendorff, 261.
3. Rudolph Olden, *Hitler the Pawn* (London 1936), 126.
4. Erich Ludendorff, *Vom Feldherrn zum Weltrevolutionär*, 13, 61.
5. *Hitler's Table Talk* (transl. N. Cameron and R. Stevens) (London 1953), 597.
6. General Friedrich von Rabenau, *Seeckt, aus seinem Leben 1918–1936* (Leipzig 1940), II, 324.

7. Görlitz, 234.
8. Rabenau, II, 328.
9. Paul Wentzcke, *Rheinkampf* (2. vols., Berlin 1925), I, 435.
10. Von Lossow's evidence, *Der Hitler Prozess* (Munich 1924), 262–69.
11. Olden, *Hitler the Pawn*, 124–25.
12. Ludecke, *I Knew Hitler*, 185.
13. Erich Ludendorff, *Vom Feldherrn zum Weltrevolutionär*, 259.
14. Karl Friedrich Novak, *Introduction to the Hoffmann Diaries*, 11.
15. John W. Wheeler-Bennett, *The Wooden Titan* (New York 1936), 253; Margarethe Ludendorff, 277–78.
16. Margarethe Ludendorff, 283.
17. Erich Ludendorff, *Hitlers Verrat der Deutschen an den römischen Papst* (Munich 1931).
18. Margarethe Ludendorff, 165–66.
19. Margarethe Ludendorff, 127.
20. Margarethe Ludendorff, 272.
21. Erich Ludendorff, *Vom Feldherrn zum Weltrevolutionär*, 13.
22. Wheeler-Bennett, *The Wooden Titan*, 436.
23. Wheeler-Bennett, "Ludendorff, the Soldier and the Politician," 201.
24. Erich Ludendorff, *The Nation at War* (transl. Dr. A. S. Rappaport) (London 1936), 24.
25. Wheeler-Bennett, "Ludendorff, the Soldier and the Politician," 201.
26. Dr. Mathilde Ludendorff, *Erich Ludendorff: Sein Wesen und Schaffen* (Munich 1940), 608.
27. *Hitler's Table Talk*, 454.

INDEX

Aachen, 32, 38–39, 41, 57–58
Adlon Hotel, 279–80
Adriatic Sea, 170
Agadir, 3, 15
Aisne River, 123, 217, 253, 262
Albania, 17, 30, 170
"Alberich" Program, 210, 218
Albert, 248, 258
Albert, King of the Belgians, 38–39, 43–45, 54
Aldeutsche Blätter, 36
Alexander, Obrenovitch, King of Serbia, 27
Allenburg, 80
Allenstein, 75, 78, 85–86, 88, 92, 96, 107–08
Altvates, Admiral Vasili, 223
Amiens, 249, 258–59, 262
Angerapp River, 67, 139, 154, 156
Annopol, 130
Antwerp, 7, 44, 123
Ardennes, 1, 6, 65
Armin, General Sixt von, 222, 252
Arras, 210, 215, 217, 241, 248, 252
Augustovo, 112
Augustovo, forest of, 157, 171
Austria-Hungary, 3–4, 11, 17–18, 27, 29–30, 33, 61–62, 109, 111, 124, 148–49, 165, 170, 197, 228, 237, 239
Avesnes, 245, 254–55, 257, 259–60

Baden-Baden, 224
Ballin, Albert, 205, 273
Baltic Sea, 18, 25, 28, 65, 112, 166, 176, 223, 233, 238
Barchon, Fort, 59
Battice, 41–42

Bauer, Colonel Max, persuades Moltke to replace Prittwitz, 64; conspires against Falkenhayn, 187; in the Kapp *Putsch,* 281–82, 285, 287; other references, 236, 289
Belgian Army, 10; weaknesses of, 43–44, 54, 61
Belgian Government, 38–39, 58–59
Belgium, 6, 9–10, 20, 22, 38, 40, 58, 63, 73, 145, 193
Belgrade, 27, 33, 170
Below, General Fritz von, 66–67, 81, 85–86, 88–90, 95–96, 156, 167
Below, General Otto von, 227–28, 245, 248
Benedict XV, Pope, 223
Berchtesgaden, 301, 305, 307
Berchtold, Count Leopold, 27, 29
Berlin, 1, 8, 12, 18, 20, 22, 28, 30–32, 35, 66, 70–73, 88, 95, 137–38, 152, 179, 187, 208, 211, 214, 225, 268–270, 272–73, 275–77, 286, 288, 296, 299, 304
Berliner Tageblatt, 28
Bernstorff, Count Johann-Heinrich von, 204
Beseler, von, Governor-General of Poland, 197
Bethmann-Hollweg, Chancellor Theobald von, declares war, 40; policies of, 30, 33, 146–47; sends message to Belgian Government, 58–59; opposes unrestricted U-boat warfare, 190–91, 201, 202–04; relations with Ludendorff, 183, 201, 217, 220; dismissed, 221; other references: 31, 188, 193, 196, 236, 261
Bialystok, 75, 115, 117, 120, 172
Bischofsburg, 76, 82–83, 85–88, 93–94

Helphand, Alexander ("Parvus"), 212–13
Henry, Prince of Prussia, 219
Hentsch, Lieutenant-Colonel, 123, 170, 239
Hertling, Count Georg von, 228, 233, 261
Hesleholmgard, 276, 278
Hess, Rudolph, 291–92
Heye, Colonel Wilhelm, 262, 265, 270, 285, 287
Himmler, Heinrich, 292, 295
Hindenburg, Frau von, 70–71
Hindenburg, Major Oskar von, 175
Hindenburg, Field Marshal Paul (von Beneckendorff und von), character and appearance of, 70–77; early career of, 71–77; appointed Commander Eighth Army, 69–70; promoted to Field Marshal, 145; appointed Chief of the General Staff, 187–88; signs Proclamation to Army, 269; elected President, 305; death of, 309; other references: 63, 82–90, 95, 98, 105–11, 122, 124–25, 131, 136–38, 146, 148, 150–53, 158–60, 165, 167, 169, 171–74, 177–86, 191–94, 202–06, 216, 219, 221, 227, 233–38, 245–47, 257–68, 271, 273, 275, 304, 307
Hintze, Admiral Paul von, 255, 261, 265–66, 298
Hitler, Adolf, 284, 291–92, 295–97, 299–300, 302–06
Hocheimer, Dr., 260
Hoffmann, Frau, 70
Hoffmann, Major-General Max, character and appearance of, 73, 93, 110–12; his early career, 73–74, 81; at Tannenberg, 79–106; relations with Ludendorff, 110, 132, 137, 183; at Brest-Litovsk, 185–86; becomes Chief of Staff, Ober-Ost, 191; strategic ideas of, 74, 89, 166–167, 178, 193, 201, 217–18; and capture of Riga, 222–23; and Russian peace treaty, 233–38; quarrels with Ludendorff, 233–35; opposes Nazis, 292; death of, 307; other references: 75–77, 83, 89–90, 94–98, 106, 125, 130–33, 138, 141–47,

152, 154, 161, 165, 168–76, 181, 184, 195–98, 204–05, 209, 217, 230–32, 243–48, 251–53, 282, 304, 306, 310, 312
Hollogne, Fort, 60
Hutier, General von, 223, 245, 247

Independent Socialist Party, 223, 270
Insterburg, 79, 122, 153, 155–56
Isonzo River, 179, 189
Ivangorod, 128, 130–32, 151
Ivanov, General, 127, 182

Jagow, Foreign Minister von, 196
Jahn, Gustav, 36
Jellicoe, Admiral Sir John, 181
Jilinski, General, 66, 75–76, 99, 112–115, 117, 120
Joachim, Prince of Prussia, 179
Joffre, General Joseph J. C., 54, 60, 217
Jura Mountains, 6
Jutland, Battle of, 181

Kahr, Ritter Gustav von, 297, 299–301, 308
Kaiser. See Wilhelm II
Kaiserschlacht, 240, 257
Kapp, Dr. Wolfgang, 281–87
Kekuela, Alexander, 212
Kemmel, Mount, 252
Kemmitz, Mathilde. See Ludendorff, Frau Mathilde
Kersten, General, 93
Kerensky, Alexander, 221, 230
Kindermord, 136, 178, 187
Kliouev, General, 85–86, 102
Kluck, Colonel-General Alexander von, 44, 60, 109–10, 123
Knox, Major Alfred, 92, 100
Kondratovitch, General, 101
Königgrätz, Battle of, 3, 71
Königsberg, 62, 66, 71, 79, 155, 161
Kovno, 117, 156, 166–67, 171–72, 174–75, 179–80, 185, 208, 270
Kreuznach, 207, 212, 215, 220, 224, 227, 233, 237, 245
Kriegsakademie, 13, 135
Krupp howitzers, 59